OEDIPUS TYRANNUS

A NEW TRANSLATION

PASSAGES FROM ANCIENT AUTHORS

RELIGION AND PSYCHOLOGY: SOME STUDIES

CRITICISM

⇶ NORTON CRITICAL EDITIONS ⇴

SOPHOCLES

OEDIPUS TYRANNUS

A NEW TRANSLATION
PASSAGES FROM ANCIENT AUTHORS
RELIGION AND PSYCHOLOGY:
SOME STUDIES
CRITICISM

➤➤➤◄◄◄

Translated and Edited by

LUCI BERKOWITZ and THEODORE F. BRUNNER

UNIVERSITY OF CALIFORNIA AT IRVINE

W · W · NORTON & COMPANY · INC · *New York*

SBN 393 04307 x (Cloth edition)
SBN 393 09874 5 (Paper edition)

Translation of *Oedipus Tyrannus* Copyright © 1966
by Luci Berkowitz and Theodore F. Brunner

Library of Congress Catalog Card No. 74–81157

PRINTED IN THE UNITED STATES OF AMERICA

1 2 3 4 5 6 7 8 9 0

Contents

v

Preface

Of the three Greek tragedians, only Sophocles embodies completely the mind and spirit of Athens in the fifth century B.C. His birth in 496 B.C. falls within a period characterized by the dissolution of tyranny and the ascendancy of Greece over the Persian Empire; in his youth and adulthood he saw the Golden Age of Athens inaugurated and promoted by the statesman Pericles; and before his death in 406 B.C. he witnessed the approaching and inevitable collapse of Athens under the strain of the Peloponnesian War.

The *Oedipus Tyrannus* was performed shortly after the great plague which paralyzed Athens in 429 B.C.† In his title character Sophocles created a man who epitomizes the hopeless human struggle against nemesis, the ever-present power which could topple in an instant the fortunes of men and cities alike. The nature of this power, the problem of guilt or innocence, the role of fate in human life—these are questions which have occupied the attention of philosophers and critics from the time of Aristotle to the present day. The essays contained in this volume were selected not only to reflect some of the answers which have been proposed to these questions, but also to present a broad sampling of the critics' approaches to the play as a piece of literature and drama. A tragedy as complex as the *Tyrannus* will, by necessity, give rise to a great many divergent interpretations. The causes of Oedipus' downfall, for instance, have been discussed and argued for centuries, and this volume presents under the heading "The Problem of Guilt" a selection of essays by twentieth-century scholars who are in considerable disagreement with one another on this point.

The translation of the *Tyrannus* presented here was originally commissioned for stage production by the Repertory Theater at the University of California, Irvine, under the direction of Robert Cohen. The director concurred with the translators in interpreting Oedipus as a character with whose suffering a modern audience could identify and sympathize, an ancient hero who was timeless and immediate, a figure of towering stature who nevertheless showed both the strengths and weaknesses of a man. This interpre-

---

†But cf. Bernard M. W. Knox, "The Date of the Oedipus Tyrannus of Sophocles," *AJP*, 77 (1956), pp. 133–147, who argues for 425 B.C. as the date of the plague. Thucydides' account of the plague in Athens is included in the section entitled *Passages from Ancient Authors*.

tation justified a translation employing twentieth-century idiom, a
language simple so as not to detract from the intrinsic power of the
play, free of Victorian embellishment, yet strong and meaningful.
Although the translation was written with a theater audience in
mind, it is hoped that it will appeal to the reading audience as
well. It is based upon the Greek edition of A. C. Pearson (Oxford,
1928).

The editors are grateful to Gordon M. Kirkwood (Cornell University) and Bernard M. W. Knox (Director, Center for Hellenic
Studies, Washington, D.C.) for their helpful suggestions on both
the translation and selected essays. A further word of thanks is
owed to the University of California which provided welcome
assistance in the preparation of this volume.

Luci Berkowitz

Theodore F. Brunner

The Text of
Oedipus Tyrannus

translated by
Luci Berkowitz
and
Theodore F. Brunner

Cast of Characters

Oedipus, Ruler of Thebes[1]

Jocasta, Wife of Oedipus[2]

Creon, Brother of Jocasta[3]

Teiresias, A Blind Prophet

A Priest

Messenger 1

Messenger 2

A Shepherd

An Attendant

Antigone }
Ismene } Daughters of Oedipus and Jocasta

Chorus of Theban Elders

---

1. Son of Laius and Jocasta; the meaning of his name is "swollen foot."

The persons, places, and divinities mentioned in the footnotes are identified with reference to their special functions in the *Oedipus Tyrannus*. For example, Hermes is identified as a god of flocks and pastures, even though his divine precincts are far more numerous, *e.g.*, commerce, trickery, music, messenger, guardian of city boundaries, etc.

2. Daughter of Menoeceus, sister of Creon, wife of Laius, mother of Oedipus.

3. Son of Menoeceus. After the death of Laius, he ruled Thebes until the arrival of Oedipus and resumed the rule of the city after Oedipus' fall.

OEDIPUS: What is it, children, sons of the ancient house of Cadmus?[4] Why do you sit as suppliants crowned with laurel branches? What is the meaning of the incense which fills the city? The pleas to end pain? The cries of sorrow? I chose not to hear it from my messengers, but came myself—I came, Oedipus, Oedipus, whose name is known to all. You, old one—age gives you the right to speak for all of them—you tell me why they sit before my altar. Has something frightened you? What brings you here? Some need? Some want? I'll help you all I can. I would be cruel did I not greet you with compassion when you are gathered here before me.

PRIEST: My Lord and King, we represent the young and old; some are priests and some the best of Theban youth. And I—I am a priest of Zeus.[5] There are many more who carry laurel boughs like these—in the market-places, at the twin altars of Pallas,[6] by the sacred ashes of Ismenus' oracle.[7] You see yourself how torn our city is, how she craves relief from the waves of death which now crash over her. Death is everywhere—in the harvests of the land, in the flocks that roam the pastures, in the unborn children of our mothers' wombs. A fiery plague is ravaging the city, festering, spreading its pestilence, wasting the house of Cadmus, filling the house of Hades[8] with screams of pain and of fear. This is the reason why we come to you, these children and I. No, we do not think you a god. But we deem you a mortal set apart to face life's common issues and the trials which the gods dispense to men. It was you who once before came to Thebes and freed us from the spell that hypnotized our lives. You did this, and yet you knew no more than we—less even. You had no help from us. God aided you. Yes, you restored our life. And now a second time, great Oedipus, we turn to you for help. Find some relief for us, whether with god or man to guide your way. You helped us then. Yes. And we believe that you will help us now. O Lord, revive our city; restore her life. Think of your fame, your own repute. The people know you saved us from our past despair. Let no one say you raised us up to let us fall. Save us and keep us

4. Son of Agenor and founder of Cadmea, the citadel which grew to be the city of Thebes (in central Greece), where the drama takes place.
5. Most supreme of the divinities; regarded as the father of gods and men alike. He was often appealed to as a dispenser of justice.
6. Title of the goddess Athena (originally the name of a friend whom she accidentally killed). Athena was god-

dess of wisdom, but of particular importance as a protectress of cities in Attica and Boeotia.
7. Referring to the shrine of Apollo, located near the river Ismenus in the vicinity of Thebes. It contained an altar made of ashes supposed to have divining powers.
8. Brother of Zeus; god of the underworld.

3

safe. You found good omens once to aid you and brought us fortune then. Find them again. If you will rule this land as king and lord, rule over men and not a wall encircling emptiness. No city wall, no ship can justify its claim to strength if it is stripped of men who give it life.

OEDIPUS: O my children, I know well the pain you suffer and understand what brings you here. You suffer—and yet not one among you suffers more than I. Each of you grieves for himself alone, while my heart must bear the strain of sorrow for all— myself and you and all our city's people. No, I am not blind to it. I have wept and in my weeping set my thoughts on countless paths, searching for an answer. I have sent my own wife's brother Creon, son of Menoeceus, to Apollo's Pythian shrine[9] to learn what I might say or do to ease our city's suffering. I am concerned that he is not yet here—he left many days ago. But this I promise: whenever he returns, whatever news he brings, whatever course the god reveals—*that* is the course that I shall take.

PRIEST: Well spoken. Look! They are giving signs that Creon is returning.

OEDIPUS: O God! If only he brings news as welcome as his smiling face.

PRIEST: I think he does. His head is crowned with laurel leaves.

OEDIPUS: We shall know soon enough. There. My Lord Creon, what word do you bring from the god?

(Enter Creon)

CREON: Good news. I tell you this: if all goes well, our troubles will be past.

OEDIPUS: But what was the oracle? Right now I'm swaying between hope and fear.

CREON: If you want to hear it in the presence of these people, I shall tell you. If not, let's go inside.

OEDIPUS: Say it before all of us. I sorrow more for them than for myself.

CREON: Then I shall tell you exactly what the god Apollo answered. These are his words: Pollution. A hidden sore is festering in our land. We are to stop its growth before it is too late.

OEDIPUS: Pollution? How are we to save ourselves?

CREON: Blood for blood. To save ourselves we are to banish a man or pay for blood with blood. It is a murder which has led to this despair.

9. Apollo was god of light, prophecy, plague and healing, purification, and justice; he was the son of Zeus and Leto and the brother of Artemis. "Pythian" was an epithet of Apollo, also describing the sanctuary, oracle, and attendants at Delphi. The term originated from the belief that Apollo slew the monster Python to gain control of Delphi, the most sacred sanctuary of Apollo in Greece, located on the southern slope of Mt. Parnassus (cf. map on p. 34).

OEDIPUS: Murder? Whose? Did the god say whose . . .?

CREON: My Lord, before you came to rule our city, we had a king. His name was Laius . . .

OEDIPUS: I know, although I never saw him.

CREON: He was murdered. And the god's command is clear: we must find the assassin and destroy him.

OEDIPUS: But where? Where is he to be found? How can we find the traces of a crime committed long ago?

CREON: He lives among us. If we seek, we will find; what we do not seek cannot be found.

OEDIPUS: Where was it that Laius met his death? At home? The country? In some foreign land?

CREON: One day he left and told us he would go to Delphi. That was the last we saw of him.

OEDIPUS: And there was no one who could tell what happened? No one who traveled with him? Did no one see? Is there no evidence?

CREON: All perished. All—except one who ran in panic from the scene and could not tell us anything for certain, except . . .

OEDIPUS: Except? What? What was it? One clue might lead to many. We have to grasp the smallest shred of hope.

CREON: He said that robbers—many of them—fell upon Laius and his men and murdered them.

OEDIPUS: Robbers? Who committed *murder*? Why? Unless they were paid assassins?

CREON: We considered that. But the king was dead and we were plagued with trouble. No one came forth as an avenger.

OEDIPUS: Trouble? What could have kept you from investigating the death of your king?

CREON: The Sphinx.[1] The Sphinx was confounding us with her riddles, forcing us to abandon our search for the unknown and to tend to what was then before us.

OEDIPUS: Then I—I shall begin again. I shall not cease until I bring the truth to light. Apollo has shown, and you have shown, the duty which we owe the dead. You have my gratitude. You will find me a firm ally, and together we shall exact vengeance for our land and for the god. I shall not rest till I dispel this defilement—not just for another man's sake, but for my own as well. For whoever the assassin—he might turn his hand against me too. Yes, I shall be serving Laius and myself. Now go, my children. Leave the steps of my altar. Go. Take away your laurel branches. Go to the people of Cadmus. Summon them. Tell them that I, their king, will leave nothing untried. And with the help of God, we shall find success—or ruin.

1. A mythological monster with a woman's head, the body of a lion, and wings, who tormented the city of Thebes with the following riddle: "What walks on four feet in the morn-ing, two feet at noon, and three feet at night?" Only Oedipus was able to offer the correct answer: "Man" (in his infancy, adulthood, and old age).

(Exit Oedipus)

PRIEST: Come, children. We have learned what we came to learn.
Come, Apollo, come yourself, who sent these oracles!
Come as our savior! Come! Deliver us from this plague!

CHORUS:
O prophecy of Zeus, sweet is the sound of your words
as they come to our glorious city of Thebes
from Apollo's glittering shrine.
Yet I quake and I dread and I tremble at those words.
Io, Delian Lord![2]

What will you bring to pass? Disaster unknown,
or familiar to us, as the ever recurring seasons?
Tell me, O oracle,
heavenly daughter of blessèd hope.

Foremost I call on you, daughter of Zeus,
Athena, goddess supreme;
and on Artemis,[3] shielding the world,
shielding this land from her circular shrine
graced with renown.
And on you I call, Phoebus,[4] Lord of the unerring bow.

Come to my aid, you averters of doom!
Come to my aid if ever you came!
Come to my aid as once you did, when you quenched
the fires of doom that fell on our soil!
Hear me, and come to my aid!

Boundless the pain, boundless the grief I bear;
sickness pervades this land,
affliction without reprieve.
Barren the soil, barren of fruit;
children are born no longer to light;
all of us flutter in agony
winging our way into darkness and death.

Countless the number of dead in the land;
corpses of children cover the plain,
children dying before they have lived,
no one to pity them,
reeking, and spreading diseases and death.

---

2. "Io" (pronounced *ee-oh*) was a cry used in invoking a god or praying for help. "Delian" was an epithet of Apollo who, traditionally, is said to have been born on the island of Delos in the Aegean Sea (cf. map on p. 34). Delos was an important center of the god's worship.
3. Daughter of Zeus and Leto; sister of Apollo; goddess of the hunt, but also of childbirth, and protectress of the young. Her shrine was commonly located in the agora, the marketplace, which was often of circular shape.
4. Epithet of Apollo meaning "bright" or "radiant," from his identification with the sun.

Moaning and wailing our wives,
moaning and wailing our mothers
stream to the altars this way and that,
scream to the air with helpless cries.
Hear us, golden daughter of Zeus,
hear us! Send us release!

Ares[5] now rages in our midst
brandishing in his hands
the firebrands of disease,
raving, consuming, rousing the screams of death.
Hear us, O goddess!
Help us, and still his rage!
Turn back his assault!
Help us! Banish him from our land!
Drive him into the angry sea,
to the wave-swept border of Thrace![6]

We who escape him tonight
will be struck down at dawn.
Help us, O father Zeus,
Lord of the thunderbolt,
crush him! Destroy him!
Burn him with fires of lightning!

Help us, Apollo, Lycean[7] Lord!
Stand at our side with your golden bow!
Artemis, help us!
Come from the Lycian[8] hills!
Come with your torches aflame!
Dionysus,[9] protector, come to our aid,
come with your revelers' band!
Burn with your torch the god
hated among the gods!

(Enter Oedipus)

OEDIPUS: I have heard your prayers and answer with relief and
help, if you will heed my words and tend the sickness with the
cure it cries for. My words are uttered as a stranger to the act, a
stranger to its tale. I cannot trace its path alone, without a sign.
As a citizen newer to Thebes than you, I make this proclama-

5. Son of Zeus and Hera; god of war, whose favorite haunt was Thrace. He was sometimes considered the bringer of plague.
6. Region east of Macedonia; a favorite haunt of Ares.
7. Epithet of Apollo; it is related to the Greek word meaning "wolf" and refers to Apollo's role as patron of flocks and killer of wolves.
8. Referring to Lycia, a region on the southern coast of Asia Minor, which was one of the haunts of Apollo and Artemis.
9. Son of Zeus and Semele, the daughter of Cadmus, and thus closely associated with Thebes; god of vegetation and fertility; he frequently haunted the countryside and mountains, accompained by woodland nymphs, satyrs, and maenads.

tion: If one among you knows who murdered Laius, the son of Labdacus,[1] let him tell us now. If he fears for his life, let him confess and know a milder penalty. He will be banished from this land. Nothing more. Or if you know the assassin to be an alien, do not protect him with your silence. You will be rewarded. But if in fear you protect yourself or any other man and keep your silence, then hear what I say now: Whoever he is, this assassin must be denied entrance to your homes. Any man where I rule is forbidden to receive him or speak to him or share with him his prayers and sacrifice or offer him the holy rites of purification. I command you to drive this hideous curse out of your homes; I command you to obey the will of Pythian Apollo. I will serve the god and the dead. On the assassin or assassins, I call down the most vile damnation—for this vicious act, may the brand of shame be theirs to wear forever. And if I knowingly harbor their guilt within my own walls, I shall not exempt myself from the curse that I have called upon them. It is for me, for God, and for this city that staggers toward ruin that you must fulfill these injunctions. Even if Heaven gave you no sign, you had the sacred duty to insure that this act did not go unexamined, unavenged! It was the assassination of a noble man— your king! Now that I hold the powers that he once held, his bed, his wife—had fate been unopposed, his children would have bound us closer yet—and now on him has this disaster fallen. I will avenge him as I would avenge my own father. I will leave nothing untried to expose the murderer of Laius, the son of Labdacus, heir to the house of Cadmus and Agenor.[2] On those who deny me obedience, I utter this curse: May the gods visit them with barrenness in their harvests, barrenness in their women, barrenness in their fate. Worse still—may they be haunted and tormented and never know the peace that comes with death. But for you, my people, in sympathy with me—I pray that Justice and all the gods attend you forever.

CHORUS: You have made me swear an oath, my Lord, and under oath I speak. I did not kill the king and cannot name the man who did. The question was Apollo's. He could name the man you seek.

OEDIPUS: I know. And yet no mortal can compel a god to speak.

CHORUS: The next-best thing, it seems to me . . .

OEDIPUS: Tell me. Tell me all your thoughts. We must consider everything.

CHORUS: There is one man, second only to Apollo, who can see the truth, who can clearly help us in our search—Teiresias.

OEDIPUS: I thought of this. On Creon's advice, I sent for him. Twice. He should be here.

CHORUS: There were some rumors once, but no one hears them now.

OEDIPUS: What rumors? I want to look at every tale that is told.

---

1. Grandson of Cadmus.

2. Mythological king of Phoenicia, father of Cadmus.

CHORUS: They said that travelers murdered Laius.

OEDIPUS: I have heard that too. And yet there's no one to be found who saw the murderer in the act.

CHORUS: He will come forth himself, once he has heard your curse, if he knows what it means to be afraid.

OEDIPUS: Why? Why should a man now fear words if then he did not fear to kill?

CHORUS: But there is one man who can point him out—the man in whom the truth resides, the god-inspired prophet. And there—they are bringing him now.

(Enter Teiresias, guided by a servant)

OEDIPUS: Teiresias, all things are known to you—the secrets of heaven and earth, the sacred and profane. Though you are blind, you surely see the plague that rakes our city. My Lord Teiresias, we turn to you as our only hope. My messengers may have told you—we have sent to Apollo and he has answered us. We must find Laius' murderers and deal with them. Or drive them out. Then—only then will we find release from our suffering. I ask you not to spare your gifts of prophecy. Look to the voices of prophetic birds or the answers written in the flames. Spare nothing. Save all of us—yourself, your city, your king, and all that is touched by this deathly pollution. We turn to you. My Lord, it is man's most noble role to help his fellow man the best his talents will allow.

TEIRESIAS: O God! How horrible wisdom is! How horrible when it does not help the wise! How could I have forgotten? I should not have come.

OEDIPUS: Why? What's wrong?

TEIRESIAS: Let me go. It will be better if you bear your own distress and I bear mine. It will be better this way.

OEDIPUS: This city gave you life and yet you refuse her an answer! You speak as if you were her enemy.

TEIRESIAS: No! No! It is because I see the danger in your words. And mine would add still more.

OEDIPUS: For God's sake, if you know, don't turn away from us! We are pleading. We are begging you.

TEIRESIAS: Because you are blind! No! I shall not reveal my secrets. I shall not reveal yours.

OEDIPUS: What? You know, and yet you refuse to speak? Would you betray us and watch our city fall helplessly to her death?

TEIRESIAS: I will not cause you further grief. I will not grieve myself. Stop asking me to tell; I will tell you nothing.

OEDIPUS: You will not tell? You monster! You could stir the stones of earth to a burning rage! You will never tell? What will it take?

TEIRESIAS: Know yourself, Oedipus. You denounce me, but you do not yet know yourself.

OEDIPUS: Yes! You disgrace your city. And then you expect us to control our rage!

TEIRESIAS: It does not matter if I speak; the future has already been determined.

OEDIPUS: And if it has, then it is for you to tell me, *prophet!*

TEIRESIAS: I shall say no more. Rage, if you wish.

OEDIPUS: I *am* enraged. And now I will tell you what *I* think. I think this was *your* doing. *You* plotted the crime, *you* saw it carried out. It was *your* doing. All but the actual killing. And had you not been blind, you would have done *that*, too!

TEIRESIAS: Do you believe what you have said? Then accept your own decree! From this day on, deny yourself the right to speak to anyone. You, Oedipus, are the desecrator, the polluter of this land!

OEDIPUS: You traitor! Do you think that you can get away with this?

TEIRESIAS: The truth is my protection.

OEDIPUS: Who taught you this? It did not come from prophecy!

TEIRESIAS: *You* taught me. *You* drove me, *you* forced me to say it against my will.

OEDIPUS: Say it again. I want to make sure that I understand you.

TEIRESIAS: Understand me? Or are you trying to provoke me?

OEDIPUS: No, I want to be sure, I want to know. Say it again.

TEIRESIAS: I say that you, Oedipus Tyrannus, are the murderer you seek.

OEDIPUS: So! A second time! Now twice you will regret what you have said!

TEIRESIAS: Shall I tell you more? Shall I fan your flames of anger?

OEDIPUS: Yes. Tell me more. Tell me more—whatever suits you. It will be in vain.

TEIRESIAS: I say you live in shame with the woman you love, blind to your own calamity.

OEDIPUS: Do you think you can speak like this forever?

TEIRESIAS: I do, if there is any strength in truth.

OEDIPUS: There is—for everyone but you. You—you cripple! Your ears are deaf, your eyes are blind, your mind—your *mind* is crippled!

TEIRESIAS: You fool! You slander me when one day you will hear the same . . .

OEDIPUS: You live in night, Teiresias, in night that never turns to day. And so, you cannot hurt me—or any man who sees the light.

TEIRESIAS: No—it is not I who will cause your fall. That is Apollo's office—and he will discharge it.

OEDIPUS: Was this *your* trick—or Creon's?

TEIRESIAS: No, not Creon's. No, Oedipus. You are destroying yourself!

OEDIPUS: Ah, wealth and sovereignty and skill surpassing skill in life's contentions, why must envy always attend them? This city *gave* me power; I did not ask for it. And Creon, my friend, my trusted friend, would plot to overthrow me—with this charlatan, this impostor, who auctions off his magic wares! His eyes see profit clearly, but they are blind in prophecy. Tell me, Teiresias, what makes you a prophet? Where were you when the monster was here weaving her spells and taunts? What words of relief did Thebes hear from you? Her riddle would stagger the simple mind; it demanded the mind of a seer. Yet, put to the test, all your birds and god-craft proved useless; you had no answer. Then I came—ignorant Oedipus—I came and smothered her, using only my wit. There were no birds to tell me what to do. I am the man you would overthrow so you can stand near Creon's throne. You will regret—you and your conspirator—you will regret your attempt to purify this land. If you were not an old man, I would make you suffer the pain which you deserve for your audacity.

CHORUS: Both of you, my Lord, have spoken in bitter rage. No more—not when we must direct our every thought to obey the god's command.

TEIRESIAS: Though you are king, the right to speak does not belong to you alone. It is *my* right as well and I shall claim it. I am not your servant and Creon is not my patron. I serve only Loxian[3] Apollo. And I tell you this, since you mock my blindness. You have eyes, Oedipus, and do not see your own destruction. You have eyes and do not see what lives with you. Do you know whose son you are? I say that you have sinned and do not know it; you have sinned against your own—the living and the dead. A double scourge, your mother's and your father's curse, will drive you from this land. Then darkness will shroud those eyes that now can see the light. Cithaeron[4]—the whole earth will resound with your mournful cries when you discover the meaning of the wedding-song that brought you to this place you falsely thought a haven. More sorrow still awaits you—more than you can know—to show you what you are and what your children are. Damn Creon, if you will; damn the words I say. No man on earth will ever know the doom that waits for you.

OEDIPUS: How much of this am I to bear? Leave! Now! Leave my house!

TEIRESIAS: I would not be here had you not sent for me.

OEDIPUS: I never would have sent for you had I known the madness I would hear.

TEIRESIAS: To you, I am mad; but not to your parents ...

OEDIPUS: Wait! My parents? Who are my parents?

TEIRESIA: This day shall bring you birth *and* death.

OEDIPUS: Why must you persist with riddles?

TEIRESIAS: Are you not the best of men when it comes to riddles?

OEDIPUS: You mock the very skill that proves me great.

3. Epithet of Apollo. The term has been explained to mean "ambiguous" with reference to the nature of the god's oracles.

4. Mountain range southwest of Thebes, on the border of Attica and Boeotia (cf. map on p. 34).

TEIRESIAS: A great misfortune—which will destroy you.
OEDIPUS: I don't care. If I have saved this land, I do not care.
TEIRESIAS: Then I shall go. [*To his servant*] Come, take me home.
OEDIPUS: Yes, go home. You won't be missed.
TEIRESIAS: I will go when I've said all that I came to say. I am not
afraid of you. You cannot hurt me. And I tell you this: The man
you seek—the man whose death or banishment you ordered, the
man who murdered Laius—that man is here, passing as an alien,
living in our midst. Soon it will be known to all of you—he is a
native Theban. And he will find no joy in that discovery. His
eyes now see, but soon they will be blind: rich now, but soon a
beggar. Holding a scepter now, but soon a cane, he will grope for
the earth beneath him—in a foreign land. Both brother and
father to the children that he loves. Both son and husband to
the woman who bore him. Both heir and spoiler of his father's
bed and the one who took his life. Go, think on this. And if you
find the words I speak are lies, *then* say that I am blind.

(*Exeunt Oedipus, Teiresias*)

CHORUS:
Who is he? Who is the man?
Who is the man whom the voice of the Delphian shrine
denounced as the killer, the murderer,
the man who committed the terrible crime?
Where is he? Where is he now?
Let him run, let him flee!
Let him rush with the speed of the wind on his flight!
For with fire and lightning the god will attack,
and relentlessly fate will pursue him and haunt him
and drive him to doom.

Do you hear? Do you hear the command of the god?
From Parnassus[5] he orders the hunt.
In vain will the murderer hide,
in vain will he run,
in vain will he lurk in the forests and caves
like an animal roaming the desolate hills.
Let him flee to the edge of the world:
On his heels he will find
the command of the god!

Confusion and fear
have been spread by the prophet's words.
For I cannot affirm, yet I cannot refute
what he spoke. And I'm lost, I am lost—
What am I to believe?
Now foreboding is gripping my heart.

5. Mountain massif in central Greece, at the foot of which Delphi was lo- cated (cf. map on p. 34); sacred to Apollo.

Was there ever a strife between Laius and Polybus' house?[6]
Can I test? Can I prove?
Can I ever believe that the name of my king
has been soiled by a murder unknown?

It is Zeus and Apollo who know,
who can see the affairs of men.
But the seer and I,
we are mortal, and blind.
Who is right? Who can judge?
We are mortal, our wisdom assigned in degrees.
Does the seer know? Do I?
No, I will not believe in the prophet's charge
till the charge has been proved to my mind.
For I saw how the king
in the test with the Sphinx
proved his wisdom and worth
when he saved this city from doom.
No! I can *never* condemn the king!

(*Enter Creon*)

CREON: My fellow-citizens, anger has impelled me to come because
I have heard the accusation which Oedipus has brought against
me—and I will not tolerate it. If he thinks that I—in the midst
of this torment—I have thought to harm him in any way, I will
not spend the rest of my life branded by his charge. Doesn't he
see the implications of such slander? To you, to my friends, to
my city—I would be a traitor!
CHORUS: He spoke in anger—without thinking.
CREON: Yes—and who was it who said that the prophet lied on my
advice?
CHORUS: It was said, but I don't know how it was meant.
CREON: And was this a charge leveled by one whose eyes were
clear? Whose head was clear?
CHORUS: I don't know. I do not judge my master's actions. But
here he comes.

(*Enter Oedipus*)

OEDIPUS: Why have you come, Creon? Do you have the audacity
to show your face in my presence? Assassin! And now you would
steal my throne! What drove you to this plot? Did you see cow-
ardice in me? Stupidity? Did you imagine that I would not see
your treachery? Did you expect that I wouldn't act to stop you?
You fool! Your plot was mad! You go after a throne without
money, without friends! How do you think thrones are won?

6. Polybus was king of Corinth and foster-father of Oedipus.

CREON: You listen to me! And when you have heard me out, when you have heard the truth, *then* judge for yourself.

OEDIPUS: Ah yes, your oratory! I can learn nothing from that. This is what I have learned—you are my enemy!

CREON: Just let me say . . .

OEDIPUS: Say one thing—say that you are not a traitor.

CREON: If you think that senseless stubbornness is a precious gift, you are a fool.

OEDIPUS: If you think that you can threaten the house of Cadmus—your own house—and not pay for it, you are mad.

CREON: I grant you that. But tell me: just what is this terrible thing you say I have done to you?

OEDIPUS: Did you or did you not tell me to send for that—that—prophet?

CREON: I did. And I would again.

OEDIPUS: Then, how long since Laius . . .?

CREON: What? I do not follow . . .

OEDIPUS: . . . Disappeared?

CREON: A long time ago.

OEDIPUS: Your Teiresias—was he—was he a prophet then?

CREON: Yes—and just as honored and just as wise.

OEDIPUS: Did he ever mention me—then?

CREON: Not in my presence.

OEDIPUS: But didn't you investigate the murder?

CREON: Of course we did—

OEDIPUS: And why didn't the prophet say anything *then*?

CREON: I do not know. It's not for me to try to understand.

OEDIPUS: You know this much which you will try to tell me . . .

CREON: What is it? I will tell you if I can.

OEDIPUS: Just this: Had he not acted under your instructions, he would not have named *me* killer of Laius.

CREON: If this is what he said, you ought to know. You heard him. But now I claim the right to question you, as you have me.

OEDIPUS: Ask what you wish. I am not the murderer.

CREON: Then answer me. Did you marry my sister?

OEDIPUS: Of course I did.

CREON: And do you rule on equal terms with her?

OEDIPUS: She has all that she wants from me.

CREON: And am I not the third and equal partner?

OEDIPUS: You are—and that is where you have proved yourself a traitor.

CREON: Not true. Consider rationally, as I have done. First ask yourself—would any man prefer a life of fear to one in which the self-same rank, the self-same rights are guaranteed untroubled peace? I have no wish to be a king when I can act as one without a throne. And any man would feel the same, if he were wise. I share with you a king's prerogatives, yet you alone must face the danger lurking around the throne. If *I* were king, I would have to act in many ways against my pleasure. What added benefit could kingship hold when I have rank and rule without the threat of pain? I am not deluded—no, I would not look for honors beyond the ones which profit me. I have the favor of every man; each greets me first when he would hope to have *your* favor. Why should I exchange this for a throne? Only a fool would. No, I am not a traitor nor would I aid an act of treason. You want proof? Go to Delphi; ask if I have brought you the truth. Then, if you find me guilty of conspiracy with the prophet, command my death. I will face that. But do not condemn me without proof. You are wrong to judge the guilty innocent, the innocent guilty—without proof. Casting off a true friend is like casting off your greatest prize—your life. You will know in time that this is true. Time alone reveals the just; a single day condemns the guilty.

CHORUS: He is right, my Lord. Respect his words. A man who plans in haste will gamble the result.

OEDIPUS: This is a plot conceived in rashness. It must be met with quick response. I cannot sit and wait until the plot succeeds.

CREON: What will you do then? Do you intend to banish me?

OEDIPUS: No. No, not banish you. I want to see you *dead*—to make you an example for all aspiring to my throne.

CREON: Then you won't do as I suggest? You won't believe me?

OEDIPUS: You have not shown that you deserve belief.

CREON: No, because I see that you are mad.

OEDIPUS: In my own eyes, I am sane.

CREON: You should be sane in mine as well.

OEDIPUS: No. You are a traitor!

CREON: And what if you are wrong?

OEDIPUS: Still—I will rule.

CREON: Not when you rule treacherously.

OEDIPUS: O Thebes! My city! Listen to him!

CREON: *My* city too!

CHORUS: My Lords, no more. Here comes Jocasta. Perhaps the queen can end this bitter clash.

(Enter Jocasta)

JOCASTA: Why do you behave like senseless fools and quarrel without reason? Are you not ashamed to add trouble of your own when your city is sick and dying? Go, Creon. Go and leave us alone. Forget those petty grievances which you exaggerate. How important can they be?

CREON: This important, sister: Oedipus, your husband, in his insanity, has threatened me with banishment or death.

OEDIPUS: Yes, for I have realized his plot—a plot against my person.

CREON: May the gods haunt me forever, if that is true—if I am guilty of that charge.

JOCASTA: In the name of God, believe him, Oedipus! Believe him
for the sake of his oath, for my own sake, and for theirs!

CHORUS: Listen to her, my Lord. I beg you to consider and comply.

OEDIPUS: What would you have me do?

CHORUS: Respect the oath that Creon gave you. Respect his past
integrity.

OEDIPUS: Do you know what you are asking?

CHORUS: Yes, I know.

OEDIPUS: Then, tell me what you mean.

CHORUS: I mean that you are wrong to charge a friend who has
invoked a curse upon his head. You are wrong to slander without
proof and be the cause for his dishonor.

OEDIPUS: Then you must know that when you ask for this, you ask
for banishment or doom—for *me*.

CHORUS:
O God, no!
O Helios,[7] no!
May Heaven and Earth exact my doom
if that is what I thought!
When our city is torn by sickness
and my heart is torn with pain—
do not compound the troubles
that beset us!

OEDIPUS: Then, let him go, although it surely means my death—or
banishment with dishonor. *Your* words—not his—have touched
my heart. But Creon—wherever he may be—I will hate him.

CREON: You are hard when you should yield, cruel when you
should pity. Such natures deserve the pain they bear.

OEDIPUS: Just go—and leave me in peace.

CREON: I will go—my guilt pronounced by you alone. Behold my
judge and jury—Oedipus Tyrannus!

(Exit Creon)

CHORUS: My queen, persuade your husband to rest awhile.

JOCASTA: I will—when I have learned the truth.

CHORUS: Blind suspicion has consumed the king. And Creon's passions flared beneath the sting of unjust accusations.

JOCASTA: Are *both* at fault?

CHORUS: Yes, both of them.

JOCASTA: But what is the reason for their rage?

CHORUS: Don't ask again. Our city is weary enough from suffering.
Enough. Let the matter rest where it now stands.

OEDIPUS: Do you see what you have done? Do you see where you
have come—with your good intentions, your noble efforts to dull
the sharpness of my anger?

7. As god of the sun, he sees and hears   to as a witness of oaths.
everything and is, thus, often appealed

CHORUS:
My Lord, I have said before
and now I say again:
I would be mad,
a reckless fool
to turn away my king,
who saved us from a sea of troubles
and set us on a fairer course,
and who will lead us once again
to peace, a haven from our pain.

JOCASTA: In the name of Heaven, my Lord, tell me the reason for your bitterness.

OEDIPUS: I will—because you mean more to me than anyone. The reason is Creon and his plot against my throne.

JOCASTA: But can you *prove* a plot?

OEDIPUS: He says that I—Oedipus—bear the guilt of Laius' death.

JOCASTA: How does he justify this charge?

OEDIPUS: He does not stain his own lips by saying it. No. He uses that false prophet to speak for him.

JOCASTA: Then, you can exonerate yourself because no mortal has the power of divination. And I can prove it. An oracle came to Laius once from the Pythian priests—I'll not say from Apollo himself—that he would die at the hands of his own child, his child and mine. Yet the story which *we* heard was that robbers murdered Laius in a place where three roads meet. As for the child—when he was three days old, Laius drove pins into his ankles and handed him to someone to cast upon a deserted mountain path—to die. And so, Apollo's prophecy was unfulfilled— the child did not kill his father. And Laius' fears were unfulfilled —he did not die by the hand of his child. Yet, these had been the prophecies. You need not give them any credence. For the god will reveal what he wants.

OEDIPUS: Jocasta—my heart is troubled at your words. Suddenly, my thoughts are wandering, disturbed . . .

JOCASTA: What is it? What makes you so frightened?

OEDIPUS: Your statement—that Laius was murdered in a place where three roads meet. Isn't that what you said?

JOCASTA: Yes. That was the story then; that is the story now.

OEDIPUS: Where is this place where three roads meet?

JOCASTA: In the land called Phocis where the roads from Delphi and from Daulia converge.[8]

OEDIPUS: How long a time has passed since then?

JOCASTA: We heard it shortly before you came.

OEDIPUS: O God, what have you planned for me?

JOCASTA: What is it, Oedipus? What frightens you?

8. Phocis was a region in central Greece, in which Delphi was located; the city of Daulia was southeast of Mt. Parnassus (cf. map on p. 34).

OEDIPUS: Do not ask me. Do not ask. Just tell me—what was Laius like? How old was he?

JOCASTA: He was tall and his hair was lightly cast with silver tones, the contour of his body much like yours.

OEDIPUS: O God! Am I cursed and cannot see it?

JOCASTA: What is it, Oedipus? You frighten me.

OEDIPUS: It cannot be—that the prophet sees! Tell me one more thing.

JOCASTA: You frighten me, my Lord, but I will try to tell you what I know.

OEDIPUS: Who traveled with the king? Was he alone? Was there a guide? An escort? A few? Many?

JOCASTA: There were five—one of them a herald—and a carriage in which Laius rode.

OEDIPUS: O God! O God! I see it all now! Jocasta, who told you this?

JOCASTA: A servant—the only one who returned alive.

OEDIPUS: Is he here now? In our house?

JOCASTA: No. When he came back and saw you ruling where once his master was, he pleaded with me—begged me—to send him to the fields to tend the flocks, far from the city. And so I did. He was a good servant and I would have granted him more than that, if he had asked.

OEDIPUS: Could we arrange to have him here—now?

JOCASTA: Yes, but what do you want with him?

OEDIPUS: I am afraid, Jocasta. I have said too much and now I have to see him.

JOCASTA: Then he shall be brought. But I, too, must know the cause of your distress. I have the right to know.

OEDIPUS: Yes, you have that right. And I must tell you—now. You, more than anyone, will have to know what I am going through. My father was Polybus of Corinth, my mother a Dorian— Merope.[9] I was held in high regard in Corinth until—until something strange occurred—something uncanny and strange, although I might have given it too much concern. There was a man dining with us one day who had had far too much wine and shouted at me—half-drunk and shouting that I was not rightly called my father's son. I could barely endure the rest of that day and on the next I went to my parents and questioned them. They were enraged at the remark. I felt relieved at their response. But still, this—this thing—kept gnawing at my heart. And it was spread about in vulgar whispers. And then, without my parents' knowledge, I went to Delphi, but Apollo did not say what I had gone to hear. Instead, he answered questions I had not asked and told of horror and misery beyond belief—how I would know my mother's bed and bring to the world a race of

9. Corinth was a city in the northern Peloponnese on the Isthmus of Corinth; it was the home of Polybus and Merope, the foster-parents of Oedipus.

"Dorian" denotes association with the inhabitants of the Peloponnese and the Isthmus of Corinth.

children too terrible for men to see and cause the death of my own father. I trembled at those words and fled from Corinth—as far as I could—to where no star could ever guide me back, where I could never see that infamous prophecy fulfilled. And as I traveled, I came to that place where you say the king was murdered. This is the truth, Jocasta—I was in that place where the three roads meet. There was a herald leading a carriage drawn by horses and a man riding in the carriage—just as you described. The man in front, and the old one, ordered me out of the path. I refused. The driver pushed. In anger, I struck him. The old man saw it, reached for his lash and waited till I had passed. Then he struck me on the head. But he paid—oh yes, he paid. He lost his balance and fell from the carriage and as he lay there helpless—on his back—I killed him. I killed them all. But if this stranger had any tie with Laius—O God—who could be more hated in the eyes of Heaven and Earth? I am the one whom strangers and citizens are forbidden to receive! I am the one to whom all are forbidden to speak! I am the one who must be driven out! I am the one for whom my curse was meant! I have touched his bed with the very hands that killed him! O God! The sin! The horror! I am to be banished, never to see my people, never to walk in my fatherland. Or else I must take my mother for a bride and kill my father Polybus, who gave me life and cared for me. What cruel god has sent this torture? Hear me, you gods, you holy gods—I will never see that day! I will die before I ever see the stain of this abominable act!

CHORUS: Your words frighten us, my Lord. But you must have hope until you hear the story from the man who saw.

OEDIPUS: Yes—hope. My only hope is waiting for this shepherd.

JOCASTA: Why? What do you hope to find with him?

OEDIPUS: This—if his story agrees with what you say, then I am safe.

JOCASTA: What did I say that makes you sure of this?

OEDIPUS: You said he told of *robbers*—that *robbers* killed the king. If he still says *robbers*, then I am not the guilty one—because no man can talk of many when he means a single one. But if he names a *single* traveler, there will be no doubt—the guilt is mine.

JOCASTA: You can be sure that this was what he said—and he cannot deny it. The whole city heard him—not I alone. But even if he alters what he said before, he cannot prove that Laius met his death as it was prophesied. For Apollo said that he would die at the hand of a child—of mine. And as it happens, the child is dead. So prophecy is worthless. I wouldn't dignify it with a moment's thought.

OEDIPUS: You are right. But still—send someone for the shepherd. Now.

JOCASTA: I shall—immediately. I shall do what you ask. But now—let us go inside.

(Exeunt Oedipus, Jocasta)

CHORUS:
I pray, may destiny permit
that honestly I live my life
in word and deed.
That I obey the laws
the heavens have begotten
and prescribed.
Those laws created by Olympus,[1]
laws pure, immortal,
forever lasting, essence of the god
who lives in them.
On arrogance and pride
a tyrant feeds.
The goad of insolence,
of senseless overbearing, blind conceit,
of seeking things unseasonable,
unreasonable,
will prick a man to climb to heights
where he must lose his footing
and tumble to his doom.
Ambition must be used
to benefit the state;
else it is wrong, and God
must strike it from this earth.
Forever, God, I pray,
may you stand at my side!

A man who goes through life
with insolence in word and deed,
who lacks respect for law and right,
and scorns the shrines and temples of the gods,
may he find evil fate and doom
as his reward for wantonness,
for seeking ill-begotten gains
and reaching after sacred things
with sacrilegious hands.
No! Surely no such man
escapes the wrath, the vengeance of the god!
For if he did, if he could find reward
in actions which are wrong,
why should I trouble to acclaim,
to honor you, God, in my song?

No longer shall my feet
take me to Delphi's sacred shrine;

1. The highest mountain on the Greek peninsula (cf. map on p. 34), considered by the Greeks to be the home of the gods. By transference the term "Olympus" is applied to the sky or heaven.

no longer shall they Abae or Olympia's altars[2] seek
unless the oracles are shown to tell the truth
to mortals without fail!
Where are you, Zeus, all-powerful, all-ruling?
You must be told,
you must know in your all-pervading power:
Apollo's oracles now fall into dishonor,
and what the god has spoken about Laius
finds disregard.
Could God be dead?

(Enter Jocasta)

JOCASTA: My Lords, I want to lay these laurel wreaths and incense
offerings at the shrines of Thebes—for Oedipus is torturing himself, tearing his heart with grief. His vision to weigh the present
against the past is blurred by fear and terror. He devours every
word of dread, drinks in every thought of pain, destruction,
death. And I no longer have the power to ease his suffering. Now
I turn to you, Apollo, since you are nearest, with prayer and suppliant offerings. Find some way to free us, end our agony! O God
of Light, release us! You see the fear that grips us—like sailors
who watch their captain paralyzed by some unknown terror on
the seas.

(Enter Messenger 1)

MESSENGER 1: Strangers, would you direct me to the house of Oedi-
pus? Or if you know where I might find the king himself, please
tell me.
CHORUS: This is his house, stranger. He is inside. But this is the
queen—his wife, and mother of his children.
MESSENGER 1: Then, blessings on the house of Oedipus—his house,
his children, and his wife.
JOCASTA: Blessings on you as well, stranger. Your words are kind.
But why have you come? What is it?
MESSENGER 1: Good news, my lady—for your husband and your
house.
JOCASTA: What news? Where do you come from?
MESSENGER 1: From Corinth, my lady. My news will surely bring
you joy—but sorrow, too.
JOCASTA: What? How can that be?
MESSENGER 1: Your husband now is ruler of the Isthmus!
JOCASTA: Do you mean that Polybus of Corinth has been deposed?
MESSENGER 1: Deposed by death, my lady. He has passed away.

2. Abae was a city in central Greece
and Olympia a city in the western
Peloponnese, where there were important
oracles of Apollo and Zeus, respectively
(cf. map on p. 34).

JOCASTA: What! Polybus dead?

MESSENGER 1: I swear on my life that this is true.

JOCASTA (*to a servant*): Go! Quickly! Tell your master. (*To the heavens*) You prophecies—you divinely-uttered prophecies! Where do you stand now? The man that Oedipus feared, the man he dared not face lest he should be his killer—that man is dead! Time claimed his life—not Oedipus!

(Enter Oedipus)

OEDIPUS: Why, Jocasta? Why have you sent for me again?

JOCASTA: I want you to listen to this man. Listen to him and judge for yourself the worth of those holy prophecies.

OEDIPUS: Who is he? What news could he have for me?

JOCASTA: He comes from Corinth with the news that—that Polybus—is dead.

OEDIPUS: What! Tell me.

MESSENGER 1: If you must know this first, then I shall tell you—plainly. Polybus has died.

OEDIPUS: How? An act of treason? Sickness? How?

MESSENGER 1: My Lord, only a slight shift in the scales is required to bring the agèd to their rest.

OEDIPUS: Then it was sickness. Poor old man.

MESSENGER 1: Sickness—yes. And the weight of years.

OEDIPUS: Oh, Jocasta! Why? Why should we even look to oracles, the prophetic words delivered at their shrines or the birds that scream above us? They led me to believe that I would kill my father. But he is dead and in his grave, while I stand here—never having touched a weapon. Unless he died of longing for his son. If that is so, then I *was* the instrument of his death. And those oracles! Where are they now? Polybus has taken them to his grave. What worth have they now?

JOCASTA: Have I not been saying this all along?

OEDIPUS: Yes, you have. But I was misled by fear.

JOCASTA: Now you will no longer have to think of it.

OEDIPUS: But—my mother's bed. I still have *that* to fear.

JOCASTA: No. No, mortals have no need to fear when chance reigns supreme. The knowledge of the future is denied to us. It is better to live as you will, live as you can. You need not fear a union with your mother. Men often, in their dreams, approach their mothers' beds, lie with them, possess them. But the man who sees that this is meaningless can live without the threat of fear.

OEDIPUS: You would be right, Jocasta, if my mother were not alive. But she *is* alive. And no matter what you say, I have reason to fear.

JOCASTA: At least your father's death has brought some comfort.

OEDIPUS: Yes—some comfort. But my fear is of *her*—as long as she lives.

MESSENGER 1: Who is *she*? The woman you fear?

OEDIPUS: Queen Merope, old man, the wife of Polybus.

MESSENGER 1: But why does *she* instill fear in you?

OEDIPUS: There was an oracle—a dreadful oracle sent by the gods.

MESSENGER 1: Can you tell me—a stranger—what it is?

OEDIPUS: Yes, it is all right to tell. Once Loxian Apollo said that I would take my mother for my bride and murder my father with my own hands. This is the reason that I left Corinth long ago. Fortunately. And yet, I have often longed to see my parents.

MESSENGER 1: Is this the fear that drove you away from Corinth?

OEDIPUS: Yes. I did not want to kill my father.

MESSENGER 1: But I can free you from this fear, my Lord. My purpose for coming was a good one.

OEDIPUS: And I shall see that you receive a fitting reward.

MESSENGER 1: Yes—that's why I came. To fare well myself by your returning home.

OEDIPUS: Home? To Corinth? To my parents? Never.

MESSENGER 1: My son, you do not realize what you are doing.

OEDIPUS: What do you mean, old man? For God's sake, tell me what you mean.

MESSENGER 1: I mean—the reasons why you dread returning home.

OEDIPUS: I dread Apollo's prophecy—and its fulfillment.

MESSENGER 1: You mean the curse—the stain they say lies with your parents?

OEDIPUS: Yes, old man. That is the fear that lives with me.

MESSENGER 1: Then you must realize that this fear is groundless.

OEDIPUS: How can that be—if I am their son?

MESSENGER 1: Because Polybus was no relative of yours.

OEDIPUS: What are you saying! Polybus was *not* my father?

MESSENGER 1: No more than I.

OEDIPUS: No more than you? But you are nothing to me.

MESSENGER 1: He was not your father any more than I.

OEDIPUS: Then why did he call me his son?

MESSENGER 1: You were a gift to him—from me.

OEDIPUS: A gift? From you? And yet he loved me as his son?

MESSENGER 1: Yes, my Lord. He had been childless.

OEDIPUS: And when you gave me to him—had you bought me? Or found me?

MESSENGER 1: I found you—in the hills of Cithaeron.

OEDIPUS: What were you doing there?

MESSENGER 1: Tending sheep along the mountain side.

OEDIPUS: Then you were a—hired shepherd?

MESSENGER 1: Yes, my son—a hired shepherd who saved you at that time.

OEDIPUS: Saved me? Was I in pain when you found me? Was I in trouble?

MESSENGER 1: Yes, your ankles are the proof of that.

OEDIPUS: Ah, you mean this old trouble. What has that to do with it?

MESSENGER 1: When I found you, your ankles were pierced with rivets. And I freed you.

OEDIPUS: Yes, I have had this horrible stigma since infancy.

MESSENGER 1: And so it was the swelling in your ankles that caused your name: Oedipus—"Clubfoot."

OEDIPUS: Oh! Who did this to me? My father? Or my mother?

MESSENGER 1: I don't know. You will have to ask the man who handed you to me.

OEDIPUS: You mean—*you* did not find me? It was someone else?

MESSENGER 1: Another shepherd.

OEDIPUS: Who? Do you remember who he was?

MESSENGER 1: I think—he was of the house of Laius.

OEDIPUS: The king who ruled this city?

MESSENGER 1: Yes. He was a shepherd in the service of the king.

OEDIPUS: Is he still alive? Can I see him?

MESSENGER 1 (*addressing the Chorus*): You—you people here—could answer that.

OEDIPUS: Do any of you know this shepherd? Have you seen him in the fields? Here in Thebes? Tell me now! Now is the time to unravel this mystery—once and for all.

CHORUS: I think it is the shepherd you asked to see before. But the queen will know.

OEDIPUS: Jocasta, is that the man he means? Is it the shepherd we have sent for? Is *he* the one?

JOCASTA: Why? What difference does it make? Don't think about it. Pay no attention to what he said. It makes no difference.

OEDIPUS: No difference? When I must have every clue to untangle the line of mystery surrounding my birth?

JOCASTA: In the name of God, if you care at all for your own life, you must not go on with this. I cannot bear it any longer.

OEDIPUS: Do not worry, Jocasta. Even if I am a slave—a third-generation slave, it is no stain on your nobility.

JOCASTA: Oedipus! I beg you—don't do this!

OEDIPUS: I can't grant you that. I cannot leave the truth unknown.

JOCASTA: It is for *your* sake that I beg you to stop. For your own good.

OEDIPUS: My own good has brought me pain too long.

JOCASTA: God help you! May you never know what you are!

OEDIPUS: Go, someone, and bring the shepherd to me. Leave the queen to exult in her noble birth.

JOCASTA: God help you! This is all that I can say to you—now or ever.

(*Exit Jocasta*)

CHORUS: Why has the queen left like this—grief-stricken and tortured with pain? My Lord, I fear—I fear that from her silence some horror will burst forth.

OEDIPUS: Let it explode! I will still want to uncover the secret of my birth—no matter how horrible. She—she is a woman with a woman's pride—and she feels shame for my humble birth. But I am the child of Fortune—beneficent Fortune—and I shall not be shamed! She is my mother. My sisters are the months and they have seen me rise and fall. This is my family. I will never deny my birth—and I will learn its secret!

(Exit Oedipus)

CHORUS:
Ah Cithaeron,
if in my judgment I am right,
if I interpret what I hear correctly,
then—by Olympus' boundless majesty!—
tomorrow's full moon will not pass
before, Cithaeron, you will find
that Oedipus will honor you
as mother and as nurse!
That we will praise you in our song,
benevolent and friendly to our king.
Apollo, our Lord, may you find joy in this!

Who bore you, Oedipus? A nymph?
Did Pan[3] beget you in the hills?
Were you begotten by Apollo?
Perhaps so, for he likes the mountain glens.
Could Hermes[4] be your father?
Or Dionysus? Could it be
that he received you as a gift
high in the mountains from a nymph
with whom he lay?

(Enter Oedipus)

OEDIPUS: My Lords, I have never met him, but could that be the shepherd we have been waiting for? He seems to be of the same age as the stranger from Corinth. And I can see now—those are my servants who are bringing him here. But, perhaps you know—if you have seen him before. Is he the shepherd?

(Enter Shepherd)

CHORUS: Yes. I recognize him. He was a shepherd in the service of Laius—as loyal as any man could be.
OEDIPUS: Corinthian, I ask you—is this the man you mean?

---

3. A woodland god; patron of shepherds and flocks; usually represented as part man and part goat.

4. Son of Zeus and Maia; god of flocks and pastures.

MESSENGER 1: Yes, my Lord. This is the man.

OEDIPUS: And you, old man, look at me and answer what I ask. Were you in the service of Laius?

SHEPHERD: I was. But not bought. I was reared in his house.

OEDIPUS: What occupation? What way of life?

SHEPHERD: Tending flocks—for most of my life.

OEDIPUS: And where did you tend those flocks?

SHEPHERD: Sometimes Cithaeron, sometimes the neighboring places.

OEDIPUS: Have you ever seen this man before?

SHEPHERD: What man do you mean? Doing what?

OEDIPUS: This man. Have you ever met him before?

SHEPHERD: Not that I recall, my Lord.

MESSENGER 1: No wonder, my Lord. But I shall help him to recall. I am sure that he'll remember the time we spent on Cithaeron—he with his two flocks and I with one. Six months—spring to autumn—every year—for three years. In the winter I would drive my flocks to my fold in Corinth, and he to the fold of Laius. Isn't that right, sir?

SHEPHERD: That is what happened. But it was a long time ago.

MESSENGER 1: Then tell me this. Do you remember a child you gave me to bring up as my own?

SHEPHERD: What are you saying? Why are you asking me this?

MESSENGER 1: This, my friend, this—is that child.

SHEPHERD: Damn you! Will you keep your mouth shut!

OEDIPUS: Save your reproaches, old man. It is you who deserve them—your words deserve them.

SHEPHERD: But master—how have I offended?

OEDIPUS: By refusing to answer his question about the child.

SHEPHERD: He doesn't know what he's saying. He's crazy.

OEDIPUS: If you don't answer of your own accord, we'll make you talk.

SHEPHERD: No! My Lord, please! Don't hurt an old man.

OEDIPUS *(to the Chorus)*: One of you—twist his hands behind his back!

SHEPHERD: Why? Why? What do you want to know?

OEDIPUS: Did you or did you not give him that child?

SHEPHERD: I did. I gave it to him—and I wish that I had died that day.

OEDIPUS: You tell the truth, or you'll have your wish now.

SHEPHERD: If I tell, it will be worse.

OEDIPUS: Still he puts it off!

SHEPHERD: I said that I gave him the child!

OEDIPUS: Where did you get it? Your house? Someone else's? Where?

SHEPHERD: Not mine. Someone else's.

OEDIPUS: Whose? One of the citizens'? Whose house?

SHEPHERD: O God, master! Don't ask me any more.

OEDIPUS: This is the last time that I ask you.

SHEPHERD: It was a child—of the house of Laius.

OEDIPUS: A slave? Or of his own line?

SHEPHERD: Ah master, do I *have* to speak?

OEDIPUS: You have to. And I *have* to hear.

SHEPHERD: They said—it was his child. But the queen could tell you best.

OEDIPUS: Why? Did *she* give you the child?

SHEPHERD: Yes, my Lord.

OEDIPUS: Why?

SHEPHERD: To—kill!

OEDIPUS: Her own child!

SHEPHERD: Yes. Because she was terrified of some dreadful prophecy.

OEDIPUS: What prophecy?

SHEPHERD: The child would kill his father.

OEDIPUS: Then why did you give him to this man?

SHEPHERD: I felt sorry for him, master. And I thought that he would take him to his own home. But he saved him from his suffering—for worse suffering yet. My Lord, if you are the man he says you are—O God—you were born to suffering!

OEDIPUS: O God! O no! I see it now! All clear! O Light! I will never look on you again! Sin! Sin in my birth! Sin in my marriage! Sin in blood!

(Exit Oedipus)

CHORUS:

O generations of men, you are nothing!
You are nothing!
And I count you as not having lived at all!
Was there ever a man,
was there ever a man on this earth
who could say he was happy,
who knew happiness, true happiness,
not an image, a dream,
an illusion, a vision, which would disappear?
Your example, Oedipus,
your example, your fate, your disaster,
show that none of us mortals
ever knew, ever felt what happiness truly is.

Here is Oedipus,
fortune and fame and bliss
leading him by the hand,
prodding him on to heights
mortals had never attained.
Zeus, it was he who removed
the scourge of the riddling maid,
of the sharp-clawed, murderous Sphinx!
He restored me to life from the brink
of disaster, of doom and of death.

It was he who was honored and hailed,
who was crowned and acclaimed as our king.

Here is Oedipus:
Anyone on this earth
struck by a harder blow,
stung by a fate more perverse?
Wretched Oedipus!
Father and son alike,
pleasures you took from where
once you were given life.
Furrows your father ploughed
bore you in silence. How, how, oh how could it be?

Time found you out,
all-seeing, irrepressible time.
Time sits in judgment on
the union that never could be;
judges you, father and son,
begot and begetter alike.
Would that I never had
laid eyes on Laius' child!
Now I wail and I weep,
and my lips are drenched in lament.
It was you, who offered me life;
it is you, who now bring me death.

(*Enter Messenger 2*)

MESSENGER 2: O you most honored citizens of Thebes, you will
mourn for the things you will hear, you will mourn for the
things you will see, you will ache from the burden of sorrow—if
you are true sons of the house of Labdacus, if you care, if you
feel. The waters of Ister and Phasis[5] can never cleanse this house
of the horrors hidden within it and soon to be revealed—horrors
willfully done! Worst of the sorrows we know are those that are
willfully done!

CHORUS: We have mourned enough for sorrows we have known.
What more is there that you can add?

MESSENGER 2: One more and only one—Jocasta, the queen, is
dead.

CHORUS: O God—no! How?

MESSENGER 2: By her own hand. But the most dreadful pain you
have not seen. You have not seen the worst. I have seen it and I
shall tell you what I can of her terrible suffering. She ran in fren-
zied despair through the palace halls and rushed straight to her
bridal bed—her fingers clutching and tearing at her hair. Then,
inside the bedroom, she flung the doors closed and cried out to

5. The Ister (the lower Danube) was
considered by the Greeks the largest
river of Europe; the Phasis is a large
river originating in the Caucasus
mountain range and flowing into the
eastern portion of the Black Sea.

Laius, long since dead. She cried out to him, remembering the son that she had borne long ago, the son who killed his father, the son who left her to bear a dread curse—the children of her own son! She wept pitifully for that bridal bed which she had twice defiled—husband born of husband, child born of child. I didn't see what happened then. I didn't see her die. At that moment the king rushed in and shrieked in horror. All eyes turned to him as he paced in frantic passion and confusion. He sprang at each of us and begged to have a sword. He begged to know where he could find the wife that was no wife to him, the woman who had been mother to him and to his children. Some power beyond the scope of man held him in its sway and guided him to her. It was none of us. Then—as if someone had beckoned to him and bade him follow—he screamed in terror and threw himself against the doors that she had locked. His body's weight and force shattered the bolts and thrust them from their sockets and he rushed into the room. There we saw the queen hanging from a noose of twisted cords. And when the king saw her, he cried out and moaned in deep, sorrowful misery. Then he untied the rope that hung about her neck and laid her body on the ground. But what happened then was even worse. Her gold brooches, her pins—he tore them from her gown and plunged them into his eyes again and again and again and screamed, "No longer shall you see the suffering you have known and caused! You saw what was forbidden to be seen, yet failed to recognize those whom you longed to see! Now you shall see only darkness!" And as he cried out in such desperate misery, he struck his eyes over and over—until a shower of blood and tears splattered down his beard, like a torrent of crimson rain and hail. And now suffering is mingled with pain for man and wife for the sins that both have done. Not one alone. Once—long ago—this house was happy—and rightly so. But now—today—sorrow, destruction, death, shame—all torments that have a name—all, all are theirs to endure.

CHORUS: But the king—does he have any relief from his suffering now?

MESSENGER 2: He calls for someone to unlock the gates and reveal to Thebes his father's killer, his mother's—I can't say it. I cannot say this unholy word. He cries out that he will banish himself from the land to free this house of the curse that he has uttered. But he is weak, drained. There is no one to guide his way. The pain is more than he can bear. You will see for yourselves. The palace gates are opening. You will see a sight so hideous that even his most bitter enemy would pity him.

(Enter Oedipus)

CHORUS:
Ah!
Dread horror for men to see!

Most dreadful of all that I have seen!
Ah!
Wretched one,
what madness has possessed you?
What demon has descended upon you
and bound you to this dire fate?
Ah!
Wretched one,
I cannot bear to look at you.
I want to ask you more
and learn still more
and understand—
but I shudder at the sight of you!

OEDIPUS: Ah! Ah! Where has this misery brought me? Is this my own voice I hear—carried on the wings of the air? O Fate! What have you done to me?

CHORUS: Terrible! Too terrible to hear! Too terrible to see!

OEDIPUS: O cloud of darkness! Cruel! Driven by the winds of fate! Assaulting me! With no defense to hold you back! O God! The pain! The pain! My flesh aches from its wounds! My soul aches from the memory of its horrors!

CHORUS: Body and soul—each suffers and mourns.

OEDIPUS: Ah! You still remain with me—a constant friend. You still remain to care for me—a blind man now. Now there is darkness and I cannot see your face. But I can hear your voice and I know that you are near.

CHORUS: O my Lord, how could you have done this? How could you blind yourself? What demon drove you?

OEDIPUS: Apollo! It was Apollo! *He* brought this pain, this suffering to me. But it was my own hand that struck the blow. Not his. O God! Why should I have sight when all that I would see is ugliness?

CHORUS: It is as you say.

OEDIPUS: What is there for me to see and love? What sight would give me joy? What sound? Take me away! Take me out of this land! I am cursed! Doomed! I am the man most hated by the gods!

CHORUS: You have suffered equally for your fortune and for your disaster. I wish that you had never come to Thebes.

OEDIPUS: Damn the man who set me free! Who loosed the fetters from my feet and let me live! I never will forgive him. If he had let me die, I would never have become the cause—the grief . . .

CHORUS: I wish that it had been this way.

OEDIPUS: If it had been, I would not have come to this—killer of my father, bridegroom of the woman who gave me birth, despised by the gods, child of shame, father and brother to my children. Is there any horror worse than these—any horror that has not fallen upon Oedipus?

CHORUS: My Lord, I cannot condone what you have done. You would have been better dead than alive and blind.

OEDIPUS: I did what I had to. You know I did. No more advice. Could these eyes have looked upon my father in the house of Hades? Could these eyes have faced my mother in her agony? I sinned against them both—a sin no suicide could purge. Could I have joy at the sight of my children—born as they were born? With these eyes? Never! Could I look upon the city of Thebes? The turrets that grace her walls? The sacred statues of her gods? Never! Damned! I—the noblest of the sons of Thebes—I have damned myself. It was I who commanded that Thebes must cast out the one who is guilty, unholy, cursed by the heavenly gods. I was the curse of Thebes! Could these eyes look upon the people? Never! And if I could raise a wall to channel the fountain of my hearing, I would spare nothing to build a prison for this defiled body where sight and sound would never penetrate. Then only would I have peace—where grief could not reach my mind. O Cithaeron! Why did you receive me? Why did you not let me die then? Why did you let me live to show the world how I was born? O Polybus! O Corinth! My home that was no home! You raised me, thinking I was fair and never knowing the evil that festered beneath. Now—now see the evil from which I was born, the evil I have become. O God! The three roads! The hidden glen! The thickets! The pathway where three roads meet! The blood you drank from my hands—do you not know—it was the blood of my father! Do you remember? Do you remember what I did then and what I did for Thebes? Wedding-rites! You gave me birth and gave my children birth! Born of the same womb that bore my children! Father! Brother! Child! Incestuous sin! Bride! Wife! Mother! All of one union! All the most heinous sins that man can know! The most horrible shame—I can no longer speak of it. For the love of God, hide me somewhere. Hide me away from this land! Kill me! Cast me into the sea where you will never have to look at me again! I beg you—touch me—in my misery. Touch me. Do not be afraid. My sins are mine alone to bear and touch no other man.

(Enter Creon)

CHORUS: My Lord, Creon is here to act or counsel in what you ask. In your stead—he is now our sole protector.

OEDIPUS: What can I say to him? How can I ask for his trust? I have wronged him. I know that now.

CREON: I have not come to mock you, Oedipus, nor to reproach you for the past. But you—if you have no respect for men, at least respect the lord of the sun whose fires give life to men. Hide your naked guilt from his sight. No earth or sacred rain or light can endure its presence. *(To a servant)* Take him inside. It is impious for any but his own family to see and hear his suffering.

OEDIPUS: I ask you in the name of God to grant one favor. You have been kinder to me than I deserved. But one favor. I ask it for you—not for myself.

CREON: What do you ask of me?

OEDIPUS: Cast me out of this land. Cast me out to where no man can see me. Cast me out now.

CREON: I would have done so, you can be sure. But I must wait and do the will of the god.

OEDIPUS: He has signified his will—with clarity. Destroy the parricide! Destroy the unholy one! Destroy Oedipus!

CREON: That was the god's command, I know. But now—with what has happened—I think it better to wait and learn what we must do.

OEDIPUS: You mean that you would ask for guidance for a man so sorrowful as I?

CREON: Surely, you are ready to put your trust in the god—now.

OEDIPUS: Yes, I am ready now. But I ask this of you. Inside—she is lying inside—give her whatever funeral rites you wish. You will do the right thing for her. She is your sister. But for me—do not condemn this city—my father's city—to suffer any longer from my presence as long as I live. Let me go and live upon Cithaeron—O Cithaeron, your name is ever linked with mine! Where my parents chose a grave for me. Where they would have had me die. Where I shall die in answer to their wish. And yet, I know, neither sickness nor anything else will ever bring me death. For I would not have been saved from death that once. No—I was saved for a more dreadful fate. Let it be. Creon, do not worry about my sons. They are boys and will have all they need, no matter where they go. But my daughters—poor creatures! They never ate a single meal without their father. We shared everything together. Creon, take care of them. Creon, let me touch them one last time. And let me weep—one last time. Please, my Lord, please, allow it—you're generous, you're kind. If I could only touch them and feel that they are with me—as I used to—when I could see them. *(Enter Antigone and Ismene)* What is that crying? Is it my daughters? Has Creon taken pity on me? Has he sent my daughters to me? Are they here?

CREON: Yes, Oedipus, they are here. I had them brought to you. I know how much you love them, how much you have always loved them.

OEDIPUS: Bless you for this, Creon. Heaven bless you and grant you greater kindness than it has granted me. Ah, children, where are you? Come—come, touch my hands, the hands of your father, the hands of your brother, the hands that blinded these eyes which once were bright—these eyes—your father's eyes which neither saw nor knew what he had done when he became your father. I weep for you, my children. I cannot see you now. But when I think of the bitterness that waits for you in life, what

you will have to suffer—the festivals, the holidays—the sadness
you will know when you should share in gaiety! And when you
are old enough to marry—who will there be, who will be the
man strong enough to bear the slander that will haunt you—
because you are *my* children? What disgrace will you not know?
Your father killed his father. And lay with the woman that bore
him and his children. These are the taunts that will follow you.
And what man will marry you? No man, my children. You will
spend your lives unwed—without children of your own—barren
and wasted. Ah, Creon, you are the only father left to them.
We—their parents—are lost. We gave them life. And we are lost
to them. Take care of them. See that they do not wander poor
and lonely. Do not let them suffer for what I have done. Pity
them. They are so young. So lost. They have no one but you.
Take my hand and promise me. And oh, my children, if you
were older, I could make you understand. But now, make this
your prayer—to find some place where you can live and have a
better life than what your father knew.

CREON: Enough, my Lord. Go inside now.
OEDIPUS: Yes. I do not want to, but I will go.
CREON: All things have their time and their place.
OEDIPUS: I shall go—on this condition.
CREON: What condition? I am listening.
OEDIPUS: That you will send me away.
CREON: That is the god's decision, not mine.
OEDIPUS: The gods will not care where I go.
CREON: Then you shall have your wish.
OEDIPUS: Then—you consent?
CREON: It has nothing to do with my consent.
OEDIPUS: Let me go away from here.
CREON: Go then—but leave the children.
OEDIPUS: No! Do not take them away from me!
CREON: Do not presume that you are still in power. Your power has
not survived with you.
CHORUS:
There goes Oedipus—
he was the man who was able
to answer the riddle proposed by the Sphinx.
Mighty Oedipus—
he was an object of envy
to all for his fortune and fame.
There goes Oedipus—
now he is drowning in waves of dread and despair.
Look at Oedipus—
proof that none of us mortals
can truly be thought of as happy
until he is granted deliverance from life,
until he is dead
and must suffer no more.

GREECE

Only the locations which are pertinent to
the *Oedipus Tyrannus* appear on this map.

Passages from Ancient Authors

HOMER

The Odyssey

[Odysseus' Recollection] †

I saw the mother of Oedipos, lovely Epicaste,
Who did an enormous deed in the ignorance of her mind
And married her son. He slew his own father
And married her. The gods soon made these things known to men.
But he suffered pains in his much-beloved Thebes,
And ruled the Cadmeians through the destructive plans of the gods;
And she went to the place of the mighty gatekeeper Hades.
She hung up a high noose from the lofty roofbeam,
Possessed by her grief. For him she left many pains
Behind her, the kind a mother's Furies bring to pass.

THUCYDIDES

The Peloponnesian War

[The Plague in Athens] ‡

As soon as summer returned, the Peloponnesian army, comprising as before two-thirds of the force of each confederate state, under the command of the Lacedaemonian king Archidamus, the son of Zeuxidamus, invaded Attica, where they established themselves and ravaged the country. They had not been there many days when the plague broke out at Athens for the first time. A similar disorder is said to have previously smitten many places, particularly Lemnos, but there is no record of such a pestilence occurring elsewhere, or of so great a destruction of human life. For a while physicians, in ignorance of the nature of the disease, sought to apply remedies; but it was in vain, and they themselves were among the first victims, because they oftenest came into contact with it. No human art was of any avail, and as to supplications in temples, enquiries of oracles, and the like, they were utterly useless, and at last men were overpowered by the calamity and gave them all up.

† From Homer, *The Odyssey*, a new verse translation by Albert Cook (New York: W. W. Norton & Company, Inc., 1967), p. 152. Copyright © 1967 by Albert Cook. Reprinted by permission of the publisher.

‡ From Thucydides, *The Peloponnesian War*, Book 2, chapters 47–52, in *The Greek Historians*, ed. by Francis R. B. Godolphin (New York: Random House, 1942), vol. 1, pp. 653–656. Reprinted by permission.

The disease is said to have begun south of Egypt in Aethiopia; thence it descended into Egypt and Libya, and after spreading over the greater part of the Persian empire, suddenly fell upon Athens. It first attacked the inhabitants of the Piraeus, and it was supposed that the Peloponnesians had poisoned the cisterns, no conduits having as yet been made there. It afterwards reached the upper city, and then the mortality became far greater. As to its probable origin or the causes which might or could have produced such a disturbance of nature, every man, whether a physician or not, will give his own opinion. But I shall describe its actual course, and the symptoms by which any one who knows them beforehand may recognize the disorder should it ever reappear. For I was myself attacked, and witnessed the sufferings of others.

The season was admitted to have been remarkably free from ordinary sickness; and if anybody was already ill of any other disease, it was absorbed in this. Many who were in perfect health, all in a moment, and without any apparent reason, were seized with violent heats in the head and with redness and inflammation of the eyes. Internally the throat and the tongue were quickly suffused with blood, and the breath became unnatural and fetid. There followed sneezing and hoarseness; in a short time the disorder, accompanied by a violent cough, reached the chest; then fastening lower down, it would move the stomach and bring on all the vomits of bile to which physicians have ever given names; and they were very distressing. An ineffectual retching producing violent convulsions attacked most of the sufferers; some as soon as the previous symptoms had abated, others not until long afterwards. The body externally was not so very hot to the touch, nor yet pale; it was of a livid colour inclining to red, and breaking out in pustules and ulcers. But the internal fever was intense; the sufferers could not bear to have on them even the finest linen garment; they insisted on being naked, and there was nothing which they longed for more eagerly than to throw themselves into cold water. And many of those who had no one to look after them actually plunged into the cisterns, for they were tormented by unceasing thirst, which was not in the least assuaged whether they drank little or much. They could not sleep; a restlessness which was intolerable never left them. While the disease was at its height the body, instead of wasting away, held out amid these sufferings in a marvellous manner, and either they died on the seventh or ninth day, not of weakness, for their strength was not exhausted, but of internal fever, which was the end of most; or, if they survived, then the disease descended into the bowels and there produced violent ulceration; severe diarrhoea at the same time set in, and at a later stage caused exhaustion, which finally with few exceptions carried them off. For the disorder which had originally settled in the head passed gradually through the whole body, and, if a person got over the worst, would often seize the extremities and leave its mark, attacking the genitals and the fingers and the toes; and some escaped with the loss of these, some with the loss of their eyes. Some again had no sooner recovered than they were seized with a forgetfulness of all things and knew neither themselves nor their friends.

The malady took a form not to be described, and the fury with which it fastened upon each sufferer was too much for human nature to endure. There was one circumstance in particular which distinguished it from ordinary diseases. The birds and animals which feed on human flesh, although so many bodies were lying unburied, either never came near them, or died if they touched them. This was proved by a remarkable disappearance of the birds of prey, who were not to be seen either about the bodies or anywhere else; while in the case of the dogs the fact was even more obvious, because they live with man.

Such was the general nature of the disease: I omit many strange peculiarities which characterised individual cases. None of the ordinary sicknesses attacked any one while it lasted, or, if they did, they ended in the plague. Some of the sufferers died from want of care, others equally who were receiving the greatest attention. No single remedy could be deemed a specific; for that which did good to one did harm to another. No constitution was of itself strong enough to resist or weak enough to escape the attacks; the disease carried off all alike and defied every mode of treatment. Most appalling was the despondency which seized upon any one who felt himself sickening; for he instantly abandoned his mind to despair and, instead of holding out, absolutely threw away his chance of life. Appalling too was the rapidity with which men caught the infection; dying like sheep if they attended on one another; and this was the principal cause of mortality. When they were afraid to visit one another, the sufferers died in their solitude, so that many houses were empty because there had been no one left to take care of the sick; or if they ventured they perished, especially those who aspired to heroism. For they went to see their friends without thought of themselves and were ashamed to leave them, even at a time when the very relations of the dying were at last growing weary and ceased to make lamentations, overwhelmed by the vastness of the calamity. But whatever instances there may have been of such devotion, more often the sick and the dying were tended by the pitying care of those who had recovered, because they knew the course of the disease and were themselves free from apprehension. For no one was ever attacked a second time, or not with a fatal result. All men congratulated them, and they themselves, in the excess of their joy at the moment, had an innocent fancy that they could not die of any other sickness.

The crowding of the people out of the country into the city aggravated the misery; and the newly arrived suffered most. For, having no houses of their own, but inhabiting in the height of summer stifling huts, the mortality among them was dreadful, and they perished in wild disorder. The dead lay as they had died, one upon another, while others hardly alive wallowed in the streets and crawled about every fountain craving for water. The temples in which they lodged were full of the corpses of those who died in them; for the violence of the calamity was such that men, not knowing where to turn, grew reckless of all law, human and divine. The customs which had hitherto been observed at funerals were universally violated, and they buried their dead each one as best he could. Many, having no proper appliances, because the deaths in their household had been so frequent, made no scruple of using the burial-place of others. When one man had raised a funeral pile, others would come, and throwing on their dead first, set fire to it; or when some other corpse was already burning, before they could be stopped would throw their own dead upon it and depart.

EURIPIDES

The Phoenician Women

[Jocasta's Prologue]†

Jocasta
You who cut your way through heaven's stars,
riding the chariot with its welded gold,
Sun, with your swift mares whirling forth our light,
evil the shaft you sent to Thebes that day
when Cadmus came here, leaving Phoenicia's shore,
he who wed Cypris' child, Harmonia,
fathering Polydorus, who in turn
had Labdacus, they say, and he had Laius.
Now I am known as daughter of Menoeceus,
Creon my brother by the selfsame mother,
my name Jocasta, as my father gave it,
Laius my husband. When he still was childless
after long marriage with me in the palace,
he went to Phoebus asking and beseeching

† From Euripides' *The Phoenician Women*, translated by Elizabeth Wyckoff, in *The Complete Greek Tragedies*, Vol. 5, Euripides, edited by David Greene and Richmond Lattimore (Chicago: The University of Chicago Press, 1959). Reprinted by permission of the publisher.

that we might share male children for the house.
But he said, "Lord of Thebes and its famed horses,
sow not that furrow against divine decree.
For if you have a child, him you beget
shall kill you, and your house shall wade through blood."
But Laius, in his lust, and drunk beside,
begot a child on me, yet when he had,
knowing his sex was sin, as God had said it,
he gave the child to shepherds to expose
in Hera's field, high on Cithaeron's rock,
when he had pinned its ankles with sharp iron
(and this is why Greece called it Oedipus).
Then Polybus' herdsman-riders took the child
and brought it home and gave it to their mistress.
She took my labor's fruit to her own breast
and told her husband that it was her own.
When his red beard was growing, my young son,
who had guessed or heard the truth, set off to learn,
at Phoebus' house, his parents. So did Laius,
seeking to learn if the child he had exposed
were still alive. They met in middle journey
at the same spot in the split road of Phocis.
Then Laius' runner ordered him away:
"Stranger, yield place to princes." But he came on,
silent, in pride. So with their sharp-edged hooves
the mares of Laius bloodied up his feet.
And so—why give the detail of disaster?—
son slew his father, and he took the team
to give to Polybus, his foster parent.
When the Sphinx bore down our city with her raids,
my husband gone, Creon proclaimed my marriage:
whoever might guess the clever maiden's riddle,
to him I should be wed. And so it happened.
It was Oedipus, my son, who guessed her song.
So he became the ruler of this land
and got the scepter of this realm as prize.
The wretch, unknowing, wedded with his mother;
nor did she know she bedded with her son.
And to my son I bore two further sons,
Eteocles and mighty Polyneices,
and daughters two. Her father named Ismene
while I before had named Antigone.
When Oedipus learned I was his wife and mother,
he had endured all suffering, and he struck
with terrible gory wounding his own eyes,
bleeding the pupils with a golden brooch.
When his sons' beards had grown, they shut him up
behind the bolts that this fate might be forgotten
which needs too much intelligence to explain it.

There in the house he lives, and struck by fate
he calls unholy curses on his children.
They shall divide this house with sharpened steel.
They were afraid that if they lived together
the gods might grant his prayers. So they agreed
that Polyneices should go, a willing exile,
while Eteocles stayed in this land and held the scepter,
to change though, year by year. Yet when Eteocles
sat safe on high, he would not leave the throne,
but keeps his brother exiled from this land.
He went to Argos, married Adrastus' daughter,
and brings the Argive force he has collected
against these very seven-gated walls,
seeking his share of the land, and his father's scepter.
I have persuaded son to come to son
under a truce before they take to arms.
I hope for peace. The messenger says he'll come.
O Zeus who lives in heaven's shining folds
save me and let my sons be reconciled.
If you are wise you should not leave a mortal
constantly wretched throughout all of life.

Religion and Psychology: Some Studies

MARTIN P. NILSSON

[The Origin of the Oedipus Myth]†

The Theban cycles were treated in post-Homeric epics of which we have some slight knowledge and were especially taken up and favored by the great tragic poets. The chief figure is Oedipus. Professor Robert has treated his myths exhaustively and has given a model piece of mythographical research in his great work *Oidipus*; here we must try to get behind the traditional myths and see what their origin and their connections with the Mycenaean age may be. I cannot share Professor Robert's opinion that Oedipus is an old depossessed god.[1] From the fact that three of the tombs and cult places ascribed to Oedipus are certainly late, Professor Robert draws the conclusion that the fourth, the tomb at Eteonus in Boeotia, was the original and old one. Oedipus is, however, no old vegetation god but simply a *Märchen*-hero, a folk-tale personage who, by vanquishing the sphinx won the hand of the queen and the kingdom, although this simple and common motif was complicated by the addition of a great many others. That his name is a descriptive one, corroborates this view. Such a mythical personage has of course no tomb; even that at Eteonus is a late creation.[2] Nor can I side with Professor Rose who takes Oedipus to be a historical personage, a prince who had been exposed as a child and who at the head of a Corinthian army conquered Thebes, slew King Laius, and wedded Queen Epikaste, his mother.[3] He fully recognizes the folk-tale elements but thinks that Oedipus is a nickname. In view of the fact that it is one of the few characteristic *Märchen* names in Greek mythology, I am persuaded that the origin of Oedipus is to be found not in history but in folk-tales.

The myth was localized at Thebes; consequently Oedipus became king of Thebes and was inserted in the genealogy of the kingly Theban house. A detailed analysis of the Oedipus cycle is out of place here, but I am bound to point to certain circumstances of importance for our subject. To begin with I remark that the

---

† From Martin P. Nilsson, *The Mycenaean Origin of Greek Mythology* (Berkeley: University of California Press, 1932, and New York: W. W. Norton & Co., Inc., 1963), pp. 102–106. Reprinted by permission of The Regents of the University of California.
1. C. Robert, *Oidipus*, I (1915), p. 44 *et seq*. For a criticism see L. R. Farnell, *Greek Hero Cults* (1921), p. 332 *et seq*.

2. Cp. my review of Robert's book in *Göttingischer gelehrter Anzeiger* (1922), pp. 36 *et seq*.
3. H. J. Rose, *Modern Methods in Classical Mythology* (St. Andrews, 1930), p. 24 *et seq*. An analysis from the point of view of folk-tale motifs is made by S. Luria in *Raccolta di scritti in onore di F. Ramorino* (1930), p. 289 *et seq*. I· prefer to leave the treasure of Thisbe out of account.

45

reception of folk-tale motifs in this cycle, just as, e.g., in the Perseus cycle, shows its popularity and age.

Concerning the ancestors of Oedipus a few words will suffice. His grandfather Labdacus is an empty name, and if the guess deriving his name from the name of the letter, *labda,* Λ, hits the mark, he is of very late origin. On the other hand, the myth in its developed form implies an important rôle for Oedipus' father.

If the myth of Oedipus told only that he guessed the riddle of the sphinx, or simply that he slew her and in reward won the hand of the queen and with her the kingdom, it would have been a very simple folk-tale of a well-known kind. But other motifs were added, drawn from the conflicts in family and ethical life of an early people: the queen was his mother and the man he slew his father. The addition of these motifs created the real Oedipus myth and its essential greatness. In a later chapter [4] we shall treat the naming of the mythical personages and we shall see that the name Oedipus belongs to a class of names, rare in Greek mythology but of frequent occurrence in folk-tales, in which the hero's name is descriptive of certain peculiar characteristics which he possesses. Oedipus signifies "the man with the swollen feet." The formation of the name is of great antiquity, showing a kind of derivation which was obsolete in the Greek language of the historic age.[5] The feature that his feet were pierced, though irrational as has been said, is bound up with the story that as a newborn child he was exposed to die, but was saved, and when grown up was recognized by his parents. This motif is on the other hand essential only in connection with the myth telling that Oedipus married his mother. That is to say, in this case, because of the formation of the name, we are able to state that the tale of the exposure of Oedipus and of his marrying his mother was joined in an age which long preceded the historical age with the folk-tale of the young man who by guessing the riddle of the sphinx won the queen and the kingdom. I confidently ascribe the origin of this myth complex to the Mycenaean age.

Folk-tales have a logic of their own which sometimes is rather penetrating, though it may seem puzzling to us. When it was asked

---

4. See below pp. 189 *et seq.*

5. H. Petersson in my above-quoted (p. 103 n. 8) review, p. 45. I repeat Petersson's convincing argument: It is evident that the first compound part of Οἰδίπους is connected with the stem in οἰδάω, οἰδέω, but the difficulty consisting in the difference of vowels (ι instead of α, ε) has not been overcome. There exists, however, a type of corresponding words and compounds such as κυδρός and Κυδιάνειρα, and this type is found in Sanskrit and Old Persian also. (See J. Wackernagel, "Vermischte Beiträge zur griech. Sprachkunde," *Programm* zur Rektoratsfeier der Universi-

tät Basel (1897), p. 8 *et seq.*) If we suppose that a Greek adjective *οἰδρός once existed, the formation of the name Οἰδίπους falls in with this type, and the existence of this adjective may be assumed with much probability, formations corresponding to it being found in other languages; e.g., Old German *eitar,* "poison," from Old Teutonic *aitra,* "Venomous tumor;" Indo-eur. *oid-ro,* Lettish *idra,* "rotten marrow of a tree." Cp. P. Kretschmer, in *Glotta* XII (1923), p. 59, but I cannot approve of his chthonic interpretation of Oedipus.

how the queen became a widow, the myth answered by applying another motif of the same kind: Oedipus had without knowing it killed his father. Thus the terrific logic of events was still more emphasized. The slaying of his father is not so essential for the myth and may have been added later; but this motif also is certainly very old,[6] and with it the cycle is established in all its essential parts. Other features are more loosely bound up with it and must be passed over here.[7] The history of Greek literature proves that this myth was perhaps the most dramatic of all Greek myths. I venture to think that in its essential parts it was already created in the Mycenaean age and attached to Thebes. The reasons for its localization at Thebes we are of course unable to discover or to guess—they may have been quite fortuitous, as often happens in localizing current tales—but a necessary condition for the recognition of this localization was that Thebes in this age was a famous town.

MEYER FORTES

[Oedipus and Job]†

Frazer on Fate

It has been said that poets can be divided into two classes. There are those who write for other poets; and there are those who write for the common reader. Anthropologists can be similarly classified. There are the purists by conviction or by habit who write only for their professional peers, and there are the anthropologists of the forum and the market-place who address themselves to the world at large. But there are also a few who seem equally at home in both worlds; and among these Sir James Frazer was and remains without rival. His influence on the progressive thought of his time is a by-word, and his writings are still held in respect bordering on awe outside professional anthropological circles. Why then has his influence among his professional successors declined in recent years? Chiefly, I think, because he was not only a great anthropologist and a man of letters, but also a moralist whose zeal in spreading enlightenment too often got the better of his scholarly judgement. That glittering prose hides too many rash conjectures. The hypotheses paraded with so much learning turn out to be little more than de-

6. The earliest mention is found in the Nekyia, *Od.*, xi. v. 273.
7. Cp. my above-quoted (p. 103, n. 8) review.
† From Meyer Fortes, *Oedipus and Job*

in West African Religion. (Cambridge, England: Cambridge University Press, 1959), pp. 7–18. Reprinted by permission of the publisher.

scriptive labels for customs and institutions; and the historical and psychological speculations used to eke them out seem naïve today. The smug contempt for the exotic beliefs and customs paraded with such gusto, and contrasted disparagingly with the 'civilized mind', repels us. Modern anthropology has largely grown away from Frazer; or rather it has outgrown him.

Yet, sooner or later, every serious anthropologist returns to the great Frazerian *corpus*. For beneath the encrustations of theory, speculation, and prejudice due to the climate of thought in which Frazer lived, there is a vision of mankind which still offers inspiration. It is a vision that takes in the whole of mankind. There lies its greatness. It shows in assiduous detail how varied and diverse are the customs and institutions of mankind. But its purpose is to bring home to us the unity behind the diversity. For Frazer this lay in supposed historical connexions or common mental habits and dispositions. Fallacious though his theories now prove to be, in principle he was right. There are uniformities and common patterns in the customs and institutions of mankind; and if we want to understand them we must take into account the common intellectual and emotional dispositions of mankind.

It would not have seemed strange to Frazer to place side by side Oedipus, Job, and the religious beliefs of a West African tribe of ancestor worshippers, as I propose to do. But what he was interested in when he lumped together, as he habitually did, the customs of the Greeks and the Hebrews, other peoples of antiquity and contemporary primitive and Oriental societies, was their most superficial descriptive features. To take an instance at random, Orestes the matricide, recovering sanity by biting off a finger, is quoted in the same breath as blood avengers among American Indians, Maori, and Africans who have to taste the blood of their victims in order to lay their ghosts.[1] That is what our informants tell us; but to see no more in these customs than diverse expressions of a fear of ghosts which acts as a curb on would-be murderers is, from today's standpoint, almost ludicrous. What is significant for us in the Orestes story is that he murdered a *kinswoman*, that this kinswoman was his *mother*, and that his expiation was to mutilate himself by *biting off a finger*. To go to such an extreme merely to taste his own blood would have been silly. The parallels that leap to mind, for an anthropologist today, are other apparently irrational mutilations of the body carried out in the context of an overt or suppressed conflict between successive generations. We think of the strange story of Moses' wife Zipporah circumcising her son with a flint to save him from being killed by Yahweh, and more particularly of the very widespread association of circumcision and other

1. J. G. Frazer, *Psyche's Task* (1913), p. 56.

forms of mutilation with the initiation of youths and maidens into adulthood.

In short, we should now use the Orestes story not as one of a miscellany of examples to illustrate a particular kind of barbarous superstition, but as a model, or paradigm, from which we might be able to derive principles applicable in other cases.

In the same way Oedipus and Job both turn up in Frazer's *Folklore in the Old Testament*, but simply to illustrate widespread 'superstitious' customs. Job is cited, curiously enough, in evidence for the statement that in the Old Testament it is the blood of a murdered man, not his ghost, which cries out for vengeance, the reference being to Job's 'appealing against the injustice of his fate ... "O earth, cover not my blood, and let my cry have no resting place"'.[2] As for Oedipus, he appears as a parallel to the story of Moses in the ark of bullrushes. He is one of the many examples of the hero who was 'exposed at birth, and was only rescued from imminent death by what might seem to vulgar eyes an accident, but what really proved to be the finger of Fate interposed to preserve the helpless babe for the high destiny that awaited him. . . .'[3]

Fate, or Destiny, is the main theme of this essay. It is mentioned in many places in Frazer's writings, and invariably in the manner I have described. There is no attempt to analyse the notion of Fate as a category of religious or philosophic thought. It is treated like any other customary belief—a belief in ghosts or in lucky and unlucky omens or in magical charms to fend off supernatural threats.

Supposing, however, that we consider the stories of Oedipus and Job from an analytical rather than a descriptive point of view. What is notable then is that they epitomize, poignantly and dramatically, two religious and ethical conceptions that seem to be mutually opposed in some respects but complementary in others. These ideas are associated with different cosmological doctrines about the universe, and different conceptions of the nature of man and his relations with supernatural powers. I think that they represent, in a clear paradigmatic form, two fundamental principles of religious thought and custom. The Oedipal principle is best summed up in the notion of Fate or Destiny, the Jobian principle in that of Supernatural Justice.

Now I am not suggesting that the whole religious system of Greece of the fifth century B.C. can be reduced to what is represented in the story of Oedipus, or that the drama of Job contains the whole of Old Testament Hebrew religion. I am concerned only with the specific conceptions embodied in the two stories.

2. Frazer, *Folklore in the Old Testament* (1918 ed.), vol. I, p. 101.   3. *Ibid.*, vol. II, pp. 438–46.

50 · Meyer Fortes

Oedipus and Job as Paradigms

The myth of Oedipus is best known to us from the Theban plays of Sophocles; and what gives these plays their tragic intensity is not the horror they arouse of patricide and incest but the 'sense of the blindness and helplessness of mankind'[4] which, as Mr Lucas notes, they convey. The catastrophe which overwhelms Oedipus is due, Mr Lucas adds, to causes that 'lie hid deep in the nature of god and man', not to any faults of his. On the contrary, he is a man of virtuous and noble character choosing self-imposed exile rather than risk slaying his supposed father, a just and benevolent king, a faithful husband and devoted father. And he has one further quality which in the end proves his downfall: his resolute pursuit of the truth. When he discovers the truth about his birth and marriage, he can only bear to live by blinding himself and so blotting out the intolerable knowledge. For his sins are so infamous that not even death could atone for them.

But it is not just a matter of his having committed them unwittingly. It is as if his actions have been thrust upon him, or he driven into them, by some agency operating outside the bounds of human knowledge and unresponsive to human conduct. He is the victim of Destiny. The question of responsibility or guilt does not even seem relevant. Much later, when as an old man he is preparing for death, in the *Oedipus Coloneus*, the question does come up and he asserts his innocence. It was an appalling Fate and not his own choosing.

The part played by the concept of Fate, which is the usual translation of the Greek word *Moira*, in early Greek religion has been much discussed by classical scholars.[5] It was clearly a very complex notion, but our authorities seem to be agreed that its original meaning was 'portion' or 'lot'. Furthermore, it seems to have had two aspects. One was the idea of Fate as an impersonal power representing the necessity and justice of the 'disposition of Nature', as Professor Dodds puts it, and supreme over both gods and men. The other was its reference to the individual. Each person is conceived of as having a particular apportionment of good and evil for his lifetime which is decided at birth; and 'this luck', to quote Professor Dodds again, 'is not conceived as an extraneous accident—it is as much part of a man's natal endowment as beauty or talent'. This is the aspect most conspicuous in the Oedipus myth. But we see there also that an individual's fate is in part determined by the fate of his parents and in turn affects that of his offspring. Profes-

4. D. W. Lucas, *The Greek Tragic Poets* (1950), pp. 133 ff. 5. E. R. Dodds, *The Greeks and the Irrational* (1951).

sor Dodds relates this to the idea, very familiar to anthropologists from its occurrence in most primitive societies, that a son's life is the 'prolongation of his father's life'. By the laws of filiation and descent, a son who inherits his father's position in society *ipso facto* inherits both his material property and debts and his moral and ritual property and debts. Normally, however, filial succession is a deliberate and willing act. When Fate steps in, as with Oedipus, it occurs by blind and to some extent vainly resisted compulsion.

There is a similarity here to the notion of witchcraft. Fate, like witchcraft, is an involuntary force and can, in the last resort, only be known in retrospect. This in itself generates efforts to discover it in advance and so to try to control it. Hence the appeal to oracles. But the oracles do not in fact enable men to master their fate. As with witchcraft, they merely help to reconcile men to its ineluctability. It is best of all, really, to accept this and not to seek arrogantly to probe destiny.

Job confronts us with a wholly different conception of man and of morality. There is no suggestion here of inscrutable influences ruling the course of an individual's life from the moment of his birth. The good and evil that accrue to a man during his lifetime are the rewards and punishments meted out by an omnipotent, personified God. But God does not act arbitrarily or capriciously. He is, as Pedersen points out, bound by a covenant with his creature, man. It is almost a contractual relationship, in which God is bound to act justly and mercifully, and man is free to choose between righteousness and sin. There is a known code of righteous conduct, and a man who has consistently followed the way of righteousness is entitled to well-being, peace of mind, happiness, and even material prosperity as a gift from the Supreme Ruler of the universe. Hence Job rejects the arguments and consolations of his friends. He will not admit that his afflictions are due to his having sinned, however inadvertently. He even feels entitled to demand of God 'shew me wherefore thou contendest with me',[6] and spurns the advice of his comforters to admit his guilt and recover his happiness by asking God's pardon.

It should be emphasized that all the characters in the story believe that God is just, that the righteous man must therefore prosper, and that 'the triumphing of the wicked is short'.[7] The question is whether Job's confidence in his own righteousness is justified or whether his calamities are evidence of unadmitted sin. And there is a still deeper question. Even if Job is justified in denying that he is wicked, does righteousness, as understood in terms of human conduct, create claims on God? Is not God all-powerful so

6. Job x. 2.   7. Job xx. 5.

that he stands above all human norms of good and bad conduct and is not bound by a concept of justice founded on a rule of reciprocal obligation? For God is not only the creator of the universe but the very source of righteousness and justice. And this is the gist of God's speech in the magnificent thirty-eighth to fortieth chapters. Man is not God's equal, and however virtuous he may feel himself to be, he cannot measure himself against God to disannul God's judgement and condemn Him in order to justify himself.

It is when he realizes the import of this speech that Job is saved. He does not admit guilt in the sense of responsibility for actions that are wicked by ordinary human standards. What he admits is having placed himself on a footing of equality with God, judging for himself what conduct is righteous and what wicked. This wrong relationship was his sin. He accepts, as he has not previously done, the omnipotence of God and his own dependence on Him. Job's God is a majestic and all-powerful father-figure, the source of his creatures' life, and in virtue of that vested with final authority over them; and reciprocally—as Job constantly pleads—with responsibility for their well-being and happiness. What Job has to learn is that God's authority is ultimate, inexplicable, not subject to coercion by obedience to rules of righteousness nor bound by contracts. Job's sufferings are like severe measures of discipline that a father might use to correct a son who, while exemplary in his conduct, was getting too big for his boots and arrogating to himself a status equal to his father's; and Job's salvation might be compared to the son's realizing and accepting his filial dependence. This means accepting paternal authority without resentment and seeing it as always benevolent in intention, even when it is used punitively. This is the essence of filial piety, and Job had been on the brink of acting in defiance of it.

GORDON M. KIRKWOOD

Oracles and Dramaturgy†

We are here interested in oracles primarily from the point of view of their place in the organization of Sophocles' plays. When so considered they deserve a place close to the matters discussed in the preceding section; they are, in fact, a special branch of the technique that we noticed there. We cannot, however, entirely overlook the possible religious element in Sophocles' use of oracles

† From Gordon M. Kirkwood, *A Study of Sophoclean Drama* (Ithaca: Cornell University Press, 1958), pp. 72–82.

and the effect that this element may have upon his plays.

Oracles, perhaps not all of them but at least all that we find in Sophocles, may be divided into three categories. They may be ways of presenting truths about the conditions of life or about human character in a way that has a religious coloring or context. For example, the oracular treatment of Cleobis and Biton and of Trophonius bears the implicit lesson that death at a moment of supreme happiness is the highest good. Oracles may also consist of advice: the answer to the Athenians that they are to trust to their wooden walls. Or, commonest of all, oracles may simply declare what will happen: Croesus, if he attacks the Persian power, will destroy a mighty empire. Such oracles are frequently ambiguous, sometimes constitute a test of character (will the man who has consulted the oracle have the sagacity to understand the answer?), but seldom, if ever, enforce events or acts of character. This last point is particularly important in connection with Sophocles. In his plays events do not take place because the oracles say that they will; on the contrary, the oracles say that events will take place because they are going to. There is no fatalism involved in the oracular utterance itself; the oracles need not say why the events will take place, and they may come about because of human character. The fulfillment of most Sophoclean oracles does, in fact, require the force of human character, though it may also involve divine will. To what extent Sophocles' use of oracles is a reflection of a personal religious outlook is impossible to say and does not matter here. What we can know beyond doubt is that in his way of handling oracles in his plays he shows a good deal of freedom of invention and a consistent tendency to dovetail oracular material with the natural outcome of character. A brief survey of the chief oracles and related phenomena in the plays will clarify these assertions.

In *Ajax* there is no oracle; but Calchas' prophetic statement that the hero is subject to the divine wrath for that one day is of the same nature. Calchas' announcement does not in the least make Ajax's suicide inevitable; he could have stayed in his tent and been safe. The suicide requires two things, the anger of the gods which caused Ajax's madness and the character of Ajax.

The oracular element in *The Trachinian Women* is interesting above all for the way in which it is handled by the playwright; we shall come back to this presently. There is really only one oracle that matters, that concerning Heracles' "rest" after a certain period of time and after the fulfillment of the final task on which he is engaged when the play begins. What is the meaning of this deceptive oracle, in which the promised rest turns out to be the peace of death? Rather than a mere prank of divine cruelty upon Heracles it seems to be an oracular statement about the character of Heracles:

the restless, ever-toiling hero can have no rest so long as his mortal life goes on. The other oracle in the play, that Heracles' death will be at the hands of one no longer living, scarcely calls for consideration; it has no religious significance certainly, and its place in the play is only that of a signal to Heracles, whereby he can know that the end of his life is at hand.

In *Antigone* Teiresias' prophecy and warning to Creon are no doubt religious and reveal the displeasure of deity with Creon's conduct. There is no question here of capricious oracular power or fate: Creon's conduct gives rise to the divine displeasure, and Teiresias' statement reports this displeasure.

In *Oedipus Tyrannus* there are two oracles: the response to Creon, reported in the prologue, and the oracle given to Oedipus in his youth. Of the first we need say little. It asserts the technical guilt of Oedipus by declaring that the murderer of Laius must be driven from Thebes. But of this there is no question and therefore the oracle has no peculiar religious power or meaning; it merely gives information. The other oracle, proclaiming that it is Oedipus' fate to marry his mother and kill his father, is the best known of all Sophoclean oracles and the one which most accounts for the common attitude that things happen in Sophocles because oracles declare that they must. Here we cannot separate the content of the oracle from its manner of presentation, for in this oracle the essential feature of Sophocles' presentation is his modification of the traditional content. According to the archaic, pre-Sophoclean, and better-known version of the oracle, a dire fate is imposed on Oedipus because of Laius' insistence on begetting a son, against the will of the gods; in fact the chain of causes sometimes goes back to an earlier offense of Laius.[1] Sophocles wanted no part of this motif of inherited guilt and therefore dropped from his version of the oracle the traditional cause—a very significant omission. (Even when in *Oedipus* the corresponding oracle to Laius is mentioned—that the son he sires is destined to slay him—there is no cause given.) The traditional cause of Oedipus' suffering is thus erased from Sophocles' play, and we must not try to spirit it back in.

To what cause Sophocles wants us to ascribe the fate of Oedipus is a problem that has elicited many and various answers and is often regarded as the key to the play. But what if Sophocles never intended there to be an answer? What if the fate of Oedipus is simply a mythological datum, to be accepted and built into the study of Oedipus without comment or solution? We can enjoy the play most fully, and best avoid misunderstanding it, if we take the

1. H. W. Parke and D. E. Wormell, *The Delphic Oracle*[2] (Oxford, 1956), 298–300. Strictly speaking, there are three oracles in the play, for the response given to Laius and that given to Oedipus are separate oracles, though the content is essentially the same.

simple approach that these questions suggest. I doubt, however, if one can read all seven of Sophocles' plays without yielding to the temptation to supply some answer to the question of Oedipus' fate. But the answer will probably be based on an impression gained from all the plays; it will therefore belong to a more subjective and more abstract realm of criticism than we are now concerned with. In the next chapter we shall find confirmation of the common view that whatever the answer may be, it must not be separated from the person of Oedipus; his fate is not independent of his character. For the moment it is relevant to emphasize that it is not the oracle that brings about the events but the events that permit the oracle. Furthermore, this famous oracle is no more sacrosanct and immutable than others that Sophocles uses: when Jocasta reports the oracle (711–714), she "knows" only the part that applies to Laius. What this means, in terms of Sophocles' use of the oracle, is that at that point in the play Sophocles wants to reveal only this half of the oracle, for it is enough to set the wheels of discovery in motion.

In *Electra* the first thing to observe is that the oracle does not concern Electra. She needs no oracular backing and is impelled by no oracular demand; her actions and her feelings spring from her own character. Therefore in this play about Electra the oracle can have only an indirect bearing; it can only tell us whether Orestes is justified in his revenge, supported by Apollo's will. In assessing Sophocles' attitude toward oracles this in *Electra* is a particularly valuable guide: whether Sophocles believes in the truth and the religious force of oracles or not, we see in this play very clearly that he is at least capable of thinking in quite different terms, even in a story where oracular influence was traditionally present. He could, had he been concerned to support the validity of oracles, have contrived to make his tragic heroine base her inflexible resolve for revenge on the need for obedience to the oracle; instead, he has her base it on her own will and her own moral judgment.

In *Philoctetes* there is no oracle but one prophecy in several installments; here, as in *The Trachinian Women*, the most interesting thing is Sophocles' way of presenting the matter, of which more presently. There is no religious value in this prophecy of Helenus, which states merely that Troy cannot fall without Philoctetes' presence in the Greek army. This is surely a commentary on Philoctetes' greatness, just as his possession of the weapons of Heracles is. (In Sophocles, Philoctetes acquired the weapons directly from Heracles, though the usual tradition was that they came to him via his father Poias.)

The very theme of *Oedipus at Colonus* is, as we have already seen, embodied in an oracle that is stated in the prologue (87–95); and this same oracle is several times repeated, or paraphrased in part, elsewhere in the play. This oracle depends on the character of Oedipus and on the recognition by deity of the power and value of that character. It is because Oedipus is what he is that he is granted the strange and great power of bestowing blessings and ruin. Here again matter and presentation are inextricable, as Letters has acutely pointed out: it is significant for Sophocles' use of oracles that he does not hesitate to attach a completely new and different paragraph to the old oracle portending disaster to Oedipus. Are we to assume that Sophocles meant us to know about this ultimate rewarding of Oedipus when he used the oracle in *Tyrannus?* Of course not. In that play it suited his dramatic purpose to have only the gloomy prophecy; in this play he wants a further, restitutive clause, and so he adds it without hesitation.

There is no reason for believing that Sophocles was tyrannized over by oracles, and no reason to suppose that the presence of numerous oracles in his plays indicates a tendency to rely primarily on the power of fate or deity, as expressed through oracles, for his view of human life. In the great majority of cases the content of the oracle tells as much about character as it does about divine will or fate. Whether or not Sophocles had a personal belief in the religious value of oracles is, of course, another matter; it is altogether probable that he did, like most men of his day, but the evidence of the plays is quite inconclusive. What matters for us as students of Sophoclean drama is the fact that oracles in the plays of Sophocles are invariably shaped to fit the dramatic context, and not vice versa. We are therefore justified in assuming that when Sophocles presents oracular information in a unique and unconventional way he is doing so for his own reasons as a dramatist, and we shall see that in two plays, *The Trachinian Women* and *Philoctetes*, he uses oracles in a way that is closely similar to his method of restriction.

In *The Trachinian Women* the oracle telling of what is to happen to Heracles comes out piecemeal and rather confusedly. In the prologue Deianeira's reference to the oracle seems to indicate that it has to do specifically with Heracles' expedition against the city of Eurytus (74–81); when next she refers to it she says only that Heracles has told her that at the end of fifteen months from the time of his last departure he will either die or live in peace thereafter (166–169); and when finally Heracles speaks of it he says merely that it was prophesied that "at this time now living and present" he would have release from toils (1169–1171). These are minor differences, but the inexactness is not without significance. More striking, and more important for Sophocles' use of oracles, is the fact that in the choral ode following Hyllus' report of his father's agony, the Trachinian maidens speak with detailed knowledge of the oracle, mentioning something that neither Deianeira nor Heracles ever refers to, that the oracle was given twelve years before its fulfillment. How did they know about the oracle? Earlier, Deianeira speaks to them as if they were strangers to the whole situation. Jebb thought that "the inconsistency of detail was simply overlooked by the poet." Possibly so; but it may be more accurate to say that the poet counted on his audience to overlook the inconsistency, while he went ahead and used whatever parts of the oracle suited his purpose at various points in the play. This is Jebb's view of the use of the oracle as a whole in the play, and I think that it is certainly right. Toward the beginning Sophocles uses it, in the mouth of Deianeira, to increase the sense of foreboding that fills her mind and is an essential part of the setting; at the end it helps Heracles tie matters together and realize that his death is at hand; in between it is used in a choral ode to grace and substantiate the chorus's reflections on what has happened.

Is this not precisely the same kind of dramatic method as in the matter of burial in *Antigone?* Just as in that play "burial" is distributed according to the necessities of the dramatic action, so here "oracle" is similarly parceled out when and as the development of the play demands.

Our final example of this aspect of Sophoclean method is the prophecy of Helenus in *Philoctetes*. Here again there is one original statement several times reported in the play, and each time a little differently, according to the exigencies of the moment. Here again there are elements of illogicality in the knowledge shown by different persons, but as in *The Trachinian Women* these illogicalities have dramatic point. The prophecy, given in its fullest form in the speech of the pseudo-merchant, declares that the Greeks will not take Troy until they bring Philoctetes, by persuasion, from Lemnos to Troy (610–613); from other versions we get the information that the weapons of Heracles are also essential (113). In addition to the prophecy, there is also certain related information concerning the disease of Philoctetes and its destined cure; whether this information is known by oracle, prophecy, or some other means is never specified.

From this body of extraordinary knowledge, Sophocles draws whatever parts he needs at any given moment, often without regard for strict probability; here again, as in *The Trachinian Women*, it is probably safer to ascribe the illogicality to Sophocles' design than to oversight. (The discrepancy between Neoptolemus' statement that the Asclepiadae will cure Philoctetes [1333–1334] and Heracles' that he will send Asclepius to do so [1437–1438] is perhaps an oversight, though even here it is not unreasonable to find a dramatic point: Neoptolemus' version of the cure is more naturalistic and less miraculous, since the Asclepiadae are the traditional physi-

cians of the Greek host; Heracles' promise to send the god of healing himself is in keeping with the exalted tone of the entire epiphany and emphasizes the divine interest in Philoctetes' destiny.)
In the prologue Odysseus speaks only of the need for the weapons
in Philoctetes' possession—they and Neoptolemus are destined to
take Troy (113)—not a word about Philoctetes. The reason is
clear: Odysseus is trying to steel the young Neoptolemus to carry
through the deception, and he quite naturally stresses the glory
that will come to him. We need not assume that Odysseus does
not know the rest of the prophecy; we are best off making no
assumptions about such matters. In the parodos Neoptolemus, in
answer to the chorus's expression of sympathy for Philoctetes'
suffering, declares that the suffering was imposed by heaven and
will end only when the hero "bends the shafts of the gods" against
Troy (191–200). In view of Neoptolemus' apparent ignorance
about Philoctetes in the prologue, this sudden revelation of knowledge not gained from Odysseus is a little surprising, though not
impossible. But why is Neoptolemus ignorant in the prologue,
knowledgeable in the parodos? Because in the prologue Sophocles
wanted to stress the influence of Odysseus over him; the youth is to
be the learner, the receiver of knowledge, not the knower. In the
parodos, on the other hand, Sophocles wants us to see him steeled
against the sympathy he would naturally feel for Philoctetes; the
knowledge displayed here by Neoptolemus helps to explain, in
terms of his character, how he is able to continue to deceive Philoctetes for so long. Also, of course, Sophocles is in this way able to
give his audience pertinent information without interfering with
the progress of the action.

Later on the bogus merchant adds the vitally important fact that
Philoctetes must come to Troy and must come willingly
(610–613). It has already been suggested that the main dramatic
purpose of this speech is its effect on Neoptolemus; so far as the
action of the play is concerned, this is the first moment at which
Neoptolemus knows this part of the prophecy, and his behavior
from this point onward indicates that his emotional reaction to the
new information is strong. Finally, when Neoptolemus at the end
has returned the bow to Philoctetes and appeals to him as a friend
to come to Troy, he needs every persuasive argument possible, and
so Sophocles grants him full and authoritative knowledge of the
prophecy and of the conditions of the healing of the wound
(1329–1335); and again we are most unlikely, when we watch the
play, to ask how it is that Neoptolemus, who began in such boyish
ignorance, can now speak with such oracular firmness and fullness.

Throughout, Sophocles uses the prophetic and supernatural
knowledge exactly as it fits his dramatic design, excluding whatever

does not suit the immediate purpose, adding and changing at will, in a manner that does not always answer to the demands of strict logic but makes excellent dramatic sense, provided we do not demand logic and strict realism in inconspicuous dramaturgical details. If we do make such demands, then Sophocles will not measure up. But neither will most of the supreme poetic dramatists. By such standards Ben Jonson and Alfieri excel Shakespeare and Sophocles.

THALIA PHILLIES FELDMAN

Taboo and Neurotic Guilt in the Oedipus Theme†

So complex are the problems of interpretation in regard to the two Oedipus dramas, the *Tyrannus* and the *Colonus*, that critics disagree as to whether Sophocles is defending or attacking the gods and traditional religious ethic, whether his protagonist is a unique individual or a symbol labeled "suffering humanity." They question, again, whether Oedipus achieves his cult status in the *Colonus* because of his great intelligence, or whether this is the result of Athenian political policy. There is, as we like to say, some truth in all these interpretations.

Among recent critics, Gerald Else, Bernard Knox, and Ivan Linforth have certain insights which are especially pertinent to the spirit of Oedipus. Else gauges more accurately than has been done before the important cultural role of blood kin relationships to the plays; Knox examines most acutely the role of mind in them, while Linforth sees the moral guiltlessness of the hero as the main issue: it is not the action of the gods and their oracles which matter so much but rather, as Knox also points out, how Oedipus thinks and feels about the nature of his pollution, and how he acts upon it. "This great issue [of pollution and moral guiltlessness]," says Linforth, "is the only religious issue of the play—if it can be called religious—and must have been of profound significance to the audience."

It is this point—Oedipus' pollution, his feelings, and their significance to his audience—which I shall consider more closely. As Linforth suggests, Oedipus' pollution is not originally an ethical problem but rather a problem of primitive belief, such as commonly vexes a society prior to the development of the ethical reli-

---

† Thalia Phillies Feldman, "Taboo in the Oedipus Theme," in *Transactions and Proceedings of the American Philological Association*, 93 (1962), 124–143. Reprinted by permission. (All but one of the author's footnotes have been omitted.) Originally published as "Taboo in the Oedipus Theme" by Thalia Phillies Howe.

gions. It is my contention that it is principally Sophocles who, in his two dramas, bridges the transition between such surviving notions surrounding primitive taboo and their elevation into a significant stage beyond, one which indicates a new, individual concern and feeling. There is evidence, however, which suggests that Sophocles is following a lead in this direction initiated by Aeschylus, the great ethical interpreter of drama. In 467 B.C. Aeschylus produced a tetralogy on the Oedipus theme which was awarded first prize. Of the salient events in that tetralogy, we know only one or two which survive in the fragments. How Aeschylus' four plays affected the Sophoclean works will be discussed later.

The two Sophoclean dramas we have, of course, in their entirety, and it is from them that most of our evidence and insights must come. They were not produced together, and in fact the *Tyrannus* was written some twenty or thirty years prior to the *Colonus*, which was presented three years after Sophocles' death in 406 B.C. In the earlier play the hero discovers that a number of years previously he has unknowingly broken two major taboos: he has committed patricide and, then, incest with his mother. The latter taboo is the great universal one, the most dreaded among all primitive societies and everywhere compounded with dire pollution. Patricide, while not so universal a taboo, was for the Greeks almost as culpable an offense, for in committing it one shed kindred blood. Thus these two taboos represented their life-and-death attitudes toward familial blood: it is sacred, and one must neither procreate with it nor destroy it. These beliefs, of immemorial practice, functioned like all taboos, as institutions and "social symbols by which the complex fabric of society is built up." Furthermore, anyone breaking these taboos disrupts not only society but the cosmic order as well, insofar as the social structure is conceived by many primitive peoples, including the early Greeks, as resident within the framework of the natural order. In the case of incest, "the fatal consequences are above all manifested in the fact that the plantations will no longer yield their produce ... The scourge it lets loose will spare no one, for famine, epidemic, hurricane, earthquake are calamities that no one can escape. Hence the need for concerted action."

This quotation does not paraphrase the opening scene of the *Tyrannus* but is taken from Lévy-Bruhl's *Primitives and the Supernatural*, which describes the universal reaction of peoples upon finding incestuous practice and its consequent pollution within the community. Reactions of this kind cannot be called moral, but they *are* full of terror. In the opening of the *Tyrannus* such an experience is plainly evident; the city of Oedipus is suffering from most of the natural disasters that would be recorded from the field millennia later by Lévy-Bruhl. But precisely how did the plague and sterility function within these two dramas, for it is significant, as Knox reminds us, that they do not appear until many years after Oedipus has committed his foul acts and that he has, furthermore, prospered in the interim? If the cosmic order is disturbed at all, it has taken an unseemly amount of time to register its disapproval. At best these rumblings of nature appear to be the last retreating thunder-roll of primitive belief. But, it may be argued, the long delay in the inevitable peripety of Oedipus, the reversal in fortune coming after so much prosperity, make this downfall even more terrible, illustrating the conventional Greek maxim, "wait to see life's ending ere thou count one mortal blest," a quotation which is, in fact, the closing chorus of the *Tyrannus* itself.

Yet, in looking deeper, it becomes clear that within the economy of the drama the plague is a limited instrument of either cosmic or divine retribution. It is all but lost sight of after the first powerful stasimon. The two subsequent references to it are oblique and brief, when Jocasta (635) and the chorus (a few lines later) have to *remind* Oedipus and Creon of the "stricken state." Nor do these tokens of physical catastrophe reappear, even when the polluted hero fails to retire from the confines of Thebes according to the terms of the curse he has himself pronounced. It is crucial to observe that Sophocles does not mention them even once in the *Colonus*. Moreover, it is noteworthy that the plague does not directly touch Oedipus or his family. Indeed, had Oedipus not made every effort to find out the truth, he might never have suffered physical harm or social exposure. The long delay in the peripety of Oedipus is meaningful not only as an illustration of a religious platitude, but it is also a very effective dramatic device on its own, serving to start the events of real importance on their necessary course.

The function of the plague appears to be more dramaturgical than religious, for Sophocles seems to imply that Athens of the fifth century no longer actually believes that plagues are the natural, automatic concomitants of taboo transgression. Such a decline in belief, however, posed a very crucial religious problem; for if primitive sanctions are no longer held to, then there would seem to be no agency to exact sanctions against those who threaten the social order by clandestine transgressions. While any inclination toward patricide can normally be kept under control simply because the outcome is usually detectable, how are the ties of kindred blood —still felt to be very sacred among the Greeks—to be protected against secret incestuous defilement?

It is Sophocles, and apparently also Aeschylus, who point to a solution by having Oedipus take an extraordinarily individual attitude toward his part in the taboo transgression, and thus denote a significant cultural change. In the *Tyrannus* Oedipus imposes upon himself the maximum penalties for taboo transgression: he would repudiate all rights of kingship, family, everything, and banish himself beyond the Theban boundaries, presumably taking with him the pollution infecting the community. It is significant that these sanctions which are so integral to the Sophoclean ethic were not imposed upon Oedipus by the community, but by the protagonist himself. These sanctions, moreover, do not occur in earlier literary references, either in Homer or even in Hesiod. In both these ancient poets Oedipus continued to rule as king until his death in Thebes and, in fact, mention is made in several passages of his funeral at that place. In one passage from the *Erga* of Hesiod there is reference to the fact that the demi-gods had perished, "fighting for the flocks of Oedipus," which would imply that he was still king and not blinded. It is only in the *Odyssey*, however, that we have some indication that Oedipus at least suffered somewhat for his unhappy deeds: "when he had slain his own father, and wedded her [Epicaste–Jocasta] *straightway* the gods made these things known among men. Howbeit he abode a lord of the Cadmeians in lovely Thebes, suffering woes through the baneful counsels of the gods, but she hanged herself—but for him she left behind many [woes] even all that the Avengers [Erinyes] of a mother bring to pass."

It is of special interest to note that in this passage, while there is specific reference to the pursuit of Oedipus by his mother's Furies, no mention is made of penalties incurred for the killing of the father. This might very possibly indicate that such transgressions against the father did not as yet incur the dgeree of social condemnation that they did in the fifth century. There is more than one indication that in progressing from the darker ages of the eighth century toward the more developed social and ethical concepts of the fifth, Greek attitudes toward acts such as Oedipus' became more severe, so that in the dramas Oedipus came to feel at least as deep concern toward his father as toward his mother. Even in an extant bit of the *Thebais*, one of the minor epics of the post-Homeric Cycle, Oedipus is represented as reigning king of Thebes, seated at a banquet with his full-grown sons and still in possession of his sight. Insofar as can be ascertained, then, in the extant literature up to Aeschylus, society did not treat Oedipus as an offender who needed punishment. Nor did he himself take any action against himself, although it is true that he was not untroubled by his acts, since he was plagued by the Furies of Jocasta.

Such an attitude of social tolerance is characteristic of societies of the kind described by Meyer Fortes in his Frazer Classical Lecture, *Oedipus and Job in West African Religion*. Fortes reports of

In the Sophoclean play, which we have complete, the chorus cannot comprehend the king's action. Twice they ask him what daemon made him do it, never imagining that he himself devised and executed this action. The first time Oedipus is still too stunned to answer coherently; but when they repeat the question, he answers:

> Apollo, friends, Apollo he it was
> That brought these ills to pass;
> But mine own hand struck the blow—
> No one [did it] but hapless I.
>
> ἔπαισε δ' αὐτόχειρ νιν οὔ-
> τις ἀλλ' ἐγὼ τλάμων.

This assertion is the climax of the play. The shocking sight of Oedipus, self-blinded and reeling from the palace, is an affirmation of personal engagement of a kind that a conventional scapegoat could never have embodied. Oedipus' independent action implies that the ethos behind the taboo must now begin to be imposed *within* the individual. And when innocent of evil intent, one must, upon involvement in a taboo situation, acknowledge a willingness to recognize and support that ethos. By his answer Oedipus challenges the basic belief that the individual can hold either his primitive daemon, his Prenatal Destiny, completely responsible, or even the later and more impersonal power of the Olympians. And in foregoing the deep comfort that attends total belief in Destiny and oracles, Oedipus instead sows the seeds of guilt-feeling which in later times will come to double fruition: first, in Judaeo-Christian times, in a strong personal sense of guilt and sin; and, in more recent times, in neurotic guilt as modern man understands the term. Curiously, as we have seen, Oedipus' emotional reactions seem closer to those of modern neurotic guilt, perhaps precisely because his reactions did not arise from the pressures of a dominant religious ethic with overriding convictions about sin. In any case, the οὔτις ἀλλ' ἐγὼ τλάμων of Oedipus signals that a great break has been made with the primitive tradition of the Greeks. Yet the break is not an abandonment of a tradition but the conversion necessary for strengthening it.

Oedipus' own reaction becomes clearer, however, if we examine further the significance of the blinding. In both the Aeschylean and Sophoclean accounts, approximately the same personal reason is given by Oedipus: he is too ashamed to look upon the members of his family, both the living and the dead. There is also the possibility offered by Rose, based on his reading of Hyginus 242, that "after such horrible, though unintentional crimes he was unworthy 'to see the light,' and so should have died." These feelings are understandable enough; but in the case of both ancient writers there are, however, cultural and psychological implications to the blinding of "profound significance" [Linforth] to the contemporary audience. In the first place, it has implications as primitive as the concept of the scapegoat, since the use of blood to cleanse pollution is frequently regarded among primitive peoples as more effective than even the most sacred water. For instance, a messenger in the *Tyrannus* states, "Not Ister, nor all Phasis' flood, I think, could wash away the blood-stains from this house." Early in that play Creon also reported from the oracle that expiation should be by "banishment *or* the shedding of blood for blood." Oedipus, of course, chose both means. We are reminded, too, of Aristotle's statement, as Professor Else reads the passage, that events pitiable and fearful should be purified by events of a like kind and by persons bound by natural ties of kinship—and here the son seeks expiation for patricide by gouging his eyes, literally "blood for blood." And how it flowed from Oedipus' eyes! ". . . not oozing drop by drop, But one black gory downpour, thick as hail." Furthermore, shedding of blood is commonly a primitive form of mourning, a piacular sacrifice for the dead, in which deliberately self-inflicted scratches and even wounds, and also hair-cutting or tearing, are used as libations for the dead.

But there are other implications to the blinding which signify how profound are Oedipus' feelings of shame. In gouging his eyes Oedipus employs a form of punishment, by facial mutilation, which was used on other sexual offenders. The centaur, Eurytion, was similarly punished for the seizure of the Lapith women, and Tiresias was blinded by Athena for observing her at her bath. These suggestions become clearer when we recall that Euripides in his drama had Oedipus blinded by Laius' servant, an act, which would also imply that they regarded Oedipus as guilty. It is Sophocles, with greater penetration, who insists that Oedipus is not morally guilty. This is clear in the *Tyrannus* and most emphatic in the *Colonus*. Yet his shame is so great that he feels compelled to externalize his internal torment. "I myself must bear the load of ills [*kaka*] that no one but I can bear," he says.

This statement reflects better than any other in the play an ethos appropriate—for better or for worse—to a mature civilization. Yet, to externalize that ethos by the act of blinding, both Aeschylus and Sophocles chose to reach into a singularly primitive level of punishment. They seem deliberately to have chosen to reinforce the new ethos by an old and, no doubt, outmoded practice, by recourse to an old-fashioned severity, as it were. It also must have been in this same spirit of religious synthesis that Sophocles utilized the device of the plague.

But Sophocles went even further in using means associated with popular, primitive belief and practice in order to reinforce his new concept of man's personal involvement with his destiny. He chose, at the end of the *Tyrannus,* to have his Oedipus prefer to depart into exile, again self-imposed, and as a scapegoat, loaded not only with the primitive pollution of old but with a new sense of horror. Since the exile, however, is a voluntary one, imposed as a great gesture of self-recognition and responsibility, a gesture powerfully willed and comprehended, Oedipus remains indestructible. He recognizes, as he states, that he has been saved for some further awesome destiny. It may be the end of the *Tyrannus* but not the end of Oedipus.

A generation later, in reopening the theme of Oedipus in the *Colonus,* Sophocles reveals the progress he had made in breaking down further the more mechanical aspects of taboo retribution, while at the same time keeping this in effective harmony with contemporary concepts of jurisprudence. Thus, instead of following through with the primitive exile, Oedipus stays in retreat. There, undistracted because of his blindness, he comes to understand fully his moral guiltlessness, though this time in legal terms. In consequence his attitude becomes one of great defiance and insistence. But, we may ask, if his guiltlessness had always been taken for granted, why should a dramatist as acute as Sophocles have championed the point so far, if it were either hackneyed or unnecessary? There must be some fresh and daring innovation that he is trying to establish before his Athenian audience. Is he claiming justifiable homicide, that a man openly attacked has the right to defend himself? In part, no doubt. But as has been pointed out, this juridical opinion had been on the Athenian statute books since Draconian times and could by now hardly have been a fresh theme for social drama. What is new is the *special kind* of justifiable homicide that Sophocles is pleading. Note that Oedipus says specifically on three occasions that he killed a man in self-defense whom he did not realize was his father. On one of these occasions he also says, "Yet am I then / A villain born because in self-defense, / Stricken, I struck the striker back again? *Even had I known,* no villainy 'twould prove." And the third time Oedipus states that *even* his father, if he could return to life "would not dissent," that is, would not blame Oedipus. What Sophocles is insistently pleading is that a man not be regarded as guilty who kills *even* his father in self-defense. Therefore, under these special conditions of justifiable homicide, patricide specifically, even the ghost of the slain father would forgive and not demand retribution. The Furies need not pursue him and, in fact, as the token of their consent to this extenuation of taboo transgression, they allow Oedipus to be enshrined in their own sacred grove of Colonus. They welcome him, however, not as the Furies, but as the Eumenides, the benign powers of Aeschylean conversion.

Yet, though Sophocles advocated, and possibly innovated, this special plea in the case of patricide, his religious temperament and or psychological understanding does not seem to have regarded the offender's involvement dissolved merely by legalistic acquittal, as in ordinary cases of justifiable homicide. Such an attitude of psychological absolution must not be encouraged in cases involving the shedding of sacred, familial blood. And so he keeps his hero tormented with horror to the very end, exclaiming when reminded of the incest by the chorus: "Ah me, it is death to hear this!" And he demonstrates this self-revulsion in one magnificent gesture: even when the ancient primitive rites of purification are officially performed after everyone is convinced of his moral and legal innocense, still Oedipus will not let Theseus touch his hand to seal his absolution. He still feels ashamed, tainted even now, not with the miasma of pollution but with the blush of unexpungeable shame:

> Give me thy hand, O Prince, that I may touch it,
> And if that is right ($\epsilon\iota\ \theta\acute{\epsilon}\mu\iota s$), kiss thy cheek.
> What say I? Can I wish that thou should'st touch
> One fallen like me to utter wretchedness,
> Corrupt and tainted with ills?
> Oh no, I would not let thee if thou would'st.

Thus the immemorial prohibitions adhering to familial behavior and blood relationships are kept more inviolate than ever. Not only are they protected by the external, legal sanctions of society; they are finally made subject by Sophocles in his figure of Oedipus to the most severe sanctions of all, to feelings of profound individual engagement, feelings for which Oedipus was accorded their contemporary form of beatification in his mystic death and burial. Those problems involving the slaying of blood-kin, which had been first stated by Aeschylus in the transformation of the Furies in his *Oresteia*, are finally resolved by Sophocles in the grove of the Eumenides at Colonus. But where in that earlier work the protagonist was supported and directed step by step by Olympian deities, Oedipus, with little more than the mixed blessing of Apollo, achieves his own wisdom. He demonstrates it by a new, individual thought and action toward religious beliefs, both primitive and Olympian. The *Colonus* is, therefore, a cultural stage beyond the *Eumenides*. It proves how an intelligent, ethical, and courageous man can not only transcend his fated misdeeds, but help society profit by the knowledge he has gained from his terrible destiny. To show this was the purpose of Greek drama.

SIGMUND FREUD

[The Oedipus Complex]†

In my experience, which is already extensive, the chief part in the mental lives of all children who later become psychoneurotics is played by their parents. Being in love with the one parent and hating the other are among the essential constituents of the stock of psychical impulses which is formed at that time and which is of such importance in determining the symptoms of the later neurosis. It is not my belief, however, that psychoneurotics differ sharply in this respect from other human beings who remain normal—that they are able, that is, to create something absolutely new and peculiar to themselves. It is far more probable—and this is confirmed by occasional observations on normal children—that they are only distinguished by exhibiting on a magnified scale feelings of love and hatred to their parents which occur less obviously and less intensely in the minds of most children.

This discovery is confirmed by a legend that has come down to us from classical antiquity: a legend whose profound and universal power to move can only be understood if the hypothesis I have put forward in regard to the psychology of children has an equally universal validity. What I have in mind is the legend of King Oedipus and Sophocles' drama which bears his name.

Oedipus, son of Laïus, King of Thebes, and of Jocasta, was exposed as an infant because an oracle had warned Laïus that the still unborn child would be his father's murderer. The child was rescued, and grew up as a prince in an alien court, until, in doubts as to his origin, he too questioned the oracle and was warned to avoid his home since he was destined to murder his father and take his mother in marriage. On the road leading away from what he believed was his home, he met King Laïus and slew him in a sudden quarrel. He came next to Thebes and solved the riddle set him by the Sphinx who barred his way. Out of gratitude the The-

† From Sigmund Freud, *The Interpretation of Dreams*, translated and edited by James Strachey (New York: Basic Books, Inc., and London: George Allen & Unwin Ltd., 1955), pp. 260–264. Reprinted by permission of the publishers. Acknowledgement is also made to The Hogarth Press, Inc., and the Institute of Psycho-Analysis, publishers of *The Standard Edition of the Complete Psychological Works of Sigmund Freud*, and to Sigmund Freud Copyrights Ltd.

bans made him their king and gave him Jocasta's hand in marriage. He reigned long in peace and honour, and she who, unknown to him, was his mother bore him two sons and two daughters. Then at last a plague broke out and the Thebans made enquiry once more of the oracle. It is at this point that Sophocles' tragedy opens. The messengers bring back the reply that the plague will cease when the murderer of Laïus has been driven from the land.

> But he, where is he? Where shall now be read
> The fading record of this ancient guilt?[1]

The action of the play consists in nothing other than the process of revealing, with cunning delays and ever-mounting excitement—a process that can be likened to the work of a psychoanalysis—that Oedipus himself is the murderer of Laïus, but further that he is the son of the murdered man and of Jocasta. Appalled at the abomination which he has unwittingly perpetrated, Oedipus blinds himself and forsakes his home. The oracle has been fulfilled.

Oedipus Rex is what is known as a tragedy of destiny. Its tragic effect is said to lie in the contrast between the supreme will of the gods and the vain attempts of mankind to escape the evil that threatens them. The lesson which, it is said, the deeply moved spectator should learn from the tragedy is submission to the divine will and realization of his own impotence. Modern dramatists have accordingly tried to achieve a similar tragic effect by weaving the same contrast into a plot invented by themselves. But the spectators have looked on unmoved while a curse or an oracle was fulfilled in spite of all the efforts of some innocent man: later tragedies of destiny have failed in their effect.

If *Oedipus Rex* moves a modern audience no less than it did the contemporary Greek one, the explanation can only be that its effect does not lie in the contrast between destiny and human will, but is to be looked for in the particular nature of the material on which that contrast is exemplified. There must be something which makes a voice within us ready to recognize the compelling force of destiny in the *Oedipus*, while we can dismiss as merely arbitrary such dispositions as are laid down in [Grillparzer's] *Die Ahnfrau* or other modern tragedies of destiny. And a factor of this kind is in fact involved in the story of King Oedipus. His destiny moves us only because it might have been ours—because the oracle laid the same curse upon us before our birth as upon him. It is the fate of all of us, perhaps, to direct our first sexual impulse towards our mother and our first hatred and our first murderous wish against our father. Our dreams convince us that that is so. King Oedipus, who slew his father Laïus and married his mother Jocasta, merely shows us the

1. [Lewis Campbell's translation (1883), line 108 f.]

fulfilment of our own childhood wishes. But, more fortunate than he, we have meanwhile succeeded, in so far as we have not become psychoneurotics, in detaching our sexual impulses from our mothers and in forgetting our jealousy of our fathers. Here is one in whom these primaeval wishes of our childhood have been fulfilled, and we shrink back from him with the whole force of the repression by which those wishes have since that time been held down within us. While the poet, as he unravels the past, brings to light the guilt of Oedipus, he is at the same time compelling us to recognize our own inner minds, in which those same impulses, though suppressed, are still to be found. The contrast with which the closing Chorus leaves us confronted—

> . . . Fix on Oedipus your eyes,
> Who resolved the dark enigma, noblest champion and most
> wise.
> Like a star his envied fortune mounted beaming far and wide:
> Now he sinks in seas of anguish, whelmed beneath a raging tide
> . . .[2]

—strikes as a warning at ourselves and our pride, at us who since our childhood have grown so wise and so mighty in our own eyes. Like Oedipus, we live in ignorance of these wishes, repugnant to morality, which have been forced upon us by Nature, and after their revelation we may all of us well seek to close our eyes to the scenes of our childhood.[3]

There is an unmistakable indication in the text of Sophocles' tragedy itself that the legend of Oedipus sprang from some primaeval dream-material which had as its content the distressing disturbance of a child's relation to his parents owing to the first stirrings of sexuality. At a point when Oedipus, though he is not yet enlightened, has begun to feel troubled by his recollection of the oracle,

2. [Lewis Campbell's translation 1524 ff.]
3. [*Footnote added* 1914:] None of the findings of psycho-analytic research has provoked such embittered denials, such fierce opposition—or such amusing contortions—on the part of critics as this indication of the childhood impulses towards incest which persist in the unconscious. An attempt has even been made recently to make out, in the face of all experience, that the incest should only be taken as 'symbolic'.— Ferenczi (1912) has proposed an ingenious 'over-interpretation' of the Oedipus myth, based on a passage in one of Schopenhauer's letters.—[*Added* 1919:] Later studies have shown that the 'Oedipus complex', which was touched upon for the first time in the above paragraphs in the *Interpretation* *of Dreams*, throws a light on the history of the human race and the evolution of religion and morality. (See my *Totem and Taboo*, 1912-13 [Essay IV].) —[Actually the gist of this discussion of the Oedipus complex and of the *Oedipus Rex*, as well as of what follows on the subject of *Hamlet*, had already been put forward by Freud in a letter to Fliess as early as October 15th, 1897. (See Freud, 1950a, Letter 71.) A still earlier hint at the discovery of the Oedipus complex was included in a letter of May 31st, 1897. (Ibid., Draft N.)—The actual term 'Oedipus complex' seems to have been first used by Freud in his published writings in the first of his 'Contributions to the Psychology of Love' (1910h).]

Jocasta consoles him by referring to a dream which many people dream, though, as she thinks, it has no meaning:

> Many a man ere now in dreams hath lain
> With her who bare him. He hath least annoy
> Who with such omens troubleth not his mind.[4]

Today, just as then, many men dream of having sexual relations with their mothers, and speak of the fact with indignation and astonishment. It is clearly the key to the tragedy and the complement to the dream of the dreamer's father being dead. The story of Oedipus is the reaction of the imagination to these two typical dreams. And just as these dreams, when dreamt by adults, are accompanied by feelings of repulsion, so too the legend must include horror and self-punishment. Its further modification originates once again in a misconceived secondary revision of the material, which has sought to exploit it for theological purposes. (Cf. the dream-material in dreams of exhibiting, p. 243 f.) The attempt to harmonize divine omnipotence with human responsibility must naturally fail in connection with this subject-matter just as with any other.

4. [Lewis Campbell's translation, line 982 ff.]

Criticism

Essays in Criticism

ARISTOTLE

From The Poetics†

The Plot: Completeness and Magnitude

I have posited that tragedy is an imitation of an action that is a whole and complete in itself and of a certain magnitude—for a thing may be a whole, and yet have no magnitude to speak of. Now a thing is a whole if it has a beginning, a middle, and an end. A beginning is that which does not necessarily come after something else, but after which it is natural for another thing to exist or come to be. An end, on the contrary, is that which naturally comes after something else, either as its necessary sequel or as its usual [i.e. probable] sequel, but itself has nothing after it. A middle is that which both comes after something else and has another thing following it. A well-constructed plot, therefore, will neither begin at some chance point nor end at some chance point, but will observe the principles here stated.

Now as for magnitude: In order to be beautiful, a living creature or anything else made up of parts not only must have its parts organized but must also have just the size that properly belongs to it. Beauty depends on size and order; hence an extremely minute creature could not be beautiful, for our vision becomes blurred as it approaches the point of imperceptibility, nor could an utterly huge creature be beautiful, for, unable to take it in all at once, the viewer finds that its unity and wholeness have escaped his field of vision—if, for example, it were an animal a thousand miles long. Therefore just as organized bodies and animals, if they are to be beautiful, must have size and such size as to be easily taken in by the eye, so plots, for the same reason, must have length and such length as to be easily held in the memory. The limit of length considered in relation to the public contests and production in sensible form has nothing to do with the art of poetry—if a hundred

† From Aristotle, *The Poetics*, translated by James Hutton (New York: W. W. Norton & Company, Inc., 1970). Copyright © 1970 by W. W. Norton & Company, Inc. Chapters 7 (excluding first sentence), 10, 11, 13, 14, 15, 16. Reprinted by permission of the publisher.

tragedies had to be presented in the contest, the performance would be timed by water-clocks, as was actually done at one time, they say. But considered in relation to the very nature of the thing itself, the limit is this: Invariably, the larger the plot is, while still remaining perspicuous, the more beautiful it is in virtue of its magnitude, or, to express it in a simple formulation: If the length is sufficient to permit a change from bad fortune to good or from good fortune to bad to come about in an inevitable or probable sequence of events, this is a satisfactory limit of magnitude.

Simple and Complex Plots

Some plots are simple, others complex; indeed the actions of which the plots are imitations are at once so differentiated to begin with. Assuming the action to be continuous and unified, as already defined, I call that action simple in which the change of fortune takes place without a reversal or recognition, and that action complex in which the change of fortune involves a recognition or a reversal or both. These events [recognitions and reversals] ought to be so rooted in the very structure of the plot, that they follow from the preceding events as their inevitable or probable outcome; for there is a vast difference between following from and merely following after.

Parts of the Plot: Reversal, Recognition, Suffering

Reversal (Peripety) is, as aforesaid, a change from one state of affairs to its exact opposite, and this too, as I say, should be in conformance with probability or necessity. For example, in *Oedipus*, the messenger comes to cheer Oedipus by relieving him of fear with regard to his mother, but by revealing his true identity, does just the opposite of this. In *Lynceus* again, Lynceus is brought on expecting to die and Danaus follows intending to put him to death, but as a result of what has gone before it turns out that Danaus is put to death and Lynceus is saved.

Recognition, as the word itself indicates, is a change from ignorance to knowledge, leading either to friendship or to hostility on the part of those persons who are marked for good fortune or bad. The best form of recognition is that which is accompanied by a reversal, as in the example from *Oedipus*. There are, to be sure, other forms of recognition—and indeed what I have just said may occur in reference to inanimate objects or anything whatever, and it is possible to discover that someone has or has not done something—but the form that has most to do with the plot, and most to do with the action, is the one I have mentioned; for a recognition joined thus with a reversal will be fraught with pity or with fear (the type of action tragedy is presumed to imitate) because misery and happiness alike will come to be realized in recognitions of this kind. Now since recognition involves more than one person, there are cases in which one of two persons already knows the other and the recognition is on one side only, and other cases in which recognition has to take place on both sides. Iphigeneia, for example, was recognized by Orestes from the sending of her letter, but a second recognition was required to reveal his identity to her.

Two elements of the tragic plot, then, are Reversal and Recognition. A third element is Suffering (*pathos*). We have said what reversal and recognition are; suffering is an action of a destructive or painful description, such as deaths that take place in the open [and not behind the scenes], agonies of pain, wounds, and so on.

The Best Form of Tragedy

Next in order after the points I have just dealt with, it would seem necessary to specify what one should aim at and what avoid in the construction of plots, and what it is that will produce the effect proper to tragedy.

Now since in the finest kind of tragedy the structure should be complex and not simple, and since it should also be a representation of terrible and piteous events (that being the special mark of this type of imitation), in the first place, it is evident that good men ought not to be shown passing from happiness to misfortune, for this does not inspire either pity or fear, but only revulsion; nor evil men rising from ill fortune to prosperity, for this is the most untragic plot of all—it lacks every requirement, in that it neither elicts human sympathy nor stirs pity or fear. And again, neither should an extremely wicked man be seen falling from prosperity into misfortune, for a plot so constructed might indeed call forth human sympathy, but would not excite pity or fear, since the first is felt for a person whose misfortune is undeserved and the second for someone like ourselves—pity for the man suffering undeservedly, fear for the man like ourselves—and hence neither pity nor fear would be aroused in this case. We are left with the man whose place is between these extremes. Such is the man who on the one hand is not preëminent in virtue and justice, and yet on the other hand does not fall into misfortune through vice or depravity, but falls because of some mistake; one among the number of the highly renowned and prosperous, such as Oedipus and Thyestes and other famous men from families like theirs.

It follows that the plot which achieves excellence will necessarily be single in outcome and not, as some say, double, and will consist in a change of fortune, not to prosperity from misfortune, but the opposite, from prosperity to misfortune, occasioned not by depravity, but by some great mistake on the part of one who is either such as I have described or better than this rather than worse. What actually has taken place has confirmed this; for though at first the poets accepted whatever myths came to hand, today the finest tragedies are founded upon the stories of only a few houses, being concerned, for example, with Alcmeon, Oedipus, Orestes, Meleager, Thyestes, Telephus, and such others as have chanced to suffer terrible things or to do them. So then, tragedy having this construction is the finest kind of tragedy from an artistic point of view. And consequently those persons fall into the same error who bring it as a charge against Euripides that this is what he does in his tragedies and that most of his plays have unhappy endings. For this is in fact the right procedure, as I have said; and the best proof is that on the stage and in the dramatic contests, plays of this kind seem the most tragic, provided they are successfully worked out, and Euripides, even if in everything else his management is faulty, seems at any rate to be the most tragic of the poets.

Second to this is the kind of plot that some persons place first, that which like the *Odyssey* has a double structure and ends in opposite ways for the better characters and the worse. If it seems to be first, that is attributable to the weakness of the audience, since the poets only follow their lead and compose the kind of plays the spectators want. The pleasure it gives, however, is not that which comes from tragedy, but is rather the pleasure proper to comedy; for in comedy those who in the legend are the worst of enemies—Orestes and Aegisthus, for example—end by leaving the scene as friends, and nobody is killed by anybody.

Pity and Fear

The effect of fear and pity may be created by spectacle; but it may also be created by the very structure of the events, and this method has priority and is the way of a better poet. For the plot should be so constructed that even without seeing the play, anyone who merely hears the events unfold will shudder and feel pity as a result of what is happening—which is precisely what one would experience in listening to the plot of *Oedipus*. To procure this effect by means of spectacle is less artistic in that it calls for external apparatus, while those who produce through spectacle something that is not terrifying but only portentous in effect have no part in tragedy at all, for not every sort of pleasure is to be sought from tragedy, but only that which properly belongs to it. And since the pleasure the poet is to provide is that which comes from pity and fear through an imitation, clearly this effect must be embodied in the events of the plot.

Let us consider therefore the kinds of occurrences that seem terrible or pitiful. Actions of this sort must of course happen between persons who are either friends to one another or enemies or neither. Now if enemy harms enemy there is nothing to excite pity either in his doing the deed or in his being on the point of doing it—nothing, that is, but the actual suffering; and the same is true if the parties are neither friends nor enemies. When, however, the tragic event occurs within the sphere of the natural affections —when, for instance, a brother kills or is on the point of killing his brother, or a son his father, or a mother her son, or a son his mother, or something equally drastic is done—that is the kind of event a poet must try for. There is of course no possibility of altering the traditional stories—I mean Clytemnestra being murdered by Orestes and Eriphŷle by Alcmeon—but it is the poet's duty to find a way of using even these traditional subjects well.

Let me say more clearly what I mean by using them well. It is possible to have the action occur with full knowledge and awareness on the part of those involved, as the early poets used to do and as Euripides did when he had Medea kill her children. It is possible also to do the awful thing, but to do it in ignorance and then discover the relationship of the victim later, as Sophocles' Oedipus does. In this case, to be sure, the deed is done outside the play, but it is done in the tragedy itself, for example, by the Alcmeon of Astydamas and by Telegonus in *Odysseus Wounded*. A third possibility is for one who is about to do one of these atrocious deeds in ignorance to discover the relationship before he does it. There are no other possibilities, for the deed has either to be done or not done and with knowledge or without knowledge. Of these situations, the worst is for someone to be on the point of doing the deed with knowledge, and then not do it. This is revolting in itself and is not tragic, since no suffering is involved. It is not employed therefore by the poets except occasionally as when Haemon in *Antigone* fails to kill Creon. The doing of the deed comes next in order. The better way is for it to be done in ignorance, with the recognition following afterwards; there is then nothing revolting in the act, and the recognition astounds us. The best situation, however, is the last mentioned. It is exemplified in *Chresphontes*, where Merope is on the point of murdering her son, when she recognizes him and desists, and in *Iphigeneia*, where the sister is about to slay her brother; and in *Hellê*, where the son is about to give his mother up to the enemy when he learns who she is.

These considerations account for the fact mentioned earlier, that not many families provide subjects for tragedies. The poets, that is, in seeking out tragic situations, discovered more by luck than by lore how to contrive in their plots the kind of situation we have described. And this obliges them to keep returning for subjects to those few houses that have had such dire events befall them.

Enough, then, has now been said about the construction of the events and what the plots should be like in tragedy; [and hence we turn next to Character].

The Characters of Tragedy

With regard to the Characters there are four things to aim at. First and foremost is that the characters be good. The personages will have character if, as aforesaid, they reveal in speech or in action what their moral choices are, and a good character will be one whose choices are good. It is possible to portray goodness in every class of persons; a woman may be good and a slave may be good, though perhaps as a class women are inferior and slaves utterly base. The second requisite is to make the character appropriate. Thus it is possible to portray any character as manly, but inappropriate for a female character to be manly or formidable in the way I mean. Third is to make the characters lifelike, which is something different from making them good and appropriate as described above. Fourth is to make them consistent. Even if the person being imitated is inconsistent and this is what the character is supposed to be, he should nevertheless be portrayed as consistently inconsistent.

There is an example of unnecessary baseness in the character of Menelaus in *Orestes*; of the unsuitable and inappropriate in the lamentation of Odysseus in *Scylla* and in the declamation of Melanippe; and of inconsistency in *Iphigeneia in Aulis*, where the Iphigeneia who begs to be spared bears no resemblance to the Iphigeneia who appears thereafter.

In the characters and in the plot-construction alike, one must strive for that which is either necessary or probable, so that whatever a character of any kind says or does may be the sort of thing such a character will inevitably or probably say or do and the events of the plot may follow one after another either inevitably or with probability. (Obviously, then, the *denouement* of the plot should arise from the plot itself and not be brought about "from the machine," as it is in *Medea* and in the embarkation scene in the *Iliad*. The machine is to be used for matters lying outside the drama, either antecedents of the action which a human being cannot know, or things subsequent to the action that have to be prophesied and announced; for we accept it that the gods see everything. Within the events of the plot itself, however, there should be nothing unreasonable, or if there is, it should be kept outside the play proper as is done in the *Oedipus* of Sophocles).

Inasmuch as tragedy is an imitation of persons who are better than the average, the example of good portrait-painters should be followed. These, while reproducing the distinctive appearance of their subjects in a recognizable likeness, make them handsomer in the picture than they are in reality. Similarly the poet when he comes to imitate men who are irascible or easygoing or have other defects of character should depict them as such and yet as good men at the same time. An example involving harshness is the way Agathon and Homer portray Achilles.

These, then, are matters to be carefully observed, as also are matters appertaining to the sense-perceptions that the poet's art necessarily entails, for in respect to these too it is often possible to miss the mark. A sufficient account of them has been given in my published discourse.

Different Kinds of Recognition (Anagnorisis)

What Recognition is in general has already been explained. To turn now to its several species, first (1) there is the form that is least artistic and, from poverty of invention, the one they use most—that is recognition by marks or tokens. Such marks are sometimes congenital, as "the lance the earth-born bear," or the "stars in Carcinus' *Thyestes,* and sometimes acquired, either something on the person, like a scar, or external tokens such as necklaces or the boat in *Tyro.* Even these, however, can be used in better or worse ways. Thus Odysseus is recognized by means of his scar in one way by the nurse and in another way by the swineherds. The recognitions by the herdsmen and all such recognitions as use tokens as proofs of identity are artistically worse, while those that occur spontaneously like the one in the Bath Scene are better. Second (2) are recognitions obviously managed by the poet and inartistic for that reason. An instance is the way Orestes in *Iphigeneia* gets himself recognized as Orestes: Iphigeneia is spontaneously recognized through the letter, but Orestes speaks for himself in terms imposed by the poet and not by the plot. The fault here is close to the one just mentioned, since he might just as well have had a few marks or tokens on him. Another example is the "voice of the shuttle" in Sophocles' *Tereus.* A third type of recognition (3) is that which comes about through memory—i.e. a person's reaction upon seeing something. Thus in Dicaeogenes' *Cyprians,* the hero bursts into tears upon seeing the picture, and in the Alcinous episode Odysseus, when he hears the minstrel, is reminded of the past and weeps; therewith in both cases they are recognized. Fourth (4) is recognition through reasoning. This is exemplified in the *Choephori*: "Someone resembling me has come; no one but Orestes resembles me; therefore Orestes has come." Another example is the recognition suggested for *Iphigeneia* by Polyidus the sophist. It would be natural, he said, for Orestes to reflect that his sister had been sacrificed and here he was himself about to be sacrificed in turn. Again, in the *Tydeus* of Theodectes, the father says that he had come in search of his son only to meet with death himself. In the *Phinidae*, the women upon seeing the place drew this conclusion about their fate: that here they were doomed to die, since this was the place where they had been exposed in infancy. There is also (5) a composite kind of recognition resulting from faulty interference by one party or the other. For instance, in *Odysseus the False Messenger*, the point that Odysseus and no one else can string the bow is something set up by the poet and is the basic premise [and it remains so] even if the messenger did say that he would know the bow which he had not seen; but having him gain recognition by this second means [i.e. by identifying the bow] on the assumption that he was going to be recognized by the first means [stringing the bow] is a fallacy.

Of all the forms of recognition, however, the best is that which springs from the events themselves, the shock of surprise having thus a probable basis. Such are the recognitions in the *Oedipus* of Sophocles and in *Iphigeneia*: it is probable that Iphigeneia should wish to send a letter. Only recognitions of this kind escape the artificiality of tokens and necklaces. Next best are recognitions that result from reasoning.

C. M. BOWRA

[Sophoclean Characters]†

The seven surviving plays of Sophocles form so small a proportion of what he wrote that it is rash to generalize from them about the nature of his art. Some of the lost plays, over a hundred in number, may have been constructed on principles quite different from those that survive. In the circumstances we can only hope that the surviving selection is somehow representative. It is at least a real selection. Whenever it was made, it was made with an educational purpose and must represent the choice of educated men who believed that it gave a fair or useful notion of Sophoclean tragedy. Moreover, despite great uncertainty about dates, this selection covers

† From C. M. Bowra, *Sophoclean Tragedy* (Oxford: The Clarendon Press, 1944), pp. 356–381. Reprinted by permission of the publisher.

some forty years of Sophocles' life. The *Ajax* seems to be earlier
than the *Antigone*, which was produced about 442 B.C., the *Philoctetes* was produced in 409 B.C., and the *Oedipus at Colonus* must
have been composed in the poet's last years. The other three plays
cannot be dated except perhaps relatively, and even about this
there is much dispute, though no one has suggested that any of
them is much earlier than the *Ajax*. The seven plays cover a wide
extent of time and differ much in construction, temper, and forma-
tive idea. Nor with Sophocles are we handicapped as with Aeschylus by possessing single plays of trilogies whose full import could be
seen only if we had all the members of a complex whole. Each of
the seven plays is at least complete in itself. Widely different as
they are, it should be possible to discover what principles underlie
them, what evidence they give about Sophocles' tragic art.

At the outset is may be well to consider a view which has won
more respect than it deserves and is still not quite discredited. It
has often been said that Sophocles is in some sense a 'purer' artist
than Aeschylus or Euripides, that he was not concerned with the
wider implications of the events which he dramatized or to draw
conclusions fom them, that he was not deeply interested in the
problems, religious or ethical or metaphysical, which his plots
might suggest, and that he had no answer for them. In so far as
Sophocles, unlike Aeschylus or Euripides, hardly refers to contemporary events, there is truth in these claims. It is also true that in
comparison with Euripides he was not impressed by the more
ingenious intellectual activities of his time or charmed by the agile
acrobatics of the Sophists. But analysis of the plays has shown that
each involves serious considerations about the nature of gods and of
men and gives a clue to what verdict should be passed on the
events dramatized. Sophocles is not a mere playwright, not a 'pure'
dramatist in the sense of one who is interested in nothing but plot
and character, whose only aim is to arouse excited anticipation
about what will happen next or enjoyment in the presentation of
vivid actions. Still less does his profound, searching, and sympathetic knowledge of the human soul justify us in thinking of him as
remote and detached. A man does not write like this unless he has
been deeply moved by the vagaries and passions which cast men up
and down. His detachment may indeed be godlike in its width of
vision and its power to create, but such a god feels for his creatures
and is deeply concerned about their destinies. The notion of the
impartial dispassionate Sophocles is so wrong that it needs a word
of comment.

It is based on two kinds of material, both interesting in their
own way but neither relevant to the conclusion which they are supposed to prove. The first consists of some ancient comments on

Sophocles. It happens that some literary critics of the Graeco-Roman age praise the beauty of his poetry and say nothing about his tragic vision or view of life. Even Dio Chrysostom, who was much interested in the ethical aspects of tragedy, praises him chiefly as a poet and quotes with approval two lines of Aristophanes:

> He used to lick the lips of Sophocles
> Smear'd o'er with sweetness like a honey-jar.

Dionysius praises the harmony of his composition, and the author of *On the Sublime*, who fully admires the majesty of his work, says nothing about its religious side. These critics admired his poetry, but that does not prove that they failed to see what lay behind it. Their judgements should not be extended to matters which they did not discuss. The theological background of Sophocles' work happened not to be their subject. Secondly, a few scraps of evidence about Sophocles' appearance and manners have been taken to be evidence about his art. The famous statue in the Lateran may be of him and may reveal a man who looks calm and dispassionate, but his looks do not always betray a poet's inmost thoughts. When Ion of Chios said of Sophocles, 'in state business he was neither clever or energetic but like one of the Athenian nobles', he tells us something about the poet's public life, which has little to do with his art, and something about his manners, which have nothing. When Aristophanes, soon after the death of Sophocles, characterised him as

> He, who was happy here, is happy there,

he described the man whom he had known, with a hint at his heroization after death, but he says nothing about his work. Phrynichus summed up his life in a similar spirit:

> How blessed Sophocles, who, dying old,
> Was old in happiness and skill of hand.
> Beautiful were his Tragedies, and many;
> And beautiful his end, who lived untroubled;

and his words get some support from Cephalus' account of the old Sophocles who has found peace of mind in his freedom from the passions of youth. These are the personal judgements of friends on a friend. They tell nothing of the experiences through which Sophocles passed in creating his tragic world and nothing of what he meant by his art. They add no more to our knowledge of his work than the contemporary description of Shakespeare as 'a handsome well shaped man, very good company, and of very ready and pleasant smooth wit' does to our knowledge of *Hamlet* and *King Lear*. For Sophocles, as for Shakespeare, what matter are the plays.

Another error is more likely than this to impose on good judges just because they feel the force of Sophocles' art and know what poetry is. It is the belief, partly due to a verbal confusion, that in the last resort Sophoclean and Shakespearian tragedy are both variants of a single form. It seems only right that Greek *tragoedia* should be similar to Elizabethan Tragedy. The words suggest it. Moreover, the two are like each other in many important respects. Both display abrupt and unforeseen changes of fortune which engage profound interest and sympathy; both display the hazards of the mortal state and the depths, no less than the heights, which human nature can touch; both are concerned with the great not merely in station but in natural endowments and force of character; both involve, sooner or later, speculations about the powers that govern the universe, about their justice or injustice, their solicitude or indifference to suffering men; both lead through crisis, agony, and disaster to an end which somehow, despite all the horror, provides peace. The similarities between Sophoclean and Shakespearian tragedy justify comparison and suggest speculations. But there are also differences, and to neglect these may lead to misunderstanding and false analogies. Sophoclean *tragoedia* is not Shakespearian Tragedy. Narrower in some respects, it is wider in others, and the differences show a real difference of conception.

The first, most obvious, distinction between the two kinds is that while Shakespeare's tragedies end in the death of the chief character or characters, only one of Sophocles' surviving plays, the *Women of Trachis*, so ends. To this we may well add the *Antigone*, in which Creon loses all that makes life worth living, and *King Oedipus*, in which Oedipus' fall is a kind of obliteration, a severance from his own past life and from the lives of other men. But of the other four plays not one has even an unhappy ending. The *Ajax* does indeed show the hero's death, but it ends with the satisfaction of honour and amends paid to him. The last three plays end in glory and triumph, however tempered such may be by the agony and shame through which they are reached. It is true that the Shakespearian Folio classes *Troilus and Cressida* and *Cymbeline* as tragedies, but this has been regarded as an eccentric foible and is not commonly accepted. It is not on these plays that critics base their views of Shakespeare's tragic art. It is also true that certain plays of Shakespeare, such as *A Winter's Tale* and even *The Tempest*, have something in common with the last plays of Sophocles in so far as their movement is through ugly passions and even gruesome situations to a quiet end. But in these plays there is an element of unreality, of remoteness from ordinary life, of magic and marvel, which is alien to Sophocles. It seems to soften the harshness of what happens, to throw a romantic light over it, even to detract from its importance. A similar art may well be observed in such plays of Euripides as the *Helen* and *Iphigeneia in Tauris* which are rightly compared to romantic comedies. But such plays have no real tragic conflict; they display no really serious issue. Therefore they are unlike those plays of Sophocles which end happily. For these are profoundly serious and arouse tragic emotions. In them Sophocles reveals a conception of tragedy to which Shakespeare provides no real parallel. It is therefore wrong to assume that his tragic art is the same as Shakespeare's.

A second difference is more fundamental. In every play of Sophocles the gods take an active, even a decisive, part. Their will is done, even though men resist it. It may work on or through the characters, but it works. The gods may participate directly in the action like Athene or Heracles, or indirectly as through Teiresias in the *Antigone* or through oracles which are invariably fulfilled. In Shakespeare, too, superhuman powers are at work. The Witches in *Macbeth* and the Ghost in *Hamlet* affect the action, but only a part of it, and that only because they appeal to something latent in those human beings to whom they appear, to the hidden ambition of Macbeth and the lurking suspicions of Hamlet. Even the malign coincidence which blasts fortunes in *King Lear* and *Othello* is not nearly so potent or so present as the divine powers which Sophocles sets to work. The evil that wrecks Lear and Othello is not in their stars but in the corrupt souls of men. Shakespeare is so untheological a poet that we do not know what his religious beliefs were, whereas it is impossible to appreciate Sophocles without seeing him against the background of the Olympian gods as the fifth century knew them. His plays are religious in a sense that Shakespeare's are not. They display directly the relations between gods and men. The field of their action is not political or national or even domestic; it is the single reality to which both gods and men belong. Nor is this accidental. The plays were performed at a religious festival. Precedent, as we know it in Aeschylus, shows that at an earlier stage tragedy was concerned with essentially religious issues. Sophocles followed precedent and propriety when he made plays about the relations of gods and men.

If this modern analogy is in some ways deceptive, we might still hope to learn something from the ancients, especially from Aristotle's discussion of tragedy in his *Poetics*. He knew and admired the work of Sophocles; much of his theory is based on *King Oedipus*; he was born some twenty years after the death of Sophocles and was well qualified to understand the plays as their author intended them to be understood. No critic, ancient or modern, compares with him for authority. He had at his disposal the author's complete works; he could approach them with his omnivorous curiosity and incomparable memory; he must have seen many of them acted and learned how Athenian actors thought that the parts should be interpreted. It is therefore no matter for surprise that his analysis of Greek tragedy dominated poetical thought for generations and gave to its study many standards and conceptions which are still current. Yet wonderfully acute and true though much of his criticism is, Aristotle does not entirely satisfy when he deals with the nature of tragedy, at least as we know it in the practice of Sophocles. At times in his desire to find a comprehensive formula he seems to neglect important factors; at other times he finds a formula which is indeed true so far as it goes, but he fails to see how much there is in it. Of course he generalizes from so vast a mass of particular cases that no formula can suit every one of them. Nor was he concerned so much with tragedy as it is as with what in his opinion it ought to be. Yet he does define tragedy and analyse its essential characteristics. We are therefore justified in applying his doctrine to the surviving plays of Sophocles.

When Aristotle says that tragedy is 'an imitation of an action that is serious' in the sense that it deals with material that is not paltry or ridiculous, there can be no quarrel with him. His definition covers the plays of Sophocles, though it may not be so apt for all the plays of Euripides. Whatever the conclusion of a Sophoclean tragedy may be, it is reached only when issues of great importance have been fought out on the stage. The mood in which these are presented, the characters who display them, the language of speech and song, all contribute to an extremely serious result. This is no pastime, but the imaginative vision of a poet who makes his art a means to present important issues with great intensity and concentration. Moreover, when Aristotle goes on to say that tragedy produces its effect through pity and fear, he may not say everything that might be said but his words are applicable to Sophocles. Pity for the characters in their illusions and their helplessness induces a mood of humility closely allied to fear, not merely when the characters come to a tragic end, like Creon, Heracles, and Oedipus, but when, like Neoptolemus and Philoctetes, they pass through great moral dangers before finding success. It is true even of Electra, in whose ultimate triumph there is still an element of horror not far from fear, and of the old Oedipus, whose end, fraught with anxieties and mysteries, awakes both pity for him and awe before the incalculable justice of the gods. And these feelings, despite the horrors that arouse them, lead to a final sense of relief and harmony even in the *Women of Trachis* and *King Oedipus*, an acceptance of the divine will and a mood of resignation, of 'calm of mind, all passion spent'. This process may well have been what Aristotle meant by 'purification'. So far his analysis is penetrating and right.

It is when he advances to more detailed matters that he suggests certain corrections.

Aristotle attaches special importance to two elements in the plot, Reversal and Discovery. So far as dramatic action is concerned, he is right. No play is really conceivable without something of each. For while Reversal means that the situation of the chief characters changes, Discovery means that something unknown is made known. Without these two elements a play would lack development and dramatic interest. They are present in all plays of Sophocles, but their significance is greater than Aristotle seems to have seen, certainly greater than he said. He defines both too carefully. First, Reversal. This he defines as 'the change from one state of things in the play to its opposite', and he means change of fortune whether from good to bad or from bad to good. It is true that the chief characters of Sophocles endure some such Reversal. While Creon, Heracles, and Oedipus pass from prosperity to misery, Electra, Philoctetes, and the old Oedipus pass from misery to something that might be called prosperity, and Ajax illustrates both changes in his fall from honour to death and in his rehabilitation after death. But Aristotle's formula does not convey the wide variety of which such changes are capable. He seems to regard them as a matter of good or bad luck. This is inadequate in two ways. First, by stressing the element of luck he omits the parts played by the characters themselves and by the gods. He seems to suggest that external circumstance, coincidence or the like, is more important than motivated action. This is untrue. Luck plays almost no part in the careers of Sophoclean heroes and heroines. Secondly, even if we do not press his words too closely, it is clear that the actual changes are by no means confined to mere good and bad fortune, to the happiness and misery of the characters. Deianira is unhappy even before her disasters begin; Electra's triumph is hardly matter for true joy even to her. It is true that Creon passes from self-satisfied contentment to utter misery and Philoctetes from obstinate misery to glory. But in most cases the reversal is something different. The question of happiness or unhappiness seems irrelevant to what really happens. When Ajax changes from mad arrogance to humble sanity, Deianira from rash hope to suicidal despair, Oedipus from confident illusion to self-abasing knowledge, Electra from hate to love, the old Oedipus from human to superhuman life, the changes are so various that no single word covers them. Most of them indeed are less of fortune than of heart, and even if they are not so much as this, what counts is not the reversal in the hero's position but the change in himself.

A similar narrowness may be found in Aristotle's treatment of Discovery. He defines it carefully as 'a change from ignorance to knowledge, and thus to either love or hate, in the personages marked for good or evil fortune'. The only Discovery he recognizes is that of one person by another, and his example of Orestes and Iphigeneia in the *Iphigeneia in Tauris* shows what he means. In Sophocles the only Discovery of this kind is between Electra and Orestes. It conforms to Aristotle's description. Brother and sister discover each other, find a new love and a new strength, and through these a change for the better in their fortunes. But in the other plays the Discoveries are not like this. It is true that Aristotle mentions Oedipus in this connexion and must refer to the scene where the Messenger recognizes Oedipus as the child whose life he saved years before on Cithaeron. But in the context this is important not because the Messenger recognizes Oedipus but because Oedipus discovers who he himself is. It is the self-discovery that matters. Because of it Oedipus blinds himself. And in most of the other plays the Discoveries are not of other persons by the chief characters but of themselves. Ajax finds that he has been the victim of insane delusions, Creon that he has acted with gross injustice, Heracles that the gods have kept him not for peace but for a hideous death, Philoctetes that he has been obstructing the divine will, the old Oedipus that he, a beggar and an outcast, has the powers of a hero. Even Electra in her discovery of her brother finds something about herself, her need for love after hatred, and the satisfaction which it brings. In each case the chief character finds something about himself, and this discovery determines the course of the play.

It seems then that Aristotle is right to attach importance to Reversal and Discovery, but that his analysis unduly limits them. If we look more closely, we see how essential both are for Sophoclean tragedy, how closely related to each other in its most crucial moments. This, too, within his limits, Aristotle saw when he said that the best form of Discovery was that attended by Reversals. The truth is that the two are intimately, even inevitably, connected, and that this connexion is fundamental to Sophocles' effects. We might even say that if Sophoclean Discovery is the discovery by a character of some vital truth about himself, Sophoclean Reversal is the reversal in his condition, both inner and outer, which attends this. Aristotle praises this combination in *King Oedipus*, and rightly, though there is more in it than he says. For when Oedipus finds out who he is, his fall is complete. The mere fact of discovery is his humiliation. Ajax' decision to kill himself arises directly from his recognition of what he has done in his madness and from the shame that he feels at it; Creon's final annihilation owes much to his discovery that he has acted like a fool; Deianira's life is ruined with her realization of her hideous mistake. So, too, in the plays that end happily Discovery promotes the end. Orestes and Electra find enough strength from their recognition of one another to proceed at once to vengeance; Philoctetes accepts his glorious destiny when he finds his true self through Heracles' intervention; the old Oedipus is ready for his passing when he has found the range of his daemonic powers and knows that he has settled his earthly claims. In each case the character's discovery of an important truth is the dramatic climax. Compared with this result Aristotle's insistence on the change to 'either hate or love' is secondary even when it occurs.

The discovery of such a truth is a severe test of those who make it. Pindar says

Trial is the test of men,

and his words may be applied to Sophoclean Discovery. Only when they know the real facts about themselves do the characters show what they really are. All of them live in some kind of illusion or ignorance until the gods force the truth on them. In their reception of it they show their worth. At the bottom of the scale are those who are so ruined by vice or brutality that they fail altogether to learn anything. Clytaemnestra neglects the dream by which the gods warn her; Creon in *Oedipus of Colonus* profits nothing by the salutary lesson which Theseus gives him. Such invincible ignorance betrays its victims as beyond hope or redemption. The others learn at least something of what happens to them. Creon in the *Antigone* realizes at least his own insignificance, and better men than he learn more and profit more. Women like Deianira and Jocasta kill themselves rather than face the consequences of their discoveries, but before they die they at least show their true selves, Deianira in her love for her home and Jocasta in her decision that her right place is with her dead husband. The men are more impressive. They suffer more, and the first shock of the truth may be, as it is for Ajax, almost annihilating. But Ajax recovers and humbles himself; Heracles accepts his hideous end with heroic fortitude; Oedipus assists the gods in their plan to humiliate him. Blows which might have broken lesser men bring out noble modesty and courage. So, too, in a different way, those for whom the discovery of the truth means a change to better times reveal their hidden strength and new forces of character. Electra, Philoctetes, and the old Oedipus show unexpected powers when at last they know what their destinies are.

The knowledge acquired by the characters is about themselves, but primarily about themselves in relation to the gods. For Sophocles this is the essential and fundamnetal knowledge. A man does not know himself or his place until he knows how he stands with the gods. This is obvious with Ajax, Creon, Oedipus, and Philoctetes. They are taught directly who they are and what they must do. When at last they understand the divine will, they have no more illusions and accept their condition. It is also true of Heracles, who forgets his sufferings and his hatred of Deianira when he knows that his death is ordained by the gods; of Electra, whose doubts and hesitations and despairs are resolved by the confidence that the gods are acting for her; of the old Oedipus, who sees on arriving at Colonus that his end is near and, when the thunder sounds, knows that he must go. This acceptance of the truth is a kind of submission, of obedience, even when it brings hope to Electra or a promise of power to the old Oedipus. The characters have learned that they must do what the gods demand, and illustrate what the Platonic Socrates means when he says that the commands 'Know thyself' and 'Be modest' are the same. They find modesty because they have learned to know themselves. So the central idea of a Sophoclean tragedy is that through suffering a man learns to be modest before the gods. Each leading character is taught by the gods the lesson which Pindar preaches to Hieron:

O find, and be, yourself!

Each learns his real state and accepts it by abandoning his illusions. To the audience the plays convey such a lesson. The characters whom they see humbled or exalted are types of men who, through ignorance or blindness of soul, have resisted their destinies. When they are finally forced to see the truth, we know that the gods have prevailed and that men must accept their own insignificance. It is this feeling which brings a sense of relief at the end of Sophoclean tragedy. Despite all the suffering and horror we feel not indignation but relief, because in spite of everything the human characters have made their peace with the gods.

The lesson is taught through suffering. Those who learn it must pay heavily for it, even if it is to bring them happiness in the end. Behind this lies the old adage that learning comes through suffering. The older poets who preached this were not always concerned with knowledge of the gods, but Sophocles was. He applies the lesson in a special way. The wisdom that man learns through suffering is that he is nothing before the gods and must conform to their will. The plays show the process and the means by which this is learned. Therefore the conflict in them is not so much between men and men as between men and gods. This is of course clear in the *Women of Trachis*, where Heracles and Deianira both struggle for ends which the gods deny to them. It is also clear in *King Oedipus*, where the conflict is between Oedipus' beliefs and the truth as it is presented by Teiresias and the Messenger. In other plays the human beings are involved in human conflicts, but even so the gods take part. Ajax resists them, and we know their will from Athene; the Atridae refuse burial, and the gods' point of view is given by Odysseus; Antigone throughout acts for the gods, and in resisting her Creon resists them and pays for it; Electra fights for the gods even at the cost of much spiritual damage to herself; in *Oedipus at Colonus* both Creon and Polynices oppose the divine will which Oedipus represents and Theseus assists; the whole trouble in the *Philoctetes* is that all the characters in their separate ways oppose the divine plan for the capture of Troy. The conflict in Sophoclean tragedy is mainly between divine and human purposes. It may, and usually does, involve conflicts between human beings, but in the last resort it arises from the differences between gods and men, from men's ignorance of their own state, or refusal to do what the gods demand.

Such a conflict has a peculiar poignancy because men must in the end lose. Since they act in ignorance, they are entitled to compassion, understanding, even forgiveness. But we must beware of thinking them noble simply because they resist the gods. The gods are always right and should not be opposed. When Hyllus or Philoctetes denounces the government of the universe, he is deluded by his passions and shows his pathetic ignorance. With Euripides it is different. His gods are of so questionable worth that those who fight against them have a kind of nobility because they resist powers who seem, and may indeed be, malign. There is real dignity when Hippolytus strives against Aphrodite or Creusa against Apollo. These gods are powerful, but their justice is dubious. Sophocles allows no doubts, no criticism of the gods. Sometimes indeed they are hard to understand, but none the less men must assume that all is as it ought to be. If divine ways seem wrong, human ignorance is to blame. In the end the gods will be proved right. The lowest kind of human being is he who is impervious to such enlightenment as the gods give. In their different ways Clytaemnestra, Odysseus in the *Philoctetes,* and Creon in *Oedipus at Colonus* show how certain passions can so harden the heart and delude the mind that generous or decent feelings die. Yet these degraded beings are still human. They are moved by familiar motives of sexual passion, ambition, and public advantage. No Sophoclean character, except perhaps Aegisthus, is so unmixedly evil as Lycus in Euripides' *Heracles.* There is no struggle in Sophocles between good and bad men except in a very limited sense. There is sometimes a struggle between the good and bad in a single man, but most commonly it is between men and the gods or those who represent their will. In this respect Sophocles presents a contrast to Shakespeare, who finds his tragic conflict between men who despite their faults are essentially noble and others who embody an active principle of wickedness. Iago, Lady Macbeth, and Goneril act on motives so devilish and destructive that there is no apology for them. They belong to the evil powers of the world, and it is against them that Othello, Macbeth, and Lear fight and fail. Sophocles' characters cannot be so divided into good and bad. They come from one mould and suffer in different degrees from the same defects.

We might explain this absence of evil characters by saying that Sophocles lacked the Christian sense of sin, or at least the sense of evil which was prominent in the Renaissance. There might be truth in this, but it is hardly relevant. Euripides could create types of unmitigated evil, and we have no right to assume that the Greeks were duller to the potentialities of wickedness than we are. Sophocles recognized a bad man when he saw one and at times produced such on the stage. But what counted with him was not the division of men into good and bad, which must always be arbitrary, but the differing degrees of illusion which obsess men. His characters might almost be graded in such a scale. At the top are Odysseus in the *Ajax*, Antigone, and Theseus. They are enlightened and wise in that they know the will of the gods or at least accept it as soon as it is shown to them. But all the other characters, except the old Oedipus, are in some way deluded. One delusion may be greater and worse than another. Oedipus' belief in his innocence is plainly less odious than Odysseus' belief in his cleverness. Yet both are false, and both lead to harm. These delusions are manifested in several ways. The kingly temper of Oedipus, the possessive love of Deianira, the obstinate resentment of Philoctetes, are all equally misguided. Such delusions become wrong when their victims are so blinded by them that they cannot or will not see the truth. Then they work a fearful havoc in the human soul, as they do in Clytaemnestra. She is no triumphant murderess, but a creature of passion who is unable to resist her desires or to forgo her gains. She is made of 'frail clay, nay but foul clay', but she is not an incarnate devil. We excuse her as we do not excuse Goneril, though we know that her punishment is right. In fact the evil characters of Sophocles are surely nearer to actual life than those of Shakespeare, whose Iago is almost a symbol of the evil which every man may find in himself. The belong to the same stock as the other characters. What differentiates them is their deafness to what the gods teach.

Since most of Sophocles' characters are built on this plan it is not easy to see what is meant by saying, as is commonly said, that they are 'ideal'. Such an adjective may be deserved by the early Odysseus, by Antigone, by Theseus, and by the old Oedipus. For these act as the gods will. But the word 'ideal' suggests a lack of individuality and life, and is more appropriate to types than to individuals. None of these are types or lack recognizable characteristics. Still less are most of the other characters 'ideal' in any ethical sense. They have great qualities, but these are often marred by faults. The alleged 'ideal' characters of Sophocles may owe something to the idealizing Hellenism of the eighteenth century, but the belief has a more reputable base in his own words, as Aristotle reports them, 'I make men as they should be, Euripides as they are'. Yet this surely means no more than that Sophocles claimed to make characters as they should be in a play, while Euripides copied life. This seems to have been what Aristotle understood him to mean. For in the section where he quotes the remark he uses it as an argument that what is not true may none the less be what it ought to be in a play, and postpones till later his discussion whether actions in a play are really good and bad, as if this were a separate consideration. The 'ideal' characters of Sophocles seem to be a mirage. At least they do not exist in his plays.

At the other extreme is the view that so far from creating 'ideal' characters Sophocles did not create characters at all, that his personages do not speak and act in accordance with any principle of personality but simply because such speech and such action are demanded by the plot. Two examples will show how this method works. Ajax, it is claimed, lies when he says that he has made his peace with gods and men. There is no reason for this lying except that the poet wishes to get him away from the Chorus and Tecmessa that he may die alone. Again, when Deianira claims that she will endure Heracles' love for Iole, she is acting dishonestly because the poet wishes to prepare the way for sending the robe. It is clear that if this theory is accepted, it is quite wrong to speak of characterization in Sophocles: for what interested him was plot, and he sacrificed characterization to this. As in many exaggerations, there is perhaps a very small grain of truth in this, though its exponent did not know it. In all great tragic poetry there comes a moment when characters cease to be individuals and become almost types of suffering humanity. In the first onrush of despair one character may speak very much like another. It is conceivable that what Lear says at the height of his tragedy might be said by Macbeth at the height of his; what Heracles says when he knows his doom is not unlike what Tecmessa says when she knows hers. But this is not what the advocate of the theory means. He maintains that there is no real characterization in Sophocles but only actions and statements that are out of situations.

It is perhaps no fatal objection to this view that it was not held by Sophocles himself. He recognized a stage in his own development when he changed his style to 'what is most expressive of character and best'. He evidently believed that he created characters and tried to make them speak in a suitable way. So most of his readers have also believed. Nor can such a belief be abandoned without good reason. If the characters can be interpreted as consistent and real, they have a right to be. Nor on close examination are the so-called inconsistencies of any importance. The alleged deceptions practised by Ajax and Deianira are illusory. The lack of clarity in Odysseus' plan to get hold of Philoctetes is not due to a lack of characterization but to his being characterized in a special way as the clever man who frustrates his own ends. The appearance of Teiresias in *King Oedipus* certainly has a wonderful dramatic value, but that does not mean that the old seer is unintelligible. He is sinister, remote, and forbidding, but that is what we might expect him to be. The theory assumes inconsistencies so gross as to make the characters absurd. But what are called inconsistencies are usually based on a misunderstanding of the text and afford small basis for so devastating a conclusion. Secondly, it is possible to imagine a drama in which character plays a small or negligible part, but Sophoclean drama is not of this kind. His characters come to their ends because they are what they are. They almost illustrate Heraclitus' words that 'character is destiny', though there is more in their destinies than character. Still, if they were not intelligible as men and women of this or that kind, their fates would have little significance and the dramatic scheme would be without interest. It is because Ajax is proud that he falls, because Philoctetes is fundamentally noble that he is at last rewarded, because the old Oedipus is superior to other men that the gods make him a *daimôn*. Their main characteristics are never out of our minds because we know that these help to determine their destinies and to explain them. Indeed it is hard to believe that the Greeks did not have so keen a sense of character as we like to claim for ourselves. The contemporaries of Herodotus and Aristophanes would look for human beings in Sophocles, and the fact that they admired him so much as they did indicates that they found them.

The world created by Sophocles has its own individuality, as have all worlds created by great artists. It is impossible to define it, but we may note some of its outstanding qualities. His personages of course belong to the great ones of the earth, kings and queens, commanders and rulers. That is natural enough; for most characters of Greek tragedy come from this class. Euripides may sometimes break its bounds and introduce his humbly born but noble-hearted Farmer into the *Electra*, but that is only another example of his tendency to break the traditional rules. There may well be a real tragedy of the humble, of men and women whose narrow compass makes their fall or failure seem no less cosmic than the fall of the great. But this was not what the Greeks practised. They were concerned with the great in station, with the heroic world which was the source of their plots and stories. Such persons were especially likely to be the victims of divine displeasure; their lofty position made their fall all the greater when it came; they could have that strength or force of character which belongs to the mighty and is of peculiar interest to the dramatist. Whatever their reasons, poets dealt with the great, and so did Sophocles. But his great have something more than birth or position. They have a real nobility of character, a natural superiority or *aretê* which displays itself in word and action. Each of his great princes, Ajax, Heracles, Oedipus, Philoctetes, is superior to other men in power to command or ability to endure or simple greatness of heart. Their superiority comes out in contrast with the qualities of men less gifted than themselves. Ajax' full stature is revealed when the Atridae, men of far baser mould, try to denigrate him. The stern masculinity of Heracles, severe and forbidding though it is, belongs to a grander order of being than the desperate uncertainty of Deianira. The kingly pride of Oedipus, ready to face emergencies and to take every responsibility, is more adventurous than the self-effacing modesty of Creon. The impressive, passionate Philoctetes shows his true worth in contrast to the cold-blooded calculating Odysseus. These heroes are alike in their *aretê*. We can understand why they hold great positions and win respect, why they face their sufferings with such endurance and their humiliations with a high sense of their own honour, why they count their reputation before everything else. They are superior beings, gifted above other men.

More surprising than Sophocles' men are his women. He certainly understood the conventional ideal of womanhood as it was held in Periclean Athens. His Tecmessa shows what poetry he found in the type, and what pathos. But she is hardly a tragic heroine. His great women are not like her and are more calculated to shock Athenian opinion than to conform to it. Antigone and Electra know that they act in the face of respectable opinion and that they are right to do so. Their resistance demands a heavy price, but nothing undermines their determination. The superiority which they display is not a woman's but a man's in its unflinching purpose and refusal to compromise. But they are driven not by desire for honour but by affection and loyalty to the dead who have been injured and to the sacred ties of their families. They break the limits proper to womanhood because the gods require it. The truly tragic heroines, Deianira and Jocasta, also break these limits, but for wrong reasons and to their own great harm. Yet in them too affection is the driving force. Deianira's love for Heracles drives her

to her desperate decision to secure him by magic, Jocasta's love for
Oedipus makes her shun the truth and then kill herself. The
women of Sophocles have this in common, that affection moves
them both to good and to ill. Even Clytaemnestra is driven to
crime by love for Aegisthus. And the women who fail to be great,
the typically modest Chrysothemis and to a lesser extent Ismene,
fail because their affections are feeble. In their desire for a quiet
life they are prepared to take no risks, even though they know that
such are demanded of them by their loved ones.

The climax of Sophoclean tragedy comes when these superior
beings pass through a change for better or for worse. When Theo-
phrastus defined tragedy as 'a revolution in heroic fortune', his
words are relevant to Sophocles. For these characters are heroic
both in the ancient and in the modern sense; they belong to the
high company of the epic world, and they have the endurance and
noble spirit which we call heroic. Sophocles peopled his tragic
world with superior beings, men of great power and character,
women of deep and tender affections. When such fall, their fall is
great. The men lose power, reputation, honour, respect, happiness,
all that they have desired and enjoyed with their strong, tenacious
natures; the women lose home, love, contentment, ease, all that has
made them happy. In their fall both men and women may be the
objects of scorn, misunderstanding, and hatred. The deaths of Ajax,
Antigone, Jocasta, and Deianira are all accompanied by one or
other of these undeserved wrongs. The wound is the sharper
because it is inflicted at the very centre of honour or affection. It is
the most noble qualities which are misunderstood, the courage of
Ajax, the loyalty of Antigone, the love of Deianira and of Jocasta.
The reversal is in more than their fortunes; it is in their lives and
what makes life worth living. So, too, in the plays which end happily, the suffering or frustrated characters find the one thing that
they most need, the satisfaction of their most hungry instinct. Electra's hatred for her mother turns into a new love for Orestes; the
resentful and lonely Philoctetes is restored in honour to the company of living men; the despised and polluted Oedipus is raised to
power and glory. The change through which the Sophoclean characters pass is not external or accidental. It concerns their innermost
natures, their essential qualities.

The suffering which is part of the tragic destiny usually arises
from some element in the souls of those who are destined to it.
Most often this is a passion which dominates the character, con-
founds the judgement, and leads to a disastrous conflict. It makes
men assert their will at the expense of truth and overpowers their
sense of reality. This passion takes different forms. In Ajax it is an
uncompromising sense of his own worth, his pride, his heroic

honour; in Deianira a desperate confidence that she can, despite all propriety and likelihood, keep her husband to herself; in Oedipus a kingly pride and high spirit which prevents him from seeing the truth; in Philoctetes a strength both in love and in hate which blinds him to his glorious destiny. In each the passion is strongly self-assertive and makes its possessor feel that he is right and that almost everyone else is wrong. It produces a special delusion which contains the beginnings of ruin. Passions like these are the portion of great characters. Plato regards the self-assertive element as fundamental to human nature and thinks that it normally works for good. Sophocles created characters in whom it may normally work for good but at times works for ill. The qualities which have raised Ajax and Heracles and Oedipus to glory are the cause of their undoing. Nor can we really say that their mistakes come from a perversion or misuse of their great qualities. The quality which makes Ajax a great soldier makes him incur the anger of the gods by his self-confidence; the passionate intensity which carries Heracles through his life of labours informs his love for Iole and drives him to the destruction of Oechalia; the temper of Oedipus has made him king of Thebes, but prevents him from seeing the truth and makes him feel his humiliation all the more when at last he knows it. In this respect the heroes of Sophocles differ from Shakespeare's. Hamlet, Lear, Othello, and Macbeth fall because of some fault in an otherwise noble nature, a fault which grows until it dominates their characters and encompasses their ruin. This fault is a real flaw, at variance with their true selves. The great men of Sophocles fall because they are what they are, because their great gifts may in the wrong circumstances be turned against them, because the gods choose to humble them by the same means which once exalted them. Even when all is well in the end, the same process is at work and great qualities create great dangers. Electra's love for her father almost ruins her nature with hate for his murderers; the generous emotional Philoctetes nearly wrecks himself by following his emotions too far. In this there is a kind of justice which is lacking in Shakespeare. If Shakespeare creates tragedy out of human weakness, out of small faults which spread and work havoc, Sophocles creates his out of human strength. The qualities which exalt a man above his fellows are those which sooner or later bring him into conflict with them and with the gods. At the worst pride may turn into madness as it does with Ajax, but even if it does not, the danger is always present and the gods may send suffering to its actual or potential victim. In Shakespeare the tragic scheme is different. The theological background is absent. He is concerned with the fall of the great, and attributes it to some weakness in them on which powers of evil play until they work destruction.

Since the conflict is with the gods, it is natural that men should be humiliated by violent and unconquerable forces. These need not be supernatural, though the madness of Ajax, the shirt of Nessus, the *daimôn* who guides Oedipus, are. But it happens that Sophocles sometimes depicts kinds of suffering from which modern sensibility shrinks. The great Heracles, racked and rotted by the Hydra's poison, Oedipus with his bleeding and blinded eyes, Philoctetes with his festering and stinking foot, are gruesome and almost unbearable. Nor did the ancients feel differently about them. At least Aristotle thought that horrors were more properly narrated than acted, and Horace followed him. Neither Aeschylus nor Euripides presents such physical horrors on the stage. Nor is it an accident that Sophocles' surviving plays have such. They could have been found in plays now lost, in the hideous catastrophes of the *Tereus* or the destruction of children on the stage in the *Niobe*. The element of physical horror was used by Sophocles to secure tragic effect. We can only guess why. It is possible that he was moved by his great sense of the difference between gods and men. The gods are immortal and ageless, free from suffering and disease, as Pindar says:

> For they are without eld and sickness,
> Without knowledge of sorrow, and have escaped
> The loud cries of Acheron's flood.

But men are easily assailed through their bodies. In these lies their strength, and when they are destroyed through them, it is a sign that their strength is gone. When Ajax kills himself with the sword that slew the cattle, when Heracles perishes through the Hydra's poison, they show that the very source of their power is the means of their destruction. When Oedipus, the great king, appears blind with blood on his face or Philoctetes is flung into senseless delirium, we see how helpless even these strong men are. It is another sign of their inferiority to the gods.

The collapse or destruction of physical strength is often accompanied by a spiritual state of great tragic import. The sufferer finds himself isolated from his kind. He may have his devoted friends and adherents, as Ajax has Tecmessa and his sailors, Electra the Chorus, the old Oedipus his daughters. But somehow these confidants stand at a distance and do not quite enter into the lives of those whom they attend. Heracles, Antigone, Electra, Philoctetes live by themselves, almost for themselves, and this isolation is all the greater when the crisis comes. At the end Heracles has no one but Hyllus; Antigone bewails her utter desolation; Philoctetes makes his last decision in solitude. Even Ajax goes out alone to die, and Electra's darkest hour is when she believes that her brother is dead and decides to exact vengeance without him. This isolation is right. These great personalities are not made for easy companionship. They demand too much, their standards are too high, for them to enter into the compromises of ordinary life. Even the old Oedipus has a forbidding majesty which keeps him apart and instils awe and fear into the men of Colonus. Such beings are alone because they are unlike others, because they are superior. When they act in defiance of ordinary rules, their isolation is accentuated still more when disaster comes. Even after death Ajax is severed from the other dead when burial is denied to him; in her rocky prison Antigone belongs neither to the living nor to the dead; when Deianira goes round her house for the last time, she feels that she is no longer a wife or a mother; Oedipus blinds himself that he may be severed from all human contacts; Philoctetes accepts the gibe of Odysseus that he must walk Lemnos alone. But after the tragic crisis and the isolation which it brings, the sufferers are restored to a kind of communion with their kind. Ajax is buried, and his spirit joins the company of honoured dead; Antigone kills herself and finds her brother in Hades; Deianira is forgiven by her son; Oedipus accepts his destiny and assists it; Philoctetes finds a new friend in Neoptolemus and then makes his peace with the Achaeans. The tragic conflict forces its victims out of the framework of organized harmonious life, but once the crisis is over, and the price has been paid, the sufferers return to some kind of order, even of union with their kind whether living or dead.

Sophoclean tragedy turns on a conflict between gods and men. For this conflict the gods have a reason. They wish to teach a lesson, to make men learn their mortal limitations and accept them. It is the lesson which Pindar draws from the story of Asclepius:

> We must ask from the Gods things suited to hearts that shall die,
> Knowing the path we are in, the nature of our doom.

This is what Sophocles' characters learn, but it is applied on a much wider scale than in Pindar's instance. When Asclepius revived a man from the dead, he broke the gods' laws and had to pay for it. His punishment is deserved. But with the exception of Creon hardly one of Sophocles' characters is in a position to avert his doom. They are so blinded by their illusions, so much the victims of their own natures and passions, that they have little freedom of choice. The sudden rush of confidence in Deianira, the growing obstinacy of Philoctetes, are beyond rational control. In Heracles and in Oedipus the doom which the gods have ordained allows no escape. No matter what they do, they will be forced to learn their lesson. Human suffering may come through men themselves, but the primal cause of it lies with the gods. Sophocles was for most purposes anticipated by Theognis, who tells Cyrnus that no man is responsible for his own weal or woe or knows what will happen: all mortal calculations are useless, for the gods carry out everything according to their own designs. Such a theology covers cases so different as Deianira and Philoctetes, Electra and the old Oedipus. It recognizes the ignorance in which men live and the power of the gods to do what they will with them.

When the gods treat men in this way, it is natural to ask if they are just. The same question occurred to Euripides, who more than once puts Apollo in the wrong and makes even real powers like Aphrodite and Dionysus destructive and heartless. There is undeniably a kind of tragedy in which man fights a futile battle against merciless superhuman powers who seek his destruction. It has its own grandeur and is the only kind of tragedy possible in an age which has ceased to believe that the gods are beneficent or rational. But such tragedies were not written by Sophocles. Philoctetes and Hyllus may cry out against divine injustice, Jocasta ascribe everything to chance, but their decisions are not final and are reversed by facts. Sophocles accepts the ultimate justice and wisdom of the gods. He would agree with Theognis that they act according to their own plans, and he would add that these plans are just. He does not always make their reasons clear, but he assumes that they have reasons, and he hints that once the divine will has been done men are better for it. This theological background does not make the plays less tragic. The sufferings may be by human standards undeserved, but they still arouse pity and fear. The gods are always right, but their victims are entitled to compassion and understanding.

Sophocles might well have stopped at the assumption that whatever the gods do is right and have made no further attempt to explain their ways. But in each case he suggests or gives an explanation for what they do. It is hard to reduce these explanations to a single belief, and perhaps it is foolish to attempt it. For Sophocles may have changed his ideas with the years. But we may in fact recognize three stages in his theology which are not absolutely different but certainly distinguishable. In the first stage, in the *Ajax* and *Antigone,* the scheme is simple and almost traditional. Ajax is punished for pride to Athene; Creon is the victim of a pride which breeds destructive infatuation. The notions are familiar from Aeschylus and need no comment. But this scheme which works well with the guilty does not suit cases where guilt is less clear and the apparently innocent or unconsciously guilty suffer. In the *Women* of *Trachis* and *King Oedipus* the gods act as they do simply to teach a lesson. It is salutary but not a punishment; it is even in its dark way a benefit. In the third stage, in the plays which end 'happily', the gods are with some care shown to be just. In the *Electra* they further the punishment of the wicked; in the *Philoctetes* a much injured man is raised to health and honour; in *Oedipus at Colonus* the gods make amends to one who has suffered greatly at their hands. There is certainly a difference between the confident trust of the last plays and the dark hints of the middle plays. In the last three the ways of the gods are presented in a way that satisfies the human conscience. Their participation in men's lives is shown to be governed by such rules as men set up for themselves; they display right and justice in the human sense of the words. At the end of his life Sophocles seems to have wished to demonstrate the justice no less than the power of the gods.

This apparent divergence of outlook may possibly indicate a real development in Sophocles' opinions. He may have passed from an Aeschylean theology to something less definite and from that to a position in which he vindicated the justice of the gods by human standards. But in the absence of so much of his work and in the uncertain state of his chronology it is dangerous to trust such a conclusion. For the different views displayed in his tragedies could after all be held by the same man without any gross inconsistency. In all three stages we might discern a general view that the gods are ultimately just both in punishment and in reward but that sometimes their reasons are not easy to discern. In fact all three positions seem to have been held by Herodotus. His Cambyses and Xerxes are examples of the presumption which the gods punish through its own infatuation; his Croesus is a good king who is humbled to learn modesty; his Cyrus is a noble but unknown man who is raised to great glory in accordance with a divine plan revealed in dreams. Greek theology had no single theory to account for the changes and chances of mortal life, and explained diverse events in diverse ways. It was possible for Sophocles, as it was for Herodotus, to use now this explanation, now that. Yet though his different views may be harmonized, we must still feel that in the last three plays Sophocles makes the power of the gods less external and more intimate than in the first four. In *Ajax* and *Antigone* the gods interfere almost from without by direct action. Ajax is driven mad by Athene; Creon is forced to repent by the evil omens and unburned sacrifices. In the *Women of Trachis* and *King Oedipus* oracles are fulfilled because they must be, but their fulfilment does not follow any plan of good in conflict with evil. The fight against them is not really wrong so long as it is ignorant. But in the last plays the gods are emphatically on the side of right against wrong. They further the just punishment of Clytaemnestra and Aegisthus, refuse to allow their plan for the capture of Troy to succeed through the unprincipled methods of Odysseus, and sustain Oedipus in his battle against dark powers of political opportunism and filial neglect. Sophocles may not have changed the main structure of his beliefs, but he seems to have deepened their meaning, to have come to see more clearly how closely the power of the gods was interwoven with human life.

In this respect Sophocles was a true successor of Aeschylus, whose trilogies were equally concerned with the relations of gods and men. It is true that Aeschylus used themes like that of an hereditary doom, which Sophocles avoided, and that he is more obviously didactic. But there is a greater difference between him and Sophocles than this, a difference in the kind of solution found to the tragic conflict. For Sophocles, as we have seen, the end is a resigned, reverent state of mind in the characters and through them in the audience. In Aeschylus the solution is more varied and more complex. In the *Oresteia* the dark issue of matricidal vengeance is solved by a new order of law and civic morality; the institution of the Areopagus embodies the conclusion that Orestes has acted rightly and been rightly acquitted, since murder must be punished. Aeschylus sees the question as one less for the private conscience than for society. In the trilogy which ends with the *Seven against Thebes* the hereditary doom which began with the impiety of Laius ends with the mutual slaughter of his two grandsons. In this there is certainly a warning against the far-reaching results of impiety, but the warning does not save Eteocles or Polynices. It concerns only the audience. And the curse, which they are forced to notice, belongs not to an individual but to a whole family for three generations. From this all too scanty evidence it is at least clear that Aeschylus followed different plans in his trilogies and did not make their conclusions conform to a single pattern. It is also probable that the ends which he found concerned the State and society more than individuals. What interested him in a tragic conflict was its effect on the world, not on a single soul. With this wide vision he could find conclusions which differed as much in temper as in content. If the *Oresteia* closes on a note of confident patriotic joy, the *Seven against Thebes* closes with a display of unfaltering doom. Sophocles works differently. His plays show what misfortune or good fortune do for the single soul and especially the modesty and acceptance which it learns. It looks as if Sophocles invented his own kind of tragedy and made it different from that of Aeschylus.

It is no less different from that of Euripides, in whose truly tragic

plays there is often a note not of resignation but of disquiet, even
of revolt. The gods' will is done and must be accepted, but with a
sense that it is wrong. Such is certainly the feeling aroused by the
Trojan Women, even to some extent by the *Hippolytus*. In the
Bacchants Dionysus has much right on his side, but he seems to
assert himself too savagely, and his final speech is neither satisfying
nor comforting. In other plays a mood of acceptance is indicated,
but it comes because of some divine intervention which overrules
what has happened. The peace which concludes the *Electra* or the
Ion comes almost in defiance of what has been done in the play. In
the *Heracles* the conclusion is due to the nobility of man and
comes in spite of the destructive gods. Euripides found no such
formula as Sophocles found, even when he dramatized without
irony or scepticism the power of gods over men. He may well have
accepted this power as a fact and made his characters accept it, but
this acceptance brings no peace of mind, no relief or satisfaction
after torments of the soul, no comfort in modesty and reverence.
Euripides is nearer to the modern world than Sophocles because his
characters move us simply by the horror of their fates and because
this horror serves no end but to inspire pity for them. That is perhaps why Aristotle's judgement that Euripides is 'the most tragic of
the poets' has been endorsed by so many. There is a finality about
his disasters which contains no consolation and seems almost to be
symbolical of the tragic condition of human life. Such things
happen, as we all know, and it may be useless to inquire too much
about them, or to expect to see them as parts in a harmonious
whole. But such is not Sophocles' way. He is not content merely to
portray evil, whether crime or waste or failure. He must relate it to
what he believes to be the scheme of things and show that it comes
from men's resistance to the gods.

For Sophocles the tragic issue arises in some breach in the divine
order of the world. No matter how the play ends, the conflict
which it shows comes because someone has gone too far and upset
the ordered harmony of life. In the *Ajax* and *Antigone* Ajax and
Creon transgress the Mean, are driven to brutal acts, and create
destruction in themselves and in others. In the *Women of Trachis*
Deianira's immodest decision to win back Heracles by magic leads
to her own and to his doom, and, more subtly, Heracles' own past
violence falls on his own head. In *King Oedipus* the great man's
violation of the divine laws is no less a breach of harmony than the
more conscious sins of Ajax and Creon. It brings disaster first to
Thebes, then to himself. In the later plays, where all ends well, the
tragic situation is caused by similar breaches of the divine order.
The crime of Clytaemnestra and Aegisthus creates a situation so

evil that it can be cured only by bloodshed; the original injustice done to Philoctetes is responsible for the collapse of the attempt to bring him to Troy; the earlier history of Oedipus, his pollution and his expulsion from Thebes, create a situation in which he curses his sons and shows all his terrible ferocity. In Sophocles the tragic situation is always some breach in the order of things, a violent discord which promotes angry passions and clouds the judgement. It does not matter whether it is made deliberately or not. The evil caused by the innocent Oedipus is little less than that caused by Clytaemnestra. What matters is that disorder is created. The essence of the tragic situation as Sophocles saw it may be symbolized in some words of his own, though no doubt they dealt with some specific and quite different situation:

> Not order but disorder, luckless one,
> It seems to be, and madness in your heart.

Some act of man destroys an existing order and substitutes disorder and madness for it. In different shapes this is the fundamental pattern of all Sophocles' surviving plays.

The tragic situation leads to a crisis which is usually violent. Then a conclusion comes either in destruction and loss or in some positive gain. In the later plays Sophocles happens to stress the gain, though there is no warrant for assuming that in old age he shrank from truly tragic catastrophes. In such cases we may well speak of reconciliation. The characters who have been at war with others or with circumstances or with themselves find peace and a new hope. Such a reconciliation is also to be felt at the end of the *Ajax*. Ajax has been at war with the gods and with men, but he has made his peace, and his burial shows that all is well. In the *Antigone* the reconciliation is sterner but hardly less satisfying. The amends which Creon pays for his work of destruction is right. He deserves what he gets; justice is done and right vindicated. His humiliation is a necessary preliminary to the re-establishment of justice in the world. In the *Women of Trachis* and in *King Oedipus* we may perhaps feel that, when all is said, there is still an unresolved discord, that such sufferings are heavier than they should be and that their cruelty is unexplained. Yet even here grave breaches are made in the divine order, and at the end they are healed. Heracles accepts his doom with heroic resignation; Oedipus takes upon himself the task of making amends. Both have broken the bounds set to men, and both end by subjecting themselves to the gods in consciousness of their own utter weakness. In each play the conflict is resolved in reconciliation. The disorder created by some untoward or violent act is ended, and harmony is restored.

R. C. JEBB

[The Characters of the *Oedipus Tyrannus*]†

A drama is itself the only adequate commentary on its persons.
It makes them live for us, or it does not. If we submit them to ethical analysis, this may be interesting to *us*, and instructive to those
who have not seen or read the piece. But, for a spectator or reader
of the play, the men and women must be those whom he finds
there. When we personally know a character in real life, another's
estimate of it is seldom more than a key to his point of view—
rarely a mental light which we feel that we can appropriate. And it
may be permitted to say in passing that this is a reason why the
reviving taste for good drama seems likely to aid in correcting a literary fault of the day which is frequently acknowledged—the tendency to adopt ready-made critical estimates of books which the
adopter, at least, has not read. No one who sees a play can help
forming some impression *of his own* about the characters. If he
reports it honestly, that is criticism; not necessarily good, but not
sham. To any one who reads this play of Sophocles with even
moderate attention and sympathy, how living is Oedipus! Common
experience proves so much; but almost every reader will probably
feel that by no attempt at analysis or description could he enable
another to see precisely *his* Oedipus: no, though the effort should
bring out 'a point or two as yet unseized by the Germans.' The
case is somewhat different, however, when a particular reading of
certain characters in a play is the ground for the attribution to it
of a tendency; then it is useful to inquire whether this reading is
right—whether, that is, these persons of the drama do indeed speak
and act in the tone ascribed to them.

And certainly one of the most interesting questions in the *Oedipus Tyrannus* concerns the intellectual position of Oedipus and
Iocasta towards that divine power of which the hand is laid so
heavily upon both. Sophocles had found in human nature itself
the sanction of 'the unwritten laws,' and the seal of faith in a
beneficence immortal and eternal; but his personal attitude towards
the 'sceptical' currents of thought in his age was never, so far as we
can judge, that of admonitory protest or dogmatic reproof. It was
his temperament to look around him for elements of conciliation, to

† From R. C. Jebb, *Sophocles: The
Plays and Fragments*, Part 1 (Cambridge, England: Cambridge University
Press, 1914), pp. xxvi–xxix. Reprinted
by permission of the publisher.

evoke gentle and mediating influences, rather than to make war on
the forces which he regarded as sinister:—it might be said of him,
as of a person in one of his own plays, οὗτοι συνέχθειν ἀλλὰ
συμφιλεῖν ἔφυ. But is there any reason to think that the *Oedipus
Tyrannus* marks a moment when this mind—'which saw life stead-
ily, and saw it whole'—was partly shaken in its self-centered calm by
the consciousness of a spiritual anarchy around it which seemed
fraught with ultimate danger to the cohesion of society, and that a
note of solemn warning, addressed to Athens and to Greece, is
meant to be heard throughout the drama? Our answer must depend
upon the sense in which we conceive that he places Oedipus or
Iocasta at issue with religion.

As regards Oedipus, it might be said that, in this particular
aspect, he is a modern character. The instinct of reverence for the
gods was originally fundamental in his nature: it appears in the first
act of his manhood—the journey to Delphi. Nor did he for a
moment mistrust the gods because the doom assigned to him was
bitter. Then he achieved a great intellectual success, reached the
most brilliant prosperity, and was ranked by his fellow-men as
second to the gods alone. He is not spoiled by his good fortune.
We find him, at the opening of the play, neither arrogant nor irreverent; full, rather, of tenderness for his people, full of reverence for
the word of Apollo. Suddenly, however, the prophet of Apollo
denounces *him*. Instantly his appeal is to the intellect. If it comes
to that, what claim has any other human mind to interpose
between *his* mind and Heaven? Is he not Oedipus, who silenced
the Sphinx? Yes, but presently, gradually, his own mind begins to
argue on the other side. No one is so acute as he, and of course he
must be the first to see any facts which tell against himself. And
now, when he is face to face with the gods, and no prophet stands
between, the instinct of reverence inborn in his noble nature finds
voice in the prayer, 'Forbid, forbid, ye pure and awful gods, that I
should see that day!' After varying hopes and fears, his own mind
is convinced of the worst. Reason, which had been the arbiter of
faith, now becomes the inexorable judge of sin, the most instant
and most rigorous claimant for his absolute abasement before the
gods.

Plainly, it would be a misreading to construe the fate of Oedipus
as a dramatic nemesis of impiety; but the case of Iocasta
is at first sight less clear. She, at least, is one who openly avows
scorn for oracles, and urges her lord to share it. It may often be
noticed—where the dramatist has known how to draw from life—
that the true key-note of a dominant mood is struck by a short
utterance on which no special emphasis is thrown, just as, in life

itself, the sayings most truly significant of character are not always long or marked. For Iocasta, such a key-note is given in the passage where she is telling Oedipus that a response from the Delphian temple had warned Laïus that he was destined to be slain by the child whom she bore to him. 'An oracle came to Laïus once—*I will not say from Phoebus himself, but from his ministers*' (v. 712). Iocasta thoroughly believes in the power of the gods to effect their will (724),—to punish or to save (921). But she does not believe that any mortal—be he priest or prophet—is permitted by them to read the future. Had not the Delphian priests doomed her to sacrifice her first-born child,—and this, without saving the life of her husband, Laïus? The iron which years ago had entered into the soul of the wife and mother has wrought in her a result similar to that which pride of intellect has produced in Oedipus. Like Oedipus, she still believes in the wise omnipotence of the gods; like him also, she is no longer prepared to accept any mortal interpreter of their decrees. Thus are the two foremost persons of this tragedy separated from the offices of human intercession, and directly confronted in spirit—one by his self-reliance, the other by her remembered anguish—with the inscrutable powers which control their fate. It is as a study of the human heart, true for every age, not as a protest against tendencies of the poet's own, that the *Oedipus Tyrannus* illustrates the relation of faith to reason.

S. M. ADAMS

Oedipus Tyrannus†

One of the penalties of any great work of art is that it lends itself to various interpretations. So it is with Sophocles' *Oedipus Tyrannus*; the play has always been admired, and in these later days has been presented in English translation by enthusiasts with inadequate understanding of Greek tragedy in general and of Sophocles in particular. One should not, however, wholly decry productions that stray from Sophoclean intention, for Oedipus will always remain a grand and tragic figure. As Sheppard writes, the play is great even under the worst conditions that a bad producer can invent; the present writer can bear him out, for he was privileged to witness *Oedipus King of Thebes* when a very skilful and competent actor played the title role in a production of the Gilbert Murray

† From S. M. Adams, *Sophocles the Playwright* (Toronto: University of Toronto Press, 1957), pp. 81–85. Copyright, Canada, 1957, by University of Toronto Press. Reprinted by permission of the publisher.

version. More recent performances also are not true to Sophocles, whatever other appeal they may possess.

Attempts have been made to say that Oedipus "stands for" something—ideal man, or all humanity, or the like; the play has been supposed to represent expiation through suffering, and the tragic hero has even been compared to later objects of veneration. No one who knows the drama of the period will entertain such thoughts—any more than he can abide a dismal prostitution that goes by the name of "Oedipus-complex." Oedipus is not "man," but Oedipus. The fact that his tragedy is far greater than theirs does not make him one with ordinary men, but sets him apart from them. We realize that normal sufferings are slight compared with his, and this affords a consolation; but he does not suffer on behalf of men or make atonement for them. He brings to light the truth of Apollo's oracles, and the full penalty he pays for this is the price exacted by his nature. The play exhibits a great man's strength, however mistaken and impulsive he may be. When it opens, he is at the apex of his power, with no knowledge of what awaits him; he falls to complete abasement. Sophocles saw that he could tell the story splendidly, showing Oedipus in his greatness and in his littleness. He also saw that his work could be relevant to the Athenian theatre, for it demonstrated that oracles always speak the truth—that nothing man can do will make them false. That, if we wish to state it, is the religious "lesson" of the play.

This drama should not be called "Oedipus Rex" or "Oedipus the King." Neither "rex" nor "king" conveys precisely the sense of "tyrannos." As we have seen, the word "tryannos" in the fifth century had a special significance for Athenians. It implied abundant wealth and power, with the consequent likelihood, if not the certainty, of hybris; and it contained the thought that anyone in the position of sole ruler was bound to fear sedition operating through bribery; he must especially suspect and fear those who are closest to him and who may therefore desire to supplant him. That is why in this play Oedipus suspects Teiresias and Creon, and so brings about the discovery of his parentage. And that is why *Tyrannus*, if it is added to the title of the play to distinguish it from the later *Oedipus Coloneus*, is appropriate indeed. For this, in its greater part, is the story of a tyrannos who prides himself on his position and behaves with the inevitable suspicion and mistrust that accompany it. It is, in fact, because Oedipus is a tyrannos that he learns the truth. What happens after the revelations come about is another matter.

For some four-fifths of its length, the play is the story of how Oedipus came to know the facts. It is true enough that in the course of the drama his whole career is set before us: the past is told and the future hinted at. Lessons or morals can undoubtedly be drawn from all of this; but these lessons have no relevance to the play qua play, and that is why practically nothing is said concerning them. They are fully treated in the *Coloneus*; in the *Tyrannus* we have primarily the course of events whereby Oedipus, starting from complete ignorance, drags the truth unwittingly to light. As Professor Webster sees, this demonstrates the certainty that what Apollo states explicitly through his oracles will in due time come to pass, and the piece is germane to the theatre. But we must recognize that all this part of the play, as a play, concerns the coming of the truth; that Oedipus brings it out because he has been placed in this position; and that only as they bear upon this "action" do past and future matter.

The question is often asked: 'Is Oedipus in some way a guilty man thus punished for his wickedness? Of course he is not. He is not evil; he is extraordinarily good. That is what makes his tragedy. But we must distinguish here between responsibility in the sense of guilt and responsibility from the dramatic point of view; and to see this difference clearly we should have in mind the substance of Oedipus' story as it is given in the play.

Years ago, as the audience already knew, Apollo through an oracle declared to Oedipus' parents, Laius and Jocasta, that a son born to them was destined to kill his father and marry his mother; it is not said that they were warned against having a child, although that is perhaps to be inferred. Thinking to circumvent the oracle, Laius and Jocasta had their new-born son abandoned at Mt. Cithaeron to die, its feet pinned together. The infant was rescued by a herdsman who took it back with him to Corinth. There the child grew to manhood, supposing himself to be the son of Polybus, King of Corinth, and his wife Merope, and called "Oedipus" because of the deformity to his feet. Taunted at a banquet with being no son of Polybus and Merope, he journeyed to Pytho to learn the truth of this; and the god gave him no answer to his question but stated that he was doomed to kill his father and marry his mother. Determined therefore never again to set foot in Corinth, Oedipus went onward and in a sudden quarrel at a cross-road killed an elderly man—his father—with all his retinue excepting one man who fled. He then came to Thebes and, on solving the riddle of the Sphinx, was hailed by that city as its deliverer from plague, and was made king; and the former king's wife—his mother—became his consort. When he learned the truth, he put out his own eyes.

In the dramatic sense, Oedipus is responsible: since this is drama, discoveries and blinding can be attributed, as they should be, to himself. As I have said, his discoveries are due to the fears and suspicions that beset a tyrannos. But these are not the cause of the self-blinding. Throughout the play, however, Oedipus is characterized by a marked impetuosity; this is perhaps especially noticeable in his story of the encounter at the cross-road, but it has been apparent always: the dramatist is consistent in his characterization. It is this impulsive haste which, at first kept in subordinate harmony with the natural emotions of the tyrannos, is then itself employed to give a personal motivation to the blinding. For Oedipus brings that blinding on himself; in offending against the seer Teiresias he has offended against Apollo, and the god exacts fitting punishment. In the dramatic sense, then, Oedipus "causes" that which happens in the play, and if we seek an Aristotelian "flaw of character" (*hamartia*) we must find it here; but, as compared with his essential virtue, this "flaw" is surely venial—and we should not look for a parallel in every Sophoclean tragic figure; we shall not find it.

This responsibility of Oedipus, although, being a matter of character, it is "moral" as well as dramatic, must not be confused with guilt. Excepting the self-blinding, nothing in the play suggests that Oedipus is to blame. It is when we contemplate his whole story apart from the drama, and not when we adopt the attitude of an audience, that we try to find in him some guilt sufficient to account for everything that has ever happened to him; and, if we fail to find this, we think of a malevolent Apollo, or of some other nameless Fate of which mankind is the helpless plaything. This is unnecessary. In the play itself, there is no suggestion that Apollo determined exposure, parricide, and incest, and no suggestion that this fortune was deserved by Oedipus himself. The oracles simply stated what was going to happen—why it should be so fated, we need not as spectators greatly care—and over his oracles the god presides. They are his business, and therein he is (if you like) remorseless; but he is both impersonal and just. As for Oedipus, what past guilt can be assigned to him? Obviously, he cannot be blamed for what happened when he was a baby, or before his birth. The most that can be said is that he pays, with his parents, the inevitable penalty for what they did; in any case, he is just "unfortunate" (δύστηνος). With regard to parricide and incest, it is asserted that Oedipus could have avoided these by refraining from killing or marrying anybody. But is this reasonable? He does not know the facts, as we do; and he has done what he thought necessary to avoid fulfilment of his oracle. To intelligent Athenians of the fifth century a "taint" could cling to him, but nothing more; he is just "unfortunate."

And we must not forget that parricide and incest, like exposure of the child, belong to the dramatic background; as Aristotle puts it, they are "outside the drama." Of course, when Oedipus learns the truth he is completely overwhelmed by the sense of his own "guilt"; but that, as we shall see, is because he is this kind of person. Self-blinding is different. Unlike the facts of parricide and incest, it has not been foretold in oracles. It is a part of the dramatic action set before us; as such, it requires dramatic motivation. Yet, even at the moment when Oedipus' impetuosity reaps this reward, it is artistically diminished, if not completely overwhelmed, by Apollo's intervention. Our sense of it recedes, and we are left with our clear perception that not through any flaw of character, but through his goodness and his strength, Oedipus feels his lot so deeply and makes his tragedy so great.

It is, indeed, the determination of Oedipus to avoid the oracle given to himself—he knows nothing of any other oracle when the play begins—that has dictated his subsequent career and led to his transient greatness. On this Sophocles has based his play. He gives us an Oedipus whose concern has been to escape pollution, an Oedipus who, far more than the average good man, abominates anything that has any savour of impiety and impurity; if he is also impetuous and a tyrannos who cannot escape the implications of that position, it is nevertheless his essential goodness that should strike us most. In what is probably its noblest form we see the contrast between man and fate. Impiety and impurity are the lot of one who hates them more than anything in the world. That is the "tragedy" of Oedipus. Beside it, the ordinary woes of man are small indeed.

This blend of the impetuous tyrannos and the man essentially good gives rise to misconceptions; there seems to be a tendency to seek in Oedipus some hybris to account for all that happens. It is not there. Oedipus has, as I have said, impetuosity; but such hybris as he shows arises solely from his position: there is a hint of it at the outset and it grows as the play advances. The dramatist has used the tyrannical position of this man, and any hybris that goes with it, simply in order to bring about the revelations. This it does; and everyone who reads or sees the play remarks on the excellence of its plot-construction. There is indeed an unremitting progress towards the goal, enlivened by moments when the truth seems certain to emerge. So steady is this progress that the play has established a sort of standard for all time. If we think of drama in general, the *Oedipus Tyrannus* is more akin to our ideals than any other tragedy the Greeks produced, and for this reason alone many will regard it as the greatest work of Sophocles.

A. J. A. WALDOCK

Drama of Dramas: The *Oedipus Tyrannus*†

Possibly the best service a critic can render the *Oedipus Tyrannus* is to leave it alone. The next best service is to seek to recover it; and the direction in which any such attempt must be made is fairly clear. The *Oedipus Tyrannus* is a very great play. It is so great a play that we are a little unwilling to believe that it could fall short, if rightly examined, of *any* of those attributes that a great tragedy might be expected to possess. Tradition has built up a list of such attributes, and criticism of the *Oedipus Tyrannus* consists largely in the effort to demonstrate that the play, if only we adopt the right point of view, really does square with every conceivable demand that could be made of it. One understands and to some extent sympathizes with the motives that underlie such criticism; yet it can only do the play a wrong. The *Oedipus Tyrannus* is so consummate in its kind that we need not pain ourselves to adjust it to any preconceived ideal of what a drama should be. By improving it we can only hurt it. Let us accept the *Oedipus Tyrannus*, with gratitude, as it is.

In an attempt to strip from the play its chief disguises let us begin with the view that it is a drama of character. It is easy to understand the powerful critical compulsions behind such a view. A tragedy without character is unthinkable, and to concede that, in a play so famous, character could have smaller importance than plot is to commit something like a grotesquerie. That Oedipus possesses a character is certain. It is not very clearly defined. It reaches us through a set of acts so few and so exceptional that we cannot estimate it very surely; but it is there. Oedipus is brave, energetic, resourceful, confident, impetuous. He is not outstandingly of the reflective type (it is odd that he should have untangled the riddle). He does not possess, as far as we can make out, an intelligence of piercing quickness or very remarkable reach. But he has at least an average mind, and he is beyond the average in his resolution and valour. In the visible action of the play we are made to see his faults as well as his virtues. He is too precipitate. It seems difficult for him, when excited, to hold more than one thing before his gaze at a time, so that he rushes into actions that are absurdly ill-judged, and that could be very dangerous for himself in their consequences.

† From A. J. A. Waldock, *Sophocles the Dramatist* (Cambridge, England: Cambridge University Press, 1951), pp. 143–168. Reprinted by permission of the publisher.

His treatment of Teiresias and Creon is grossly unfair and is based on suspicions that are almost childish. All this is true. Yet when we examine his conduct in the past—the conduct that, by degrees, has brought him to this ruin—do we find in it very much to criticize? He was living happily in Corinth, the son (as he thought) of Polybus and Merope, until a chance encounter brought into his mind a doubt and a worry. A roisterer at a banquet shouted to him: 'You are not really your father's son.' He questioned his parents. They did their best to reassure him, but rumours continued to spread and he could not dismiss the matter from his mind. In the end he went, for his own satisfaction, to Delphi. The result was surprising and distracting. He was disappointed in the knowledge he sought, but received in its place dire warnings of other woes to come. He was fated, he learnt, to defile his mother's bed and to become the slayer of his father. Shocked, he decided there and then to put miles between himself and his country.

So far, what can fairly be said against him? We should be careful how we pose the problem. It is not quite proper to put the question in this form: whether a man of another character would have acted differently. The question is rather this: whether the character of Oedipus can reasonably be charged with his downfall—whether, in a sufficiently emphatic and pointed way, it can be seen as the source of his troubles. The question, in familiar phrase, is whether he brought his misfortunes on his own head. (In the *Trachiniae* there was something of a parallel.) It may be conceded readily that there are certain types of people who would have solved the problem of Oedipus in an instant—cunning people who, hearing what he heard, would have fended off calamity for ever. Uriah Heep would certainly have done so—Destiny would have been no match for Heep. One can imagine other types of men, pigeon-livered and lacking in gall, who would have rushed forthwith into a hermitage or taken to the desert spaces. It is easy to think of any number of effective rejoinders to the formulated threats of the oracle—the simplest would have been plain suicide. But all this is rather beside the point and does not prove that Oedipus, in a human way of speaking, was ill-advised in the line he took. Critics who stand or fall by character adopt curious manoeuvres here. Some have as good as said that if Oedipus had been a more lackadaisical person he would have found himself in no trouble at all, for if he had been endowed with a carefree character he would not, in the first place, have been stung by the taunt; in that case, he would not have questioned his parents, he would not have resorted to the oracle, he would not, therefore, have found himself at the cross-roads, and the later disasters would not have had a chance to develop. This is a very neat illustration of the absurdities that sometimes follow from believing that, in every play worth its salt, we simply must show that 'character is destiny'. In strict aesthetics this, no doubt, ought to be so, but in fact we do not always see it. The implication of the view just mentioned is that Oedipus pays a price for being normal. He suffers because he has natural feelings, because he is a man who is fond of his parents and who likes to think that his social status is respected; because he has enough initiative and energy to try to find out the truth for himself. There was nothing extraordinary in his action; in view of the persistent rumours it was natural for him to be worried, natural to consult the oracle. (In similar circumstances to-day he would have visited some office of records.) It is true that he is not acute. The oracle leaves him with a difficult problem. He does not sit down like a chess-player and ponder his retort to all possible moves. If he had, it would possibly have struck him that the man who jeered at the banquet might just conceivably have been speaking the truth. Suppose Polybus and Merope were not really his parents; then he will not be securing himself by abandoning Corinth but will be rushing into unknown perils. But the oracle has placed the emphasis so cunningly that Oedipus does not appear to us to be stupid; nor, in plain fact, would acuteness have helped him. The oracle would not answer his question directly, but *seemed* to warn him against the direst dangers at Corinth, and there was no reason why he should think it malevolent. If we imagine ourselves in his situation we must see that he is forced to make a plunge in the dark. He cannot *know* who is speaking the truth, or how much of the truth is being spoken. As he is a man of normal impulses who wishes to proceed with his life, all he can do is to make a guess. He plumps for what seems the right course of action, and this course is assuredly as reasonable as another.

What, next, of the affray at the cross-roads? Here, again, many men would have eluded the peril. (Sir Andrew Aguecheek, for one, would have eluded it.) Oedipus is, no doubt, impetuous. The indignities to which he is subjected sting him, and in a moment or two he has 'slain them all'. Looking down on this affair from our vantage point it is not difficult for us to see that Oedipus's behaviour was rash. If he had been eminently of the planning type he would long before this have compiled a handlist of everything that he must not do; and would have so wisely drilled himself that it would have been almost automatic to refrain. But again, let us remember his assumptions, and the appearance that the drama gives to these happenings. A novel might have made a point of his folly; the mere fact is that the play does not. Simply, he has not yet seriously thought that his father could be any other than Polybus. He knows no reason why his parents should have lied, nor has the oracle sug-

gested that they did; the *suggestion* of the oracle is otherwise. So
he runs into the terrible trap; but trap, surely, is the right word to
use. It is true that he has been somewhat impetuous; it is true that
he has been less than supremely reflective. He has not triple-plated
himself against Destiny, has not been alert for every possible
ambush. Equally, Destiny has not played fair. To say, of his conduct so far, that 'his destiny lay in himself' is merely to do obeisance to a shibboleth. It caricatures the struggle. That cunning,
relentless enmeshment, that ruthless, secret campaign—what
chance has he had against this? To talk of him as deciding his fate
is to distort this picture to absurdity, to burlesque what so clearly
has been happening.

The deed at the cross-roads was unfortunate; so was his marriage
with the widow of Laius; marriage, also, should have been on his
black list. But, again, we must not consider this in the abstract; it is
the impression of the drama that counts. We do not feel that he
was inexcusably rash—do not feel that he was very injudicious. Let
us remind ourselves once more of his case. He has heard certain
bodeful things; it is obvious that he must take care. Well, he has
made his dispositions—dispositions that, in all the circumstances,
are logical and reasonably safe. We have no right, as we read this
drama, to blame him for taking *some* risks. (Indeed, as we read the
drama, there is not the slightest temptation to blame him; the
blame comes later—in criticism—when we have a little withdrawn
from the play.) He feels, and is justified in feeling, that he has
taken fair measures of security; to have made the security absolute
would have meant resigning himself to a half-life; more accurately,
perhaps, it would have meant a retirement from life *in toto*. He
prefers to accept that margin of danger, and, with moderate luck,
all would have been well. He fails because of the odds against him.
Who would have thought that out of ten million women Jocasta
was the one foreordained for his undoing? It is the feeling of these
odds against Oedipus that is the essential feeling of the drama.

And that is why insistence on character seems to me at every
point a mistake. It is a truly damaging mistake, because it amounts
to a kind of blasphemy against the special greatness of this play. It
seeks to depress that greatness and bring another sort of greatness
to the front. Critics feel that they must deprecate plot—that to
do otherwise is a kind of betrayal, is being somehow false to their
charge. So the tenor of the argument is often that, though the plot
(needless to say) is wonderful, the *Oedipus Tyrannus* does not
depend on it. (One expects constantly to meet the explicit assertion that the play could have done quite as well without it.) At any
rate, it is 'overridden', is, when all is said, an 'accessory'. 'In the
Tyrannus,' says Mr Webster, 'story is still important and excit-

ing' but is not, he implies, the main business; there are higher glories than the story, more respectable merits than the mere plot. If I may repeat without offence what I have said, there is a kind of blasphemy in such sayings. To disparage the plot of the *Oedipus Tyrannus*—a play that is plot *in excelsis*! Here is one of the supreme stories of the world—and we speak, apologetically, of the story! Of course there is character in the play—without character there could not be plot. But to make of this plot a subsidiary thing!—it seems to me a critical malfeasance.

But perhaps there is some other way of rescuing the drama from the deep damnation of dependence on plot. What, for example, of the religious strain? Can we find a profound 'moral insight'? Is there some 'eternal' significance in the tragedy?

Mr Bowra has a generalized theory of the nature of the Sophoclean plays. He thinks that they are essentially plays about the relation between gods and men. It is not so much men and men as men and gods who are in conflict. There exists a 'divine will' for men; for various reasons men oppose it, and the plays show them paying the penalty.

I feel quite sure, for my own part, that as a generalized theory this will not do. Without twisting the obvious facts, how can the *Antigone* be brought within it? We know where right lies in the *Antigone*; in that sense we know where the gods stand. To some extent they indicate their feelings, and they make their weight felt indirectly in the action. But the contest that we hear and feel is the contest between Antigone and Creon. Or, for another example, take the *Electra*. Mr Bowra says, 'Electra fights for the gods even at the cost of much spiritual damage to herself'. This may be true in part. (I am doubtful of the extent of the spiritual damage; this seems to me largely the creation of critics.) But grant that Electra fights for the right—fights, if we like, for the gods; does this mean that the play we see is a conflict between gods and men? That is just to reject the visible play, to brush it aside for what we think is its import. It is the very mark of Sophoclean drama that the conflicts it presents are human; to speak of these human conflicts as if they were, after all, subordinate issues—as if their chief value were to lead us to the veritable matters behind them—surely this is like abolishing drama. The human conflicts are not concessions, mere sops to our thirst for an action; they are the stuff of which plays are made.

I do not think, then, that Mr Bowra's theory can hold; one merely has to look at the plays to see that he is not describing them truly. But the *Oedipus Tyrannus* might seem, at first sight, the one exception; it is certainly, of all the plays, the one to which Mr Bowra's theory applies most nearly. Here, for once, there is cer-

tainly a suggestion of a conflict between a man and the gods. There
are invisible Powers in the background and there is a secret game
that they are playing; our consciousness of all this is intense. Oedipus has quarrels in the course of the drama; he is in conflict with
this person and that. But no human being is his enemy; his enemy
is this malevolent Unknown. Here, for once, Mr Bowra's pattern
seems to fit; here one man is in conflict with the gods.

The question is, then, of the meaning. Has Sophocles a deep
design? Is he trying to tell us something about the nature of man
and the universe? If he is, then assuredly we must listen; and, if we
find that he has some such Truth to communicate, we must be prepared to revise our impressions. Plot, then, will lose some of its
lustre. Great as the play is as pure story, we cannot claim that the
story is paramount if there is this Truth underlying the action.

There is only one way, of course, to answer the question and
that is to examine the play; and we must examine the play *by itself*.
If there were really a pattern of tragedy in Sophocles, then we
should be justified in looking for it here. If the other six plays were
so uniform that we could say with reasonable confidence, 'this is
the kind of thing that you find in Sophocles, this is the pattern
that life bears to his eyes', then we should expect to light on this
pattern. But no such uniformity exists. Nothing prohibits us from
approaching the *Oedipus Tyrannus* with a perfectly open mind;
and nothing ought to make us uneasy if we were to find it in some
respects unique.

I think that in some respects it is really exceptional—that while
the other plays show various resemblances, this one stands apart
from them all.

For example, Mr Bowra affirms that 'for Sophocles the tragic
issue arises in some breach in the divine order of the world'. Sophocles' heroes 'have resisted their destinies' and it is for this ignorance
or stubbornness that they are humbled. Such formulae sound mod-
erately plausible and may seem justified in this play or that. But
how are we to apply them to the *Oedipus Tyrannus*? 'Men who have
resisted their destinies.' Has Oedipus resisted his destiny? He has
heard his awful destiny announced. He most certainly has not
rushed to fulfil it; he has strained every nerve to avoid it. Does this
mean, then, that he has committed a wrong? In his case can the
formula mean *anything*? Mr Bowra says that in Sophocles a man
cannot hope for salvation until he has learned the ultimate wisdom
that he must 'do what the gods demand'. In its application to Oedipus is there even a grain of sense in this dictum? Oedipus has fled
from his destiny, has tried frantically to elude his Pursuer, only to
find, like a coursed hare, that his every move has been countered,
and that every exit has been cunningly blocked. What affinity has a

picture like this with the sort of tragedy that Mr Bowra is discuss-ing—in which men learn the virtues of obedience and are taught to renounce their illusions? Oedipus has no illusions—except those that the gods have enforced on him. He certainly 'sees the truth' in the end, but has he ever tried not to see it? He would have given his soul to have seen it. We must admit that he is like other heroes in that he learns his own insignificance; that lesson is fully brought home. But how obvious it is that there is no parallel between the tragic problem he faces and those problems that Mr Bowra has in mind! He is confronted with a dreadful future; the sins he is doomed to commit are such as gods and men will execrate. If these deeds are ever performed, then the divine order will certainly be broken; but he is the very last who wishes it broken. In Mr Bowra's view, the tragic conflict arises because 'someone has gone too far and upset the ordered harmony of life'. Well, who is it who has gone too far? It is the gods who have gone too far. What real point is there in saying that 'the evil caused by the innocent Oedi-pus is little less than that caused by Clytaemnestra'? The gods have caused Oedipus to cause it. The spectacle that this play presents is that of a man fleeing blindly from evil, and of hands reaching out to catch him and clutch him and force him to do it. When he has done evil he is polluted; he understands that thoroughly and accepts the taboo. But these gods whose cry is for order, what spe-cimens of hypocrisy they are if they impute the disorder that has arisen to their victim; and how muddled must be Sophocles' think-ing if that is the view he himself takes—if that is the way he *reads* this drama of his own creation!

It is better not to believe it. As I say, we are under no compul-sion to make this play accord with a scheme; the situation will not be desperate if we should in the end have found no formula to fit it. Better to leave the play nakedly unclassified than to tug and strain at the formulae in a vain effort to induce them to cover it. How much tugging and straining is needed Mr Bowra, I think, has sufficiently exhibited. Or take the problems that arise in the sequel. The play shows Oedipus at bay. As the dread coincidences multiply he refuses for a long while to see. If we cast about for reasons for this slowness we can put forward this 'fault' or that to explain it. We can say, for example, that he is proud. That, indeed, is what Mr Bowra says: Oedipus has 'a kingly pride and high spirit which prevents him from seeing the truth'. Other tragic heroes have 'pas-sions' that 'overpower their sense of reality', and this we may take to be Oedipus' passion. So once more we succeed in bringing him into a scheme. A little later, however, the position is different. Pres-ently, the truth is just beyond the edge of his consciousness, and the sense of this makes him restive. He has seemed to hang back from seeing the truth, now he strives forward in the effort to see it. All who are round him are frightened; they beg him to question no further. If he had stopped short at this point—if, surmising some horror in the offing, he had come to a lightning decision and resolved to let everything rest—then, conceivably, all would have been well. (We do not know, of course, what the gods would have done; it is hard to think that they would have taken defeat quite so easily.) Oedipus, in any case, is not that kind of a man. He feels, of a sudden, hemmed in and responds by pressing outwards for air. He has the nobility to *wish* to know, to be resolute to put the matter to the test; let the frame of things disjoint, he'll find out what these secrets are. So again, he is 'proud' and 'high-spirited', though now with an opposite result. Before, his pride made him slow, now it makes him too quick. He was in fault for not perceiving the truth; now he is in fault because he is too urgent to see it. Whatever he does, Oedipus cannot escape from his critics; the formulae have him enmeshed; he can act in contrary ways, but every act betrays tragic passion. The lesson of these contradictions is clear; it is simply that the proportions in such criticism are all wrong. The play is not about the faults of Oedipus. It may be conceded that he has his failings, but these are merely incidental to the pattern. Bluntly, in the *Oedipus Tyrannus* the hero's faults are of little account. The play is too busy with another thing—with another all-powerful impression; and in the shadow of this other impression the hero's deficiencies fade into nothingness.

But what, again, of the gods? What moral can be read into their doings? What Truth does the drama enshrine? I would suggest that if critics answered this question immediately after they asked it they would often hesitate and waver. But between the asking of the question and the answering of it much elaborate discussion often intervenes, so that the shock of the answer is cushioned. Mr Bowra, for example, begins in this way: 'Sophocles' play is so grand and so tragic that it is easy to misinterpret his fundamental ideas'—easy to find explanations for the downfall of Oedipus that are not really Sophocles' at all. Such a statement seems quite impeccable. We respond in instant sympathy and put ourselves into a condition of readiness. A *priori*, nothing could seem more likely than that so grand and tragic a play should have treasures of meaning to reveal. If Mr Bowra intends presently to uncover them we shall be all eyes to see what comes forth. 'A story like this can hardly fail to invite some kind of explanation, and it is legitimate to look for Sophocles'. The tragic collapse of Oedipus cries for comment or justification.' Again we give provisional assent. We agree that it is by no means improbable that Sophocles had ideas on the subject; and when Mr Bowra goes on to assert confidently that he had, we at least wait eagerly to hear.

Then follow a dozen or so pages of discussion, at the end of which Mr Bowra is ready with his answer; and this is what he finds in the play: 'King Oedipus shows the humbling of a great and prosperous man by the gods. This humbling is not deserved; it is not a punishment for insolence, nor in the last resort is it due to any fault of judgment or character in the man. The gods display their power because they will.' In between question and answer there have intervened, as I say, a dozen pages full of very interesting commentary. But there, at the beginning, was the naked question, and here is the naked answer.

Mr Bowra has one more thing to add. The gods act 'because they will', but at least they accomplish something; they give man 'a salutary lesson', and with this we reach bedrock at last. There is nothing deeper in the play than this, we are at the end of explanation, this is the ultimate moral of the drama. It seems, to speak bluntly, a fiasco. The meaning that had to be probed for, all the care to keep on the track, the patient following of clues, the rejection of inadequate hypotheses—to find this at the end of the search! We have trusted Sophocles, for this! I do not think there is the slightest immoderation in suggesting that, in that case, Sophocles has been wasting our time. It would have been far better, for all concerned, if we had never once thought of a significance. That a member of humankind should be put through such sufferings as these for no other ascertainable reason than that he and we should learn to be modest—should be warned (as Mr Bowra expresses it) not to be confident, should be made to feel less secure!—it seems altogether too much. Yet that, apparently, is the sum total of the meaning; that is the 'fundamental idea' that we sought for, that is the last word on the story. It is clear, of course, that we need never have sought for it, for this is precisely what is said in the tag. 'Count no man happy till dead' (in other words, 'we never know what may happen, do not be too sure of your luck, life has its ups and downs, there is many a terrible fall—take note how all these truths are illustrated in the story of Oedipus!'). Mr Bowra at least concedes that 'after the hideous and harrowing events this finale . . . may seem a little tame'. Tame is assuredly the word. It is completely and utterly negligible—a flourish at the end of a letter, a piece of scrollwork absently drawn; a few perfunctory words to signal that the play is over, hardly meant to be listened to but to be drowned in the rustle of departure.

But what of the gods themselves? With what credit do they emerge? Of course with no credit at all. They have picked out a man to humble him, not because he deserves to be humbled, but in order that he may be an example to others. Oedipus is to be taught his utter insignificance so that mankind in general may be chastened. There is no proof that mankind needs chastening; nothing is offered to suggest that man needs this particular rod. Simply, the gods have taken a whim to chasten. And yet Mr Bowra finds it possible to say that 'Sophocles shirks none of these difficulties.' Sophocles, I would suggest, knew well that he could not afford even to look at them; it was more than his play was worth to allow these difficulties two seconds of attention. *Nothing* can excuse the gods and Sophocles knew it perfectly well. That is why, in this play, he eschews thinking—why he makes no effort to explain, why he keeps so clear of philosophical embroilment, why he is so careful to allow nothing to divert him from the one thing with which he is concerned: that one thing being, of course, the writing of drama.

The theories so far discussed may be described as attempts at normalization. If it could be shown that this play was a tragedy of character, or if it could be shown that some profound religious truth underlay it, critics would feel much easier about its indisputable greatness. The greatness would seem better based; and no doubt it would, in fact, be so. But nothing whatever is to be gained by forcing the play into a pattern. It has its own wonderful quality; we only disguise and injure this quality when we try to turn it into another.

There have been various other attempts to bring the play into closer alignment with a type. For example, critics may shy from religion and may deprecate the use of the word 'explain'. To many, as to Mr Sheppard, it has seemed on the whole safer to admit that Sophocles has no solution to offer—that he is not claiming to hold the key of the riddle. The evil is there, he presents it, and with that his obligation is ended. He does not seek, like Aeschylus, to justify it; and he has none of the presumption of Euripides, who dared to challenge the powers who caused it. Sophocles is relatively detached. But critics are not quite content to stop at this point. Sophocles may be reserved and dispassionate, but after all it should be possible to show that he too had his thoughts about the universe. He may not tell us much about the gods, but what of the nature of things—has he not something to tell us about that? The nature of things is the cue. Let us suppose that the hero is not just *Oedipus*, a mere man who for inscrutable reasons has been picked out for special attention by the gods. Let us suppose that he stands for something—'human suffering' will conveniently do. Let us also depersonalize the gods—treat them a little abstractly by referring rather to the 'universe of circumstance as it is'. Immediately the play seems lifted; once more a new dignity accrues. It is unnecessary to argue for a thesis, we need not maintain that the play makes a point; but to have embodied human suffering—there already is an achievement. To have given dramatic expression to the universe of circumstance as it is—no work accomplishing that could be thought of as destitute of content.

This is a neat manoeuvre, but quite as illegitimate, in my opinion, as the others. It is just one more way of smuggling significance into the *Oedipus Tyrannus*; just one more expression of the feeling that this work, by hook or by crook, must be made to mean something; just another attempt to prove that the work really is universal. But the action of this play is exceptional; no argument can alter that. Oedipus is a world-wonder in his suffering, in his peculiar destiny he is a freak. He is a man selected out of millions to undergo this staggering fate; that is why his story is so fascinating. It fascinates because it is rare; because on any rational assessment his story—as far as we are concerned—is impossible. We can imagine it all so vividly, we can live in every one of his emotions; yet we should as reasonably fear to be hit by a thunderbolt as to be embroiled in his particular set of misfortunes. And if Oedipus, by the extreme rarity of his destiny, is outside the common lot of mankind, so is the special malignance that strikes him a thing quite apart from the universe of circumstance as it is. Circumstance has its practical jokes and its sinister-seeming moods, but a concatenation of malevolences on this scale is an absolutely unparalleled thing. The gods who really do stand for circumstance are very much milder beings and need cause no great affright. That is why it is so misleading to reduce this play to the normal. Mr Sheppard says that the dramatist is 'facing the facts', and that he is asking his audience to face them; Sophocles' 'work as a tragedian is to face the facts of life'. No doubt many tragedians do this—do recognize this as their task; and it may be that in some other tragedies Sophocles himself is facing the facts; but not in the *Oedipus Tyrannus*. Here the terror of sheer coincidence is vital; to suppress that terror here is to rob the play of its essence. We have here a chain of events so abnormal that they edge into the sphere of the miraculous. We have no feeling here of the nature of things; what we feel is an *interference* with nature. The play quintessentializes misfortune; it is an epigram in ill-luck.

It is a pity to spoil this quality by damping down the abnormal; and so, I think, with lesser matters, we should be careful in our strivings for naturalism, for even in details it is easy to do harm. For example, it is dangerous to tinker with the joinery-work of the plot. All words of praise seem drab for the plot of the *Oedipus Tyrannus*: There is, of course, nothing in Sophocles to match it, nothing that comes within hail of it. But its extraordinary cleanness of line was not won without finesse. We must not make unfair exactions, or sight the work from improper angles. There is that recapitulation early in the play—the passage of question and answer by which we are reminded of past events. It is somewhat naïve technique, especially as the questioner has to be Oedipus, and no matter how it is managed plausibility can hardly be saved. I have already suggested that we risk making things worse if we try to square the absurdities of this passage with the demands of realistic psychology. To explain such a sequence as this is, quite strictly, to tamper with the drama, for the last thing that Sophocles desired was that we should pause and test the passage. He knew (none better) its hollowness; he does not wish us to knock on it and sound it and then set about trying to strengthen it; he wishes us to hurry along. As I have said, what he is really proposing is a tacit agreement: if we will concede him this slight improbability then he undertakes to economize on his workmanship. After all, neither Sophocles nor the reader wishes to dally over expository details, but somewhere a place must be found for these basic preparatory facts. The earlier they are mentioned the better; and on the whole the simplest method (certainly the one that wastes least time) is to put them in the form of question and answer. So Oedipus suddenly becomes very dull. He admits to having heard tell of his predecessor, but for the rest is vagueness itself. There is no real way to explain this; but if we merely make the slight concession at the outset we can take all the difficulties in our stride.

It is much the same in some later sequences where the hero's reactions are rather slower than life. Bit by bit the evidence gathers, and Oedipus is in the position of one who is suddenly involved in a grim intelligence test. His performance is far from outstanding. Yet by hypothesis he is an anxious man. Recent years have perhaps lulled his fears, but it would be natural to imagine that they are still there, quiescent. One would expect that at the slightest warning his whole being would become quiveringly intent. Instead, his wits seem flaccid; he lags noticeably in putting two and two together. The pattern of the truth eludes him until every last thread is in place. I do not think that the unlikelihood is important. Once again we make a slight concession, and the power of the action is so great that any check of this sort becomes trifling. But the situation is the same as before in that no good is done by explaining. Jocasta, scoffing at oracles, gives Oedipus a proof of their shallowness; it was foretold of Laius that he should die by the hand of his child; in fact, he was killed by robbers; and the child was not three days old when it was put out to perish on a mountain, with its ankles pinned together. Ankles pinned together! Oedipus hears these words, and yet, strangely, they give him no hint, start no associations moving in his mind. He harks back to what Jocasta said about cross-roads—that has set deep memories a-tremble. Mr Sheppard says that this is in character; Oedipus 'becomes absorbed with any idea which seizes him, and neglects for the moment every other thought'. No doubt he is a man rather like that; yet I do not think that the explanation is sufficient; there is still some oddity left. The plain truth is that Oedipus has to be slow—rather slower than any quirk of temperament will account for. Quick wits would have meant no drama, and Sophocles is again finessing. We do not much notice the slowness; it is only when we reflect that we perceive how strange it is that Oedipus should pass over these clues. So, later, the Corinthian messenger declares that Polybus was not really his father; it was this messenger himself who found Oedipus and carried him, a babe, to Corinth. And where was it, precisely, he found him? 'In the folded vales of Cithaeron.' Cithaeron! But again he fails to take the import of the word. He is brooding now on the question of his birth—fears it may turn out to be servile. He follows this blind alley of thought while Jocasta has already leapt to the truth. Again, character will not fully suffice; we are dealing with dramatic finesse.

Finally, if one examines the play one comes across many little adjustments that make for smoothness of line, though by canons of meticulous realism most of them would be hard to defend. Some are beautifully concealed. How many readers check at what Jocasta says about the servant in vv.758–60? Oedipus has learnt from her that there was one survivor from that affray at the cross-roads; it was he, of course, who brought the tidings; and Oedipus naturally wishes to know where this most important witness may be found. 'Is he now in the house?' he asks. Jocasta replies that he is not; she says that as soon as he arrived from the cross-roads 'and saw thee in possession of the kingdom' some strange fear or reluctance came over him and he asked to be sent away, 'far out of sight of this town'. This, of course, is extremely odd; the slave certainly lost no time on the way, yet when he comes to Thebes he finds Oedipus already installed. Sophocles indulges here in a slight foreshortening. This memory of Jocasta's is quite impossible—the thing she recalls could not have occurred; on the other hand it is very good drama. This strange behavior of the herdsman makes a notable piece in the pattern. Things are beginning to slip into place for Jocasta: she is deeply uneasy now.

Or take the management of the agents and envoys. If all this had been happening in life, about four of these would have been needed. There would have been the man who escaped from the cross-roads; there would have been the man who took away the child; there would have been the man who received the child; and there would have been the man who brought the message from Corinth. Sophocles reduces them to two, by identifying the first with the second, and identifying the third with the fourth.

We concede this move easily enough; and do those sundry 'punc-

tualities' cause us much deeper distress? Dr Norwood thinks that
some of them do. In a sense, the two shepherds just mentioned
hold the fate of Oedipus in their hands; their paths must converge
at Thebes—they must arrive within the same hour—to precipitate
the full disclosure. Each holds half of the riddle, and if one or
other had been absent the whole truth need not have emerged.
(There is a pretty case here of what may be described as dramatic
supercession. The old Theban was, of course, originally summoned
to pronounce on the circumstances of the slaying; but by the time
he arrives on the scene the importance of this has faded into the
background; the vital issue now is: who gave him the infant to
expose?) That the Corinthian messenger should arrive so pat is, of
course, the sheerest coincidence, and I doubt whether we do the
play a service by trying to smooth it over. Dr Norwood, to save the
day, suggests that we might consider whether coincidence itself is
not natural; life, after all, does include accidents; so that, in a sense,
all that Sophocles is doing is 'mirroring the facts' of life; and perhaps this was his very intention. I would suggest that it is utterly
obvious that Sophocles had no such idea in his mind. Life here is
far from his thoughts; he is merely trying for a neat construction.
He knows that he is being a little incredible but he can count on
us (he feels) to co-operate. Again, it is a mutual pact; we allow
him the leeway he requires and refrain from vexatious objections;
he, on his part, tightens his plot and saves us many moments of
dullness.

Or consider, for a final instance, the disclosure by Oedipus of his
birth. 'My father was Polybus of Corinth, my mother the Dorian
Merope.' He makes this announcement to the Queen, and proceeds
to tell her why it was he left Corinth. So he has never mentioned
the matter before: what an unconcerned pair they have been! We
can say, with Mr Sheppard, that it is merely the 'grand manner'
again. That may be a part of the truth; the touch of formality in
such utterances certainly makes their reception the easier. But in
this case it is surely not the whole of the truth. The technique is
essentially transparent: Oedipus relates these things to Jocasta
because somehow they must be told. Mr Sheppard comments on
the passage: 'Of course Jocasta knows that he is supposed to be the
son of Polybus.' I do not think that this is strictly true. It might be
true if we were dealing with history, but because we are dealing
with a drama the truth is slightly different. The question of Jocasta's knowledge or ignorance does not really enter the drama; it is
left, so to speak, a blur; Sophocles deliberately smudges that point.
What Mr Sheppard does in this comment is to attempt to re-draw
that smudge; but Sophocles does not wish it re-drawn. The matter
at issue here may be trifling, but the principle behind it is vital;

when dramatists blur some detail it is because they desire it blurred; when they take pains not to raise a question then that question is *not in the play.*

What, then, is to be our verdict on this drama? What shall we say of this close-knit web of ironies that constitutes the *Oedipus Tyrannus?*

The chief problems that I have discussed resolve themselves largely, it may be, into questions of emphasis; but these are of the utmost importance. The character of Oedipus is not itself in dispute; the question is of the emphasis that this character has received in the play. I do not think for my own part that the portrayal of Oedipus is a masterpiece; it seems to me rather absurd to suggest that he is the 'best-drawn character in Sophocles'. I doubt whether we ever *feel* his nature quite as we feel the nature of Antigone—or, indeed, as we feel the nature of the aged Oedipus himself. We recognize that he has this or that quality, but do we ever quite reach the core? And his qualities have to some extent to adapt themselves to the exigencies of the plot. There is not a perfect coherence between that sagacious Oedipus of the past and this present unpredictable Oedipus whose brain seems so often befogged and who is swayed so easily by his passions. Oedipus is an assembly of qualities; they are a little loosely collected, and there is no clear *soul* in the man that makes qualities largely irrelevant; unless we are content just to speak of nobility. He becomes clearer to us after his downfall; we begin then really to see him, and perceive that his structure is truly heroic. But his character is not the point of the play.

It is the same with the different 'theses' that have been seen as underlying the drama. We know little of Sophocles' religion. When we sum up what we know of his beliefs we find them meagre in number and depressingly commonplace in quality. He thought it was best to commit no injustice and, on the whole, to avoid excess. He believed that there are ups and downs in fortunes, and that men are never secure. (An account of Shakespeare's religion would produce somewhat similar results.) There is religion in the *Oedipus Tyrannus* but it is not all crucial in the drama. Mr Webster holds the opinion that Sophocles set great store by oracles. It may well be, of course, that he did. But I would suggest that there is a simple reason for the frequency of oracles in his plays: they are excellent story-material. And as for the oracles here, it is surely quite preposterous to say that 'Sophocles wrote the *Tyrannus* to defend what was for him, as for Socrates, one of the basic facts of religion'.

He did not write it for that, nor did he write it in a laborious attempt to prove that the gods like giving men lessons; nor did he write it in order to explain. After all, how could he explain? Oedipus is indisputably a victim; that fact is at the very heart of the drama. 'O Zeus, what hast thou willed to do unto me?'—this is the central cry of the play. A thorough thinking through of the facts could have led only to an indictment of the gods. Sophocles draws back from such an indictment. But this is merely an abstinence, and does not bestow 'meaning' on the drama. There is no meaning in the *Oedipus Tyrannus*. There is merely the terror of coincidence, and then, at the end of it all, our impression of man's power to suffer, and of his greatness because of this power.

The theme is not, then, universal. The theme of Lear is universal; but what the *Oedipus Tyrannus* rests on is a frightful groundwork of accident. Its driving forces are not feelings (though the object of nearly all criticism of the play is to prove, by desperate measures, that they are). There is feeling enough in the play, but other forces than feeling produce it. It is best to take it as it is. It is so great in its kind that we hurt it in trying to help it.

How did its special qualities arise? As I suggest, we may perhaps observe in Greek drama an especial responsiveness to themes; it moulds itself to its themes, reflects their merits and defects, with a somewhat exceptional readiness. We have here a most unusual theme, a theme superbly suited to all that Greek drama could do best. It works through a passive situation; but the passive situation, because of the peculiar nature of this case, becomes instinct with dramatic life. Hardly anything happens, beyond people arriving with news. We watch how the pieces of a puzzle fall one by one into place. Yet can one think of a drama so vibrant with the sense of event?

We needed four or five of the other six tragedies to take the full measure of Sophocles, but, as dramatist, he is here at his bourn. This is the unapproachable play.

ALBIN LESKY

[*Oedipus*: An Analytic Tragedy]†

The *Oedipus* has been called an analytic tragedy, since the decisive events have all occurred before the play opens and the toils of fate have already been drawn round Oedipus. His attempts to shake

† From Albin Lesky, *A History of Greek Literature*, translated by James Willis and Cornelis deHeer (New York: Thomas Y. Crowell Company, Inc., and London: Methuen & Co. Ltd., 1966), pp. 285–288. Copyright © 1957, 1958 by A. Francke, Bern; English translation copyright © 1966 by Methuen & Co., Ltd., London. Reprinted by permission of the publishers.

and tug at the net, only to entangle himself more and more in its meshes and finally to encompass his own destruction, are depicted in this play with a mastery of concentration and compactness that has not its like in dramatic writing. The devices with which the poet achieves this effect are very simple. Laius, king of Thebes, being alarmed by an oracle, had his newly born son exposed in the wastes of Cithaeron. The servant who had this order to obey gave the child to a Corinthian shepherd, who took it back to Corinth to his king Polybus. Both persons, the shepherd and the servant, have other important functions in the course of the action. Such economy of force as this makes possible the extremely close texture of the dramatic structure. The servant who should have exposed the child is the only one who later came back from the fatal encounter at the Phocian crossroad. It was there that Oedipus, fleeing from the Delphic oracle that he should kill his father and marry his mother, slew the aged Laius in an angry quarrel. The Corinthian shepherd reappears in the piece as the messenger who at a significant moment brings the news of Polybus' death.

It is the critic's right and duty to recognize such poetic devices as these. The book which Tycho von Wilamowitz has written on Sophocles does so to the full, and draws attention to several difficulties in the plays which present themselves when we think them over afterwards. Much can be learned from such analysis, but it should never make its rules absolute and deny to works of dramatic art the right to be a law to themselves.

With a deadly logic Oedipus' road leads him into darkness and desolation. At the beginning he answers the complaints of the city with kindness and sympathy. At any moment Creon is expected, having gone to Delphi to ask why the plague is thus devastating Thebes. He reports the god's reply, demanding expiation for the murder of Laius. With eager energy Oedipus seizes on the Delphic pronouncement, which refers to himself. The blind seer Tiresias is summoned, but will not speak. Finally, irritated beyond endurance by Oedipus' false suspicions, he denounces the king: he, the blind man, denounces the reputedly sharp-sighted king with being himself the murderer and living in fearful incest. So sudden and so contrary to all appearances is this revelation that no one takes it seriously, least of all Oedipus. His quick brain follows another and a devious path. He suspects a plot hatched by Creon to make himself king. He is soon ready to pronounce sentence of death, and Jocasta has to come between them to prevent a fatal issue. She comforts her husband by deriding oracles and the crafts of seers. Did not Apollo prophesy that Laius would be killed by his own son? Yet the son died on Cithaeron, and Laius was slain by robbers at a crossroad. In this play every attempt to find comfort is a step towards catastrophe.

Oedipus recalls in terror his sudden act at the Phocian crossroad: but Jocasta spoke of robbers, or more than one man. This is now his hope, and the servant who alone survived that meeting and is now living in the country will be able to give confirmation. Meanwhile a messenger comes from Corinth to announce the death of Polybus, whom Oedipus still reckons as his father. Again Jocasta feels able to laugh at Apollo's prophecies, and Oedipus also thinks that he has escaped the destiny of being his father's murderer. But there is still the second part of the prophecy, that he should marry his mother; and his mother is still alive in Corinth. Now comes another fatal attempt to set Oedipus' mind at rest. The messenger tells what he knows of Oedipus' birth. He was only stepson to Polybus and Merope; he was found exposed on Cithaeron, where one of Laius' servants gave him to the Corinthian. The veil is now torn from Jocasta's eyes. She tries to stop Oedipus enquiring further, but her efforts to halt the wheel of fate are in vain. She goes back into the palace in despair. Once again the hasty mind of Oedipus rushes to a false conclusion: Jocasta is probably afraid that he may be of low birth, but he is proud (what a height of tragic irony!) to call himself a child of fortune. This expression gives the chorus its theme for an ode which once again strikes a note of rejoicing before the catastrophe. How many are the gods who sweep over the mountains! One of them may have fathered their beloved king. Then comes the servant, the survivor of the Phocian encounter, the same who was to have exposed the child. It is not easy to make him speak, but at last all the awful truth is revealed to Oedipus. He rushes into the palace, finds Jocasta hanged, and blinds himself with the pins of her brooches so as to close for ever the fountain of sight. He staggers back onto the stage, takes a moving farewell of his daughters and prepares to go into poverty and exile.

To understand this great work we must first clarify a question which is hardly a question nowadays. Is Oedipus atoning for guilt? Aristotle (*Poet.* 13. 1453 a 10) traces his overthrow to a mistake (ἁμαρτία τις). Since immediately before this he expressly excludes moral obliquity (κακία καὶ μοχθηρία), it is clear that his mistake was not one involving wickedness. This condemns all the unworthy attempts that have been made to turn this drama into one of sin and atonement and to reduce the unparalleled intensity of its tragic feeling to a mere story with a moral. The action at the crossroad, where Oedipus in sudden fury killed an old man who was unknown to him, could not be reckoned a terrible crime, certainly not in Greek eyes. Oedipus' quick brain also, which so often outruns itself, is not in its nature blameworthy: its significance consists only in its contrast with the frightful power of the gods which goes its way inexorably for all the wit and will of men. The gods are so very much the more powerful, they shatter human fortune with such deadly certainty, that some scholars have seen nothing else in the play, and have called it a drama of destiny. Many have gone further and have said the same of Greek drama as a whole. There is no point in discussing such mistaken notions here: even of the *Oedipus* they express only half the truth. The king of Thebes is not a fainéant, who awaits his fate passively; he goes boldly to meet it and grapples it with a burning passion for the truth and a readiness to suffer that make him one of the greatest figures of the tragic stage. The old servant hesitates before the final appalling disclosure: 'God help me, but I am about to tell you dreadful tidings'. Oedipus answers: 'And I about to hear them: but hear them I must'. The verse declares both his fate and the greatness of his soul. Tycho von Wilamowitz and others have disputed Sophocles' ability to draw 'complete characters'. Now it is true that the way in which the dramatist puts his figures before us is different from the individual character-drawing of modern drama. (We cannot consider the question whether the dominance of the psychological element in this kind of art is an unmixed advantage.) Nor can we deny that there are particular passages in which the management of the scenes took precedence in the minds of ancient dramatists over consistency in the presentation of individual character. But it is far more important to remember that Sophocles drew his characters from the pre-existing realm of myth, characters not in the modern psychological sense, but great personal figures whose traits are attached to one central feature. Free of all purely accidental and individual elements, they stand before us in their great essential qualities, an imperishable heritage. Oedipus is one of these.

In this drama also the noble soul with its unqualified determination is set off by the type that is ready always to weaken and compromise; to 'take life as it comes' is Jocasta's great maxim (979): the strongest possible contrast to the path that Oedipus treads.

In the *Oedipus* also the gods play a very large part. But what kind of gods are they who bring men to the depths of ruin without knowing why it all happens? Are we to understand the gods as cruel beings to whom man is a plaything? This is the view embodied in Hofmannsthal's treatment of *Oedipus and the Sphinx*, but it has nothing to do with Sophocles. It will be noticed that in this play, which depicts the extremity of suffering without offering any interpretation of human fate such as Aeschylus gives, we find a choral ode (864) which sings of the eternal divine laws that originate in the highest heaven. At the end of this play also we might say, 'Here is nothing that was not Zeus'. The divine governance, inaccessible to mortal thought, fulfils itself in an appalling manner, but remains always valid and deserving of reverence. When Sophocles wrote this drama, the sophists were already in full cry after everything that tradition held sacred. He expressed his rejection of the new iconoclasm as clearly here as in the first stasimon of the *Antigone*.

The *Oedipus* does not merely express the tragic with greater purity than any other play in European literature; it enables us to recognize in a special way that phenomenon of tragic pleasure which Hölderlin embodied in his famous epigram to Sophocles:

> Manche versuchen umsonst, das Freudigste freudig zu sagen,
> Hier spricht endlich es mir, hier in der Trauer sich aus.

The undeniable fact that we go home from a performance of the *Oedipus* with a feeling of elevation, even of pleasure, is very hard to explain. But part of the explanation is that in all the grief and horror the poet never for a moment leaves out of sight a great cosmic order, which remains eternally valid through all changes and all individual suffering.

WERNER JAEGER

[Sophocles and the Tragic Character]†

The sense of beauty that produced the men and women of Sophocles arose from a vast new interest in the *souls* of tragic characters. It was a manifestation of the new ideal of areté, which for the first time emphasized the central importance of the *psyché*, the 'soul', in all culture. In the course of the fifth century the word *psyché* acquired a new overtone, a loftier significance, which reached its fulness in the teaching of Socrates. The soul was now objectively recognized as the centre of man's life. From the soul came all men's actions. Long before, sculptors had discovered the laws that shape and govern the body and had studied them with the greatest enthusiasm. In the 'harmony' of the body they had rediscovered the principle of cosmos apprehended by philosophers in the structure of the universe. With that principle in mind the Greeks now turned to the exploration of the soul. They did not see it as a chaotic flow of inner experience, but subjected it to a system of laws, as the only realm of being which had not yet incorporated the ideal of cosmos. Like the body, the soul obviously had rhythm and harmony. Thus the Greeks reached the idea of a soul-structure.

† From Werner Jaeger, *Paideia: The Ideals of Greek Culture*, Vol. 1, translated by Gilbert Highet (New York: Galaxy Books, Inc. and London: Basil Blackwell, 1965), pp. 279–280; 284–285. Copyright 1939 by Oxford University Press, Inc. Renewed 1967. Reprinted by permission.

One is tempted to find its first clear expression in Simonides' description of areté as 'built foursquare in hand and foot and mind'. But it was a long way from that inchoate idea of the life of the soul as analogous to the physical ideal of athletic perfection, to the theory of culture which Plato no doubt rightly ascribes to the sophist Protagoras. That theory was a completely logical development of the idea that the soul can be formed like the body—an idea which has ceased to be a poetic image and become an educational principle. Protagoras said that the soul can be educated into true *eurhythmia* and *euharmostia*, rhythm and concord. The right rhythm and harmony are to be produced in it by the influence of poetry embodying these standards. Even in this theory the ideal of forming the soul is approached from a physical point of view; but Protagoras conceives the process to resemble sculpture, the work of a plastic artist, rather than athletic training, as Simonides had done. The standards of eurhythmia and euharmostia are likewise borrowed from the world of visible physical existence. Only in classical Greece could the concept of culture have been inspired by the sculptor's art. Even Sophocles' ideal of human character clearly betrays its sculptural origin. At that period education, poetry, and sculpture affected one another deeply—none of them could have existed without the others. Educators and poets were inspired by the sculptor's effort to create an ideal figure, and took the same path towards the ἰδέα of humanity; while the sculptor or painter was led by the example of education and poetry to look for the soul in every model he used. The focus of interest for all three was the higher value which now attached to humanity. The Athenian mind has now become anthropocentric; humanism has been born—not the emotion of love for all other members of society, called *philanthropia* by the Greeks, but intellectual search for and interest in the true nature of man. It is especially significant that now for the first time tragedy shows women as well as men, as worthy representatives of humanity. Apart from such subordinate feminine characters as Clytaemnestra, Ismene, and Chrysothemis, Sophocles' power of drawing strong noble human beings is seen at its highest in many of his tragic heroines—Antigone, Electra, Dejanira, Tecmessa, Jocasta. After the great discovery that man was the real object of tragedy, it was inevitable that woman also should be discovered.

Like Aeschylus, Sophocles thinks of drama as the instrument through which men reach a sublime knowledge. But it is not τὸ φρονεῖν, which was the ultimate certainty and necessity in which Aeschylus found peace. It is rather a tragical self-knowledge, the Delphic γνῶθι σεαυτόν deepened and broadened into a comprehension of the shadowy nothingness of human strength and human happiness. To know oneself is thus for Sophocles to know man's powerlessness; but it is also to know the indestructible and conquering majesty of suffering humanity. The agony of every Sophoclean character is an essential element in his nature. The strange fusion of character and fate is nowhere more movingly and mysteriously expressed than in the greatest of his heroes, to whom he returned once again at the very close of his life. It is Oedipus, a blind old man begging his way through the world, led by his daughter Antigone—another of Sophocles' most beloved figures. Nothing reveals the essence of Sophoclean tragedy more deeply than the fact that the poet grew old, as it were, along with his characters. He never forgot what Oedipus was to become. From the first, the tragic king who was to bear the weight of the whole world's sufferings was an almost symbolic figure. He was suffering humanity personified. At the climax of his career Sophocles proudly exerted all his powers to show him staggering under the tempest of ruin. He presented him at the very moment when he calls down curses on himself and in despair wishes to destroy his own life, as he has destroyed the light of his eyes with his own hand. And he snapped the thread, as he did in *Electra*, at that climactic moment when the character of the hero was tragically complete.

It is therefore highly significant that shortly before his death Sophocles took up the tale of Oedipus once again. It would be a mistake to expect the second drama to solve the problem of the first. If we were to interpret old Oedipus' passionate self-defence, his repeated claim that he acted unwittingly, as an answer to the question *Why?* we should be misunderstanding Sophocles, treating him, in fact, as if he were Euripides. Neither destiny nor Oedipus is acquitted or condemned. Yet in the later play the poet seems to look on life from a greater height. *Oedipus at Colonus* is a last meeting with the restless old wanderer, just before he reaches his goal. Despite misfortune and age, his noble character is unbroken, its impetuous violence still unquenched. By knowing his own strength and nobility, he has been helped to bear his own agony, the inseparable companion of his long years of exile, clinging to him until the last. There is no place for sentimental pity in this harsh portrait. Yet Oedipus' agony has made him venerable. The chorus feels its terror, but its grandeur even more; and the king of Athens receives the blind beggar as an honoured and illustrious guest. An oracle has said that Oedipus will find his final repose in Attica. But his death is veiled in mystery: he goes away, without a guide, into the grove, and is never seen again. Strange and incomprehensible as the road of suffering along which the gods have led him, is the miracle of release which he finds at the end. 'The gods who struck you down now lift you up.' No mortal eye may see the mystery: only he who is consecrated by suffering may take part in it. Hallowed by pain, he is in some mysterious way brought near to divinity: his agonies have set him apart from other men. Now he rests on the hill of Colonus, in the poet's own dear homeland, in the eternally green grove of the Kind Spirits where the nightingale sings from the branches. No human foot may tread in that place, but from it there goes out a blessing over all the land of Attica.

FRIEDRICH NIETZSCHE

[The Triple Fate of Oedipus]†

Sophocles conceived doomed Oedipus, the greatest sufferer of the Greek stage, as a pattern of nobility, destined to error and misery despite his wisdom, yet exercising a beneficent influence upon his environment in virtue of his boundless grief. The profound poet tells us that a man who is truly noble is incapable of sin; though every law, every natural order, indeed the entire canon of ethics, perish by his actions, those very actions will create a circle of higher consequences able to found a new world on the ruins of the old. This is the poet's message, insofar as he is at the same time a religious thinker. In his capacity as poet, he presents us in the beginning with a complicated legal knot, in the slow unraveling of which the judge brings about his own destruction. The typically Greek delight in this dialectical solution is so great that it imparts an element of triumphant serenity to the work, and thus removes the sting lurking in the ghastly premises of the plot. In *Oedipus at Colonus* we meet this same serenity, but utterly transfigured. In contrast to the aged hero, stricken with excess of grief and passively undergoing his many misfortunes, we have here a transcendent serenity issuing from above and hinting that by his passive endurance the hero may yet gain a consummate energy of action. This activity (so different from his earlier conscious striving, which had resulted in pure passivity) will extend far beyond the limited experience of his own life. Thus the legal knot of the Oedipus fable, which had seemed to mortal eyes incapable of being disentangled, is slowly loosened. And we experience the most profound human joy as we witness this divine counterpart of dialectics. If this explanation has done the poet justice, it may yet be asked whether it has exhausted the implications of the myth; and now we see that the poet's entire conception was nothing more nor less than the luminous after-image which kind nature provides our eyes after a look into the abyss. Oedipus, his father's murderer, his mother's lover, solver of the Sphinx's riddle! What is the meaning of this triple fate? An ancient popular belief, especially strong in Persia, holds that a wise *magus* must be incestuously begotten. If we examine Oedipus, the solver of riddles and liberator of his mother, in the light of this Parsee belief, we may conclude that wherever soothsaying and mag-ical powers have broken the spell of present and future, the rigid law of individuation, the magic circle of nature, extreme unnatural-ness—in this case incest—is the necessary antecedent; for how should man force nature to yield up her secrets but by successfully resisting her, that is to say, by unnatural acts? This is the recogni-tion I find expressed in the terrible triad of Oedipean fates: the same man who solved the riddle of nature (the ambiguous Sphinx) must also, as murderer of his father and husband of his mother, break the consecrated tables of the natural order. It is as though the myth whispered to us that wisdom, and especially Dionysiac wisdom, is an unnatural crime, and that whoever, in pride of knowledge, hurls nature into the abyss of destruction, must himself experience nature's disintegration. "The edge of wisdom is turned against the wise man; wisdom is a crime committed on nature": such are the terrible words addressed to us by myth.

JOHN JONES

[The *Tyrannus*: Action and Actors]†

It is much easier to state, even to state convincingly, that the *Antigone* concerns a burying than to make effective contact with the work of art; for the discipline which we must consciously invoke in order to resist our instinctive adjectiving of action—making action qualify and reveal interesting truths about the indi-viduals who promote it—is itself hostile to the relaxed and penetra-ble attentiveness which art demands. *Oedipus the King* is more accessible than the *Antigone*, and this is principally because the single action which it imitates (the self-discovery of Oedipus) is able to command the modern imagination as the burying of Poly-neices cannot. It has been said that *Oedipus the King* possesses the merits of a good detective story. The point of the comparison is not

† From John Jones, *On Aristotle and Greek Tragedy* (New York: Oxford University Press, and London: Chatto and Windus Ltd., 1962), pp. 200–213. Copyright © 1962 by John Jones. Re-printed by permission of the publishers.

merely the piecemeal disclosure of hidden facts, nor the process of investigation, but a kind of mental innocence; Sophocles unfolds a cat-and-mouse situation of great horror while leaving the obvious psychological resources of anguish and dread and recurring false hopes strangely unexploited. This suggests such highly stylised modern forms as the detective story and the cowboy film where, because of a withdrawal of human interest which leaves the action naked, we witness death and pain lightheartedly.

But the comparison ends there, on the threshold of the Sophoclean play's seriousness. This seriousness is hard to experience since action's proper wealth of meaning for the fifth-century Greek is virtually irrecoverable: to say the *Oedipus the King* is like a good detective story is to suggest that the cat-and-mouse horrors are not there at all, when in fact they rest in the action: the interrogations by which Oedipus exposes the truth about himself have a sublime impersonal malignity such as a series of forced moves at chess would impart if the game possessed tragic relevance to life. Furthermore, to say that *Oedipus the King* is like a good detective story is to ignore the differentiation of action and plot upon which the *Poetics* depends. Aristotle's intellectualist vision of the lucid form which the artist coaxes out of rough circumstance must not be directly imposed on Sophocles, of course; but still a general correspondence exists between the Aristotelian form and that life-situation from myth which Sophocles's play defines and re-defines, compresses, reduces, renders essentially, epitomizes. "He shall be found"—so the blind seer Teiresias declares—"at once brother and father to the children of his house, son and husband to the woman who bore him, murderer of his father and successor to his father's bed." Teiresias is a prophet; he speaks for the god and his words disclose the hard bedrock truth of the situation. The vulgar notion of prophecy as the power to predict future events must be absorbed within a wider and juster conception of god-inspired exposure of the myth's essentials; otherwise we fail to give due prominence to the fact (vital to the religious ambience of *Oedipus the King*) that the stage-figures groping forward in the play's action are brought sharply up against something that was there before.

As the dreadful truth unfolds, the people in the play recall the terms of Teiresias's prophecy—with very striking iteration, but without pointed reference to the seer himself; they are falling upon the truth, only in a very secondary sense confirming a prediction, and we should place their mortal encounter with this adamantine quasi-substance in a context of the "Great Time" investing Sophoclean humanity, and of life's cruel margin which is called Necessity. And so they nurse the essential facts with strange unmorbid concentration. A messenger describes how Queen Jocasta, on the point

of suicide, "bewailed the marriage in which, unhappy lady, she had
borne a twofold race—husband by husband, children by her child";
and how Oedipus burst into the palace, asking "where he should
find the wife that was no wife, but a mother who had borne his
children and himself".

The same concentration is maintained by the newly blind Oedipus:

> Those three roads, that secret valley, that wood and narrow pas-
> sage where the roads met and where I spilt—for the dust to
> drink up—my father's blood, and mine. . . . That marriage which
> gave me life, then gave life to other children from my seed; and
> created an incestuous kindred of fathers, brothers, sons, brides,
> wives, mothers. . . .

He summons his young daughters to him:

> Where are you, my children? Come here—come to your broth-
> er's hands . . . which are the hands of a man who, seeing noth-
> ing, understanding nothing, became your father by her that bore
> him.

He contemplates the wretched life in store for them:

> What misery is lacking? Your father killed his father and got
> children by his mother, and you two are the fruit of the womb
> which once held him—

this series of declarations culminating in the demonstrative choral
gesture ("Behold, citizens of Thebes—this is Oedipus") with
which the play ends, and which the Chorus have themselves anticipated:

> Alas, renowned Oedipus! The one ample haven enfolded son and
> father; coming to your bride you found your own beginning.
> How was it, unhappy one, that the furrow which had received
> your father's seed received yours also without mark of protest, all
> this time?

Such definitional fondling of the truth, so far from being mor-
bid, is the means to restoration, and almost an act of peace.
When Sophocles's text has been given a fair hearing we respond
to the co-operative endeavour of the outward-turning masks in
their advance towards full discovery of Oedipus. Our experience
is of something decisively accomplished.

The play opens with the city of Thebes prostrate in a passion of
despair because of a mysterious pestilence or blight which is
destroying its citizens and all living things there. A group of suppliants has assembled to ask Oedipus to save the city. They
approach him not merely because he is their king but also because

he saved Thebes once before, when the monstrous Sphinx was oppressing her, and they naturally turn to him now. Great stress is laid on Oedipus's fame and proven virtuosity as a problem-solver; his finding the answer to the Sphinx's riddle after all others had failed is repeatedly cited as a reason for believing that he will again rescue the city. His task is to find out what has angered heaven to the point of visiting Thebes with pestilence, and then to make amends; and this task he successfully performs. This last point (which has been almost totally ignored) is very relevant to the final sense of accomplishment. Thebes is put right with her gods, and the religious institutions of oracle and prophecy are vindicated.

Oedipus's first step towards saving his city is to send Creon, his wife's brother, to consult the oracle of Apollo. On his carefully staged return Creon's first words are that he brings good news; the god declares that their troubles will end when they detect and punish the murderer of Laius, who was king of Thebes before Oedipus and died at the hand of an unknown assailant when on his way to Delphi. Their present sufferings are due to the defilement they have incurred by unwittingly harbouring the murderer.

And so the search begins. Of course, there is irony in the long struggle to reach the truth, and especially in the successful outcome; but it is an irony whose force and tone will be misapprehended so long as all judgment of the play is required to come to terms with the hero's tragic fate, making the play's meaning and message primarily those which it has for him, or even in relation to him as an independent dramatic *exemplum*. Oedipus's solitary eminence, which is undeniably dominant and impressive always, may be rendered in the critical language of Character and psychological individuation (isolating Oedipus by way of the pains and problems that assault the hero's consciousness), or of action: in the latter case we say that Oedipus stands alone because of the extent— unique in Greek drama—to which he carries the action single-handed. The true Sophoclean standpoint is suggested by a glancing reference in the *Antigone* to Oedipus's "sins brought to light by his own search"; Oedipus does the work in this success-story, and *Oedipus the King* maintains throughout an extraordinary intimacy between the substantive sins themselves—their religio-moral quality, the subjective innocence of the wrongdoing and adjacent themes—and the sinner's action in laying them bare. A kind of godly faithfulness is lent to Oedipus's exertions by the fact that his progressive self-exposure is suspended in a mesh of oracle and prophecy; in fact it *is* the movement of these god-inspired pronouncements towards fulfilment, and its accomplishment *is* their final vindication. The process and its completion matter supremely.

We have noted Teiresias's words and the answer with which

Creon returned from Delphi. Another and deeper oracular layer is exposed by the Chorus:

> I will go no more to Apollo's inviolate shrine at the navel of the world, nor to the temple at Abae, nor to Olympia, if these oracles fail in fulfilment so that each man's finger points at them. . . . The old prophecies about Laius are losing their power: already men are dismissing them from mind, and Apollo is nowhere glorified with honours. Religion is dying.

They are referring to an earlier oracle or oracles which Laius received from Apollo's ministers at Delphi. Jocasta has already stated their content which was that Laius would one day be killed by the child of his marriage with herself. The reason for the Chorus's dismay is that these oracles appear to be utterly discredited; Jocasta's baby died at birth (as everyone supposes), and when Laius finally came to be murdered the accepted story was that "foreign robbers" were responsible. When Sophocles makes his Chorus of Theban elders declare that "religion is dying" because of the apparent non-fulfilment of the oracles, we should allow them to mean what they say. This is the Chorus which indicated their religious despair by asking (and we used the question in order to distinguish Sophocles's piety from Aeschylus's): "Why should I take part in the sacred dance?" Theirs is the voice of Theban religious practice; they lend the present crisis a full and obvious urgency.

It is therefore an ultimately fortunate thing that the parricide and incest should be established, and that the construction of events now prevailing, the humanly more comfortable but religion-wasting construction, should be refuted. The outcome of the play is a dreadful necessity, paradoxically divine and also embracing Oedipus's individual fate since yet another oracle has pronounced, this time in answer to Oedipus himself, that (as he reports)

> I must live in incest with my mother, and bring before my fellow men a family they will not bear to look upon, and kill the father who begat me.

By exposing the full horror of the situation Oedipus demonstrates that things have come out right; nature follows the divine plan, experience is sanctified. And the long search which achieves this is his own: we are defining the sense in which the role of Oedipus is heroic.

If these facts within the Sophoclean play have not received attention, it is largely because of the presupposition that dramatic action is bound to be crude and dull and mechanical when it is determined from above—in the present case by oracle and prophecy. The outraged individual of Romantic criticism is again to the fore, in consideration of Oedipus's sins; not only did he proceed in ignorance that the old man whom he attacked (after extreme provocation) was his father, and that the woman whom he subsequently married was his mother, but he was fated to do these things. The question of acting in ignorance need not detain us, since for Sophocles in this play, as for Aeschylus, psycho-physical defilement follows the deed without regard to intention. But the divine binding of Oedipus to his fate has a daunting and detailed rigidity which the inherited curse and prophecy seem never to impart in Aeschylus. It suggests the determined movement of the stars which is a leading image of Sophoclean mutability. And indeed the stage downfall of Oedipus is the acting out of that lyrically fore-shadowed mutability—but only in part, since the circling Bear is used by Sophocles to present a single cyclical movement bringing sorrow to one and joy to another. Romantic concentration on the figure of the king blinds us to the plight of Thebes and its final remedy; the city's terrible sickness, which overshadows everything else at the beginning of the play, is the result of harbouring a defilement, and it is cured by that single process of self-discovery leading to expulsion from the city which we incline to think of solely as Oedipus's tragedy.

The final impression of accomplishment is at one with the doubleness characterising Sophoclean mutability; the Chorus's vision of Oedipus "with his life reversed"—the thematic strand which criticism has gathered up gratefully—issues from a corporate consciousness occupied with divine fulfilment and the city's health; and the play comes to rest in a conclusion adequate to their anxieties. We return to our earlier insistence that the relationship of prosperity and adversity within the mutability-rhythm is symphonic rather than antithetical, its application at this moment being that the image of Oedipus falling as Thebes rises must be judged insufficient—insufficient and also misleading in that a number of false conclusions flow from it. In particular, it is impossible to invoke the late-classical Wheel of Fortune (or anything like it) without reducing Oedipus's downfall, and the saving of Thebes together with her religion, to complete aesthetic penury: we then have a mechanical and determinist scheme of no interest, both on the universal plane of mutability—the Bear's course is fixed—and in the plot of *Oedipus the King*, which simply follows the course laid down for it in Apollo's oracle.

That Sophocles is not at all like this is a mystery experienced at the outset in the bright lyrical freedom investing his images of mutability; and the fullest human reflection of this mystery, we have already observed, is the binding of Oedipus to his fate. One or two considerations are relevant. Oedipus's dramatic solitude—the solitude of the single-handed sustainer of the action—co-exists with a high measure of social integration. His relation to the people of Thebes is quasi-paternal; he calls them "my children" in the first words of the play; he insists that he is carrying the sorrows of the whole city on his shoulders. And it follows that our symphonic apprehension of opposite fortunes must be pursued within his single destiny: the sense in which his downfall means his city's salvation is immediate and intimate. It is true that Oedipus does not console himself, when disaster strikes him down, with the thought that his ruin is inextricably bound up with his city's deliverance from the killing plague. But the genius of this play is not compensatory. In any case, the spectator's point of view is not his. And when we do examine his own attitude, something of interest emerges.

Oedipus surveys his sins in two different ways. On the one hand he laments the pollution into which he has blundered. He has a lot to say about his ignorance of the true circumstances, but his motive in this is not to deny or even to mitigate culpability. He is exposing a might-have-been (or rather, a would-not-have-been: the analogy suggests itself of Antigone declaring the circumstances in which she would have left a relative unburied); he is saying that he would not have killed Laius or married Jocasta if he had known who they were. This situation-rooted simplicity is fundamental, it must not be perverted into false moral sophistication.

On the other hand Oedipus has an attitude to his sins which is narrowly institutional. Early in the play, when he is setting out to solve the mystery of Laius's death, he pronounces a solemn religious curse upon the unknown murderer, and this curse is treated as a fixed point of religio-moral reference as the story unfolds. Therefore *Oedipus the King* accommodates the formal curse on the sinner alongside the fact of his sin. The seer Teiresias, who is the first to state the truth, proceeds by way of directly accusing Oedipus of the polluting deeds, and at the same time charges him to "abide by the decree of your own mouth". Later, when it begins to dawn on Oedipus himself that the old man whom he killed long ago was none other than Laius, he cries out: "Unhappy me! It seems I have just been placing myself under a dreadful curse—and never knew". And later again:

> Suppose this stranger had any blood-connection with Laius—
> then who is now more miserable than the man before you, who
> more loathed of heaven? Neither stranger nor citizen is allowed
> to receive him; no one may speak to him; all must repel him
> from their homes. And it was my mouth and nobody else's that
> laid this—this curse—upon me.

He also refers his final expulsion, when it occurs, to this initial curse (which was coupled with a command to the people of Thebes not to shelter or have social or religious communication with the murderer): "noblest of Thebans, I have doomed myself to banishment by my command that all should thrust out the man of sin . . ."; and a messenger describes how Oedipus shouted out for somebody to unbar the palace gates, "purposing to expel himself from the land—at once, so as not to bring the house under his own curse".

Thus a double representation of Oedipus's sins persists throughout; the curse and the discovered acts of pollution are two ways of stating the single fact of his guilt, and so far from the curse being absorbed within the parricide and incest (when these are established), it continues to the end, undiminished. It is plain from Oedipus's manner of shifting between "I was fated" and "I have doomed myself" that he regards both representations as adequate to his case, and we should surely be mistaken in supposing that he manipulates them advisedly. They are nothing more than modes of statement lying at hand, probably not even conceived as alternatives. The importance for us of this double representation resides in the sins themselves; the whole colour of unwitting guilt is changed when we observe the guilty sufferer apprehending himself as heaven's victim and, at the same time and indifferently, as self-doomed. The individual is no longer simply set upon from above, and a crude unilinear determinism gives place to something not entirely unlike the complex of human freedom and divine omnipotence in ordinary Christian belief—something that mystifies the observer from afar, an apparently pointless binocular agility.

Further, Oedipus's representation "I have doomed myself" does not indicate his surrender to a kind of trick, as though he had set a trap and then fallen into it himself; for the curse is a trap (if we are to save this analogy) in which only the guilty man can be caught. Moreover, it is a trap created and maintained by an expressive act of self-realisation within the play—by the king's utterance of a formal religious curse, and for this reason the language of self-doom cannot be pressed too literally. Our tendency to be repelled by what seems mechanical and unfeeling is due in part to a falsely limited understanding of the ritual act's externality; underestimating the principle of the self's presence in the "mere" deed, we resent the spectacle of his self-uttered doom bearing down on the human agent senselessly, inhumanly, from behind and beyond him.

These are points of substance for the entire unitary action of *Oedipus the King*, as well as for Oedipus's conception of his guilt; given due prominence they modify our experience of discontinuity between the world of human affairs and the dense tissue of oracle and prophecy controlling (but not only controlling) that world. And so the corporate consciousness surprises us, as Oedipus's does, by its enfolding within acknowledgment of responsibility the alien, the superhuman and the uncontrollable. When Oedipus warns Teiresias to mind his words since he is too weak to save himself from punishment, the seer twice answers that he is strong in the truth which he holds; he indicates what has already been noted—that prophecy is present possession of the invincible truth, and he invites its general application to Thebes and her troubles: disclosure of what lies ahead is secondary to exposure of what lies within, and contemplation of what lies within evokes in the diseased community, as in its king, the double response of a helpless victim and of one who is blameworthy. The Chorus carry the play's omnipresent doubleness upon a corporate voice of timorous, oscillatory conjecture.

In this manner, as it seems to me, the single distinct action in which Oedipus lays bare his own sins and discovers who he is escapes from critical entanglement with a fase humanity, and floats free into a Sophoclean independence and self-poise. Humanity is not banished; it colours the action in precisely the fashion of the great central irony of Oedipus's ignorance of what he is doing: this fulfils the apparently artless function (in relation to the automatic guilt of pollution) of keeping alive awareness of a situational might-have-been; of suffusing the parricide and incest in solemn religious contemplation of that mere absence of knowledge in the human individual but for which these horrors would never have been perpetrated. Ironical this surely is, and altogether Sophoclean; and to Sophoclean irony we must join the even more popular subject of *hubris*. "I will start afresh," says Oedipus at the beginning of his search, "and once again bring dark things to the light". How are we to take this reference to his solution of the Sphinx's riddle, and this promise to repeat his success? The usual procedure (vaguely devised and executed) has been to assemble his two or three assertions of this kind and to inflate them, along with his remarks about the fallibility of human prophecy, into a hubristic correlative of the ruin that overtakes him. But this is patently unacceptable—not because the fault is incommensurate with the punishment, but because it bears no relation to the actions from which guilt and suffering flow. It is futile to think in terms of a peremptory, self-confident autocrat who stumbles in his pride, when Sophocles takes pains to show us that Oedipus received Apollo's oracle with pious seriousness and left his home and family in an attempt to escape its fulfilment; the intelligible connection which we observe, for example, between Macbeth's half-stifled ambition and his crimes and tormented conscience, is simply not to be found, nor anything like it.

That this entire method is misconceived becomes plain from a moment's consideration of the underlying necessity that the god's word shall prevail. Then why (it may be asked) does Sophocles bother to create Oedipus peremptory and self-confident? The broad Aristotelian answer is the correct one: a multi-coloured portrait is more interesting than a portrait in monochrome. In other words, a hubristic colouring to Oedipus's search for the murderer is what Sophocles is aiming at; the moral import of his proud confidence is carried in the *laying bare* of his sins; it is not supposed to throw light on, or be in some way adequate to, the sins themselves. In this respect we must approach the play with modest expectations. Oedipus's solution of the Sphinx's riddle, that feat which is stressed throughout, has only the limited significance that it places him on a high eminence of achievement and reputation as a mystery-solver. He is in a position which Greek Tragedy habitually surrounds in an atmosphere of religious dread, because it is very difficult, so the Greeks believed, to excel and still to avoid *hubris*.

Oedipus fails to avoid *hubris*: he is confident of his own success, he is quick to accuse Teiresias and Creon of plotting against his royal person and station, he remarks with near-contempt the falli-bility of the god's human ministers (while retaining an entirely respectful attitude towards the god himself); and it is a sufficient indication of the gulf dividing Sophocles from ourselves that the hubristic taint to Oedipus's search affords the dramatist and his audience a satisfying commentary on the action. A second and almost equally alien function of Oedipus's lonely eminence is to initiate the double reversal in which he and Teiresias, and he and Creon, are involved. Oedipus first appears as a man of paranormal vision, able to discern that which is obscure to others; at the end, the teleological blindness of his common humanity has been declared through his blundering against the hard and hidden truth, and is paralleled in his self-inflicted physical blindness. Teiresias is introduced in the helplessness of blind old age; he is taunted by Oedipus for his want of eyes; he utters the prophecy that Oedipus shall end his days "a blind man, who now has sight". Oedipus cries out when he begins to suspect the truth: "I dread the seer can see", and it is part of the final vindication of the divine order that all are brought to realise that Teiresias can see indeed.

Hence the double reversal in which Oedipus moves from sight to blindness and Teiresias from blindness to sight. The relationship between these two individuals elaborates the primary double rever-sal in the fortunes of the city and its king. So does that between

Oedipus and Creon. After Oedipus has publicly accused him of
treachery, Creon declares: "It is not right to pronounce bad men
good at random, or good men bad." His words point to the end of
the play where, in the moment of full revelation, Oedipus discovers
himself "most vile" (*kakistos*) and Creon, in immediate juxtaposi-
tion, "most noble" (*aristos*). The seeming traitor becomes the
city's upright king (Creon succeeds Oedipus with an instant demonstration of just authority) while the king falls to the level of
blind exiled beggar, the proven source of corporate pollution.

This festooning of quasi-mathematical symmetries is germane to
dramatic intention and effect throughout *Oedipus the King*, working at the level of overall oppositions and transverse movements,
and evident also in details of phrasing. We recognise Creon's
"Don't judge bad men good or good men bad" for a characteristic
Sophoclean turn, and one which we do not readily respond to; the
utterance seems irrelevant in its first part (since Creon is here
merely defending himself—saying that he is a good man who is
being judged bad) and woodenly sententious in its entirety. But
"Don't judge bad men good" has a hidden reference, which an
audience familiar with the myth will have seized on, to Oedipus's
as yet unexposed sins: the symmetry is fast maturing on the stage,
and what strikes us as sententious and generalised will have grati-
fied imaginations that were in love with structural proportion. So
pervasive is this quasi-mathematical mode of Sophoclean Tragedy
that it sometimes produces a paralysis of taste and intelligence in
the profssional classical scholar, so that in Jebb's very literate (if
dated) translation of *Oedipus the King* we come across grotesque
contortions like "a solitary man could not be held the same with
that band" and "how can my sire be level with him who is as
nought to me?". It is a pleasant irony that the scholars who are
busy impressing on us the continuities of our cultural tradition
should so clearly refute themselves in their instinctive vestigial honesty towards the strange texts they are rendering.

D. W. LUCAS

[The Drama of Oedipus]†

There was once a collision in a fog between a liner and an aircraft carrier in the Mediterranean; one of the carrier's aircraft exer-

† From D. W. Lucas, *The Greek Tragic
Poets* (London: Routledge and Kegan
Paul Ltd., 1950, and New York: W. W.
Norton & Company, Inc., 1964), pp.
150–151. Reprinted by permission of
Routledge and Kegan Paul, Ltd., and
Dufour Editions, Inc. All rights reserved.

cising above the fog, and powerless to intervene, could see the converging mastheads of the two vessels and the disaster in which their courses must end. That is a type of situation to which the term 'dramatic' is applied; it is by no means the only kind of drama, but it is a recognizable category, and no plot could be better raw material for such a drama of 'the convergence of the twain' than that supplied by the myth of Oedipus.

Oedipus was famous for his cleverness, yet this cleverness serves only to enmesh him in a net of illusion. He starts, through no fault of his own, from a false premise; he does not know who he is, that is his *hamartia*. Tiresias tells him of his guilt, and he jumps, not indeed unreasonably from the evidence in his possession, to the conclusion that Creon and Tiresias are conspiring against him. Jocasta intervenes to stop the quarrel between her husband and her brother, but in attempting to show the absurdity of the charge that he had murdered Laius she gives him a clue to his guilt. The final discovery depends on putting together the evidence of two parties each of whom knows only half the truth. The Theban Herdsman knows that the child he was ordered to expose was Jocasta's and that Laius was killed by Oedipus; he does not know that Oedipus was the child. The Corinthian Herdsman knows that Oedipus is the baby that he received from the Theban Herdsman. When the two are brought together, the pieces of the puzzle fit. Nothing could exceed the brilliance and dexterity with which Sophocles handles his material so as to extract the last ounce of drama from it.

Some readers may find these claims highly irritating, for it is possible to look at the play in another way. The actual story is puerile, the antecedents of the play are full of impossibilities, and the play itself contains not a few things which will not bear looking into; Oedipus's ignorance about his predecessor, his failure to respond to the plainest hints in spite of early doubts about his parentage, and the extreme irritability of Tiresias which leads to such momentous indiscretion, all these can be made the subject of easy wit, which would be justified if Oedipus was intended to be a Sherlock Holmes. The answer is that when the play is acting we do not think of looking into these things, and Sophocles never troubled himself to provide answers to questions which were not going to enter the mind of his audience. The simple and poetic fancy which contrives the folk-tale is puerile when judged from a certain angle; Sophocles, if less simple, is still moving in the world of poetry, and his plays can only be seen or read by those who are prepared to enter that world leaving all irrelevant cleverness behind.

The question of the guilt of Oedipus has been much discussed; here we are troubled by fundamental differences between primitive and sophisticated thought. Though things were moving fast when the *Oedipus* was written, men were finding great difficulty in escaping from the notion that certain acts brought with them a physical contamination as definite as the infection conveyed by contact with a leper. To this sort of guilt intention is irrelevant, though the Greeks at all times distinguished between acts done willingly and under compulsion. The incestuous parricide is a pariah; it is futile to try to analyse the horror felt by Oedipus and the Chorus at the discovery, but is is clear that they did not feel the purity of his intentions to be relevant. In the *Oedipus Coloneus* written many years later Oedipus does feel this, but he still thinks that his touch conveys contamination. It is not, however, allowable to infer anything about the ideas implicit in an earlier play from the views expressed later in the poet's life.

BERNARD M. W. KNOX

[Oedipus and God]†

When the priest, in the opening scene, tells Oedipus that he regards him not as "equated to the gods" but as "first of men," he is attempting, by means of this careful distinction, to clarify and correct an ambiguity inherent in his own speech and action. The beginning of the play suggests in both verbal and visual terms that Oedipus is in fact regarded as "equated to the gods." The priest of Zeus and selected young priests have come as suppliants to the palace of Oedipus; their action is parallel to that of other groups who, the priest tells us (19), have gone in supplication to the twin temples of Athena and the fire oracle of the Theban hero Ismenus. "You see us here," the priest says to Oedipus, "sitting in supplication at your altars" (*bōmoisi tois sois*, 16). This is an extraordinary phrase for a priest to address to a *tyrannos*, and it did not escape the eye of the ancient commentators; "They come to the altars built in front of the palace as to the altars of a god," says the scholiast. It is not until many hundred lines later (and after many events and revelations) that we find out from Jocasta that "your altars" are the altars dedicated to Lycean Apollo (919).

The equation is one that Oedipus does not reject. His first question to the suppliants contains an ambiguous pronoun (*moi*, 2) which suggests two different meanings for the sentence as a whole: "Tell me, what is the meaning of this supplicatory attitude?" or

† From Bernard M. W. Knox, *Oedipus at Thebes* (New Haven: Yale University Press, 1957), pp. 159–184. Copyright © 1957 by Yale University Press. Reprinted by permission of the publisher.

"What is the meaning of this attitude in which you supplicate me?" And at the end of the chorus' appeal to the gods, an ode which is liturgical in form, Oedipus addresses the chorus in words which, like his opening sentence, betray acceptance of the attitude towards him implicit in the tableau and speeches of the opening scene. "You are praying. And what you are praying for, if you are willing to hear and accept what I am about to say . . . you will receive . . ." The words Oedipus chooses are symptomatic of a god-like attitude. They accept and promise fulfilment of the choral prayer (which was addressed to Athena, Artemis, Apollo, Zeus, and Dionysus) and are phrased in what is a typical formula of the Delphic oracle. "You are praying to me for Arcadia," the Pythian priestess answered the Spartans, according to Herodotus; "What you are praying for is a big thing. I shall not give it to you." "You come praying for good government," she said to Lycurgus; "I shall give it to you."

These pointers would not have gone unrecognized in fifth-century Athens, for Oedipus is a *tyrannos* and the comparison of *tyrannis* to divine power is a commonplace of Greek literature. "He praises *tyrannis*," says Adeimantus in Plato's *Republic*, "as equal to godhead." The possessor of the ring of Gyges, in Glaucus' fable in the same work, is described as possessed of power to carry out any imaginable (and unlawful) act, and the catalogue of his powers concludes with the words, ". . . and act in other respects like one equal to the gods among men."

The individual *tyrannos* is equal to the gods in his power, his prosperity, and his success. The *polis tyrannos*, Athens, assumes this same quasi-divinity; in the Periclean speeches in Thucydides the city replaces the gods as the object of man's veneration and devotion. In the three magnificent and lengthy speeches attributed to Pericles in the first two books of the *History*, the word *theos*, "god," does not occur even once. The nearest thing to religious feeling which is to be found in them occurs in that section of the Funeral Speech where Pericles calls on the Athenians to "contemplate daily the power of the city and become lovers of Athens." "Athens," he says, in words more appropriate for a god than a state, "Athens alone comes to the test superior to report. Athens alone affords the attacking enemy no cause for annoyance at the character of the enemy by whom he is beaten and to the subject no cause for blaming his master as unworthy to rule."

The city which thus in fifth-century Athens becomes the object of man's veneration is in the first place the creation of man, of his "attitudes which enable him to live in communities" (*astynomous orgas*), as Sophocles puts it in the chorus of the *Antigone*. If Athens can be spoken of in worshiping tones, what of man, who created the city? The development of the new humanist view tended inevitably towards the substitution of man for god as the true center of the universe, the true measure of reality; this is what Protagoras meant by his famous phrase, "Man is the measure of all things." The rationalistic scientific mind, seeking an explanation of reality in human terms and assuming that such an explanation is possible and attainable, rejects the concept of God as irrelevant. If reality is fully explicable in human terms, the gods will automatically be disposed of when the complete explanation is worked out; meanwhile the important thing is the search for the explanation. The question of the existence or nonexistence of the gods is secondary and must be postponed; it is also a blind alley, for the answer to the question depends on the answer to another question, which the human intelligence *has* some hope of answering. "About the gods," so ran the opening sentence (all that we have left) of Protagoras' famous book *On the Gods*, "I have no means of knowing whether they exist or do not exist or what their form may be. Many things prevent [the attainment] of this knowledge, the obscurity [of the subject] and the fact that man's life is short." The word translated "obscurity" (*adêlotês*) disposes of the subject of the gods as one which does not allow of scientific method: nothing can be "made clear," "proved" (*dêlon, dêloun*). Everything connected with the gods is *adêlon*; they are, by their nature and by definition, beyond the reach of scientific understanding and discussion. And the concluding phrase—"the shortness of human life"—is not, as at first appears, a cynical quip at the impenetrability of the subject and consequent futility of discussion about it; it is the serious statement of a man who sees other things to be understood which *can* be understood by the efforts of the human intelligence, though one man's life may not be long enough to reach the goal. "Life is short," runs the first Hippocratic aphorism, "the art long"; here is the same feeling of pressure—there is so much to be learned, so little time to learn it. For such an attitude the existence or nonexistence of the gods is not the most urgent question; it is in fact a question to be excluded. And this is precisely what Plato makes Protagoras say in the *Theaetetus*, where Socrates imagines the great sophist reproving him and his fellow debaters for the irrelevancy of their discussions. "There you sit in a bunch making speeches, and bringing into the discussion the gods, while I exclude [*eksairo*] from both spoken and written discussion the whole question of their existence or nonexistence."

With the gods excluded from discussion, and man the measure of all things, man's attempt to understand his environment and nature, if successful, will make him "equated to the gods." "The doctor who is also a philosopher," says the Hippocratic treatise *On*

Decorum, "is the equal of the gods." "Many are the wonderful and terrible things," sang the chorus of the *Antigone,* "and nothing more wonderful and terrible than man." But man with the attainment of complete understanding would be more than the equal of the gods, for if the scientific explanation of the universe made the concept of divine power unnecessary or demonstrably false, man would be revealed as the creator of the gods. This final stage is represented by a famous dramatic fragment of Critias, the leading spirit of the Thirty Tyrants; it describes the invention of the gods by a man of wisdom and intelligence whose object was to stabilize society by imposing on erring human beings an inescapable superior and a fear of superhuman vision and retribution.

> There was a time when the life of man was undisciplined, beast-like, and subject to superior strength, when there was no reward for the good and no punishment for the wicked. Then it was, in my opinion, that men made laws as correctors, so that Justice would be *tyrannos* ... and have violence as its slave. A punishment was administered to anyone who acted wrongly. Then, when the laws prevented them from open acts of violence, they did them secretly. At that point, it seems to me, some man of deep wisdom and intelligence [*sophos gnomên*] invented [*ekseurein*] for mankind the fear of the gods . . . this was his reason for introducing divinity.

But long before Critias wrote these words which carry the doctrines of the enlightenment to a cynical extreme, the hopeful mood of its early stages—the vision of man in a universe he could fully understand and perhaps eventually control—had vanished. The Athenian confidence in their city's unconquerable destiny and fifth-century man's dream of a world understood and controlled by human intelligence—both alike collapsed in the horrors of the unexpected and inexplicable plague, in the growing misery and anarchy caused by the relentless and senseless war. The Protagorean "liberal" program of educating man to political justice was revealed as an idealistic illusion by the *Walpurgisnacht* of butchery and cynicism which Thucydides clinically analyzes in his accounts of the political massacres on Corcyra and the Athenian "negotiations" with Melos. The universe seemed to have been revealed not as a cosmos, an order, governed either by gods or by discoverable natural laws, but as a desperate chaos, governed by blind chance. "Whatever turns out contrary to calculation," said Pericles in the speech made just before the outbreak of the war, "we are accustomed to attribute to chance." He is reminding the Athenians that in spite of their financial and technical superiority to the enemy they may suffer setbacks. But his remarks were grimly prophetic. Too many things "turned out contrary to calculation"; the plague, which Pericles describes as "sudden, unexpected, and happening contrary to all calculation," was only the forerunner of a series of events which seemed to mock human calculation or foresight of any kind.

The plays of Euripides reflect the growth in Athens of an increasingly reckless feeling that, as Jocasta puts it, "the operation of chance governs all things." Even in the prewar *Alcestis* (438 B.C.) Euripides prophetically expounds the desperate mood of the war years in the philosophizing of the drunken Heracles. "The course of chance—no one can see where it will go—this is not a thing which can be taught, or captured by technique ... Enjoy yourself, drink, calculate that this day's life is yours—the rest belongs to chance." In the later plays the mood is grimmer. This same Heracles, in a different Euripidean play, is struck by a series of calamities which defy human expectation and rational explanation; he rejects the solution which this terrible situation seems to call for, suicide, and determines to go on living, but in a world which he redefines as one subject to inexplicable chance. "Now, it seems, I must act as a slave to chance." Menelaus, in the Euripidean *Orestes*, describes his situation in the same terms: "Now it is necessity that the wise should be slaves to chance." The most uncompromising expression of this terrible doctrine is put into the mouth of Hecuba in the *Troades*, as she mourns over the mangled body of the child Astyanax. "Any mortal man that, seeming to prosper, rejoices as if his prosperity were solidly based, is a fool. For the turns of chance are like those of a crazed man, leaping now this way, now that ..."

This chance, which the Euripidean characters identify as the governing force of the universe, is clearly the philosophical "chance" of Thucydides, an abstraction of the absence of any causality comprehensible in human terms. But it was only to be expected, in fifth-century Greece, that this abstraction which now seemed to many the dominant factor in human life should be personified, should become in fact a god, or rather (since the word *tyche*, "chance," is feminine in Greek) a goddess. So Oedipus calls himself "the son of chance" (*paida tês tychês*), and Ion, in Euripides, addresses Chance as a divine being. "O you who have changed the fortunes of tens of thousands of mortals before now, making them unfortunate and then prosperous, Chance ..."

This personification was not unprecedented; in fact the unprecedented thing was the philosophical abstraction. Chance, in the older Greek poets and even in Herodotus, is often personified, and usually, far from indicating an absence of causality and order, it is associated with divine dispensation. In Herodotus' account of the founding of the Scythian royal line (a story told him by Greek colonists in Pontus), Heracles, driving the cattle of Geryon, comes to Scythia, and while he is asleep his cattle vanish "by divine chance" (*theiai tychêi*, iv. 8). It is, in other words, no chance at all, and the result of the disappearance of the cattle, the birth of Scythes, son of Heracles and the first Scythian king, was as the phrase indicates the divine purpose behind the apparently fortuitous disappearance of the cattle. So also in the Herodotean account of the founding of the Cypselid tyranny at Corinth (v. 92), the child Cypselus, later to be *tyrannos* of Corinth, is spared by his ten appointed execution- ers because when the first man of the ten took hold of the child, "by divine chance" it smiled, and the man had not the heart to kill it, nor had the others. The child "chanced" to smile, but this was not blind chance, for if the child had been killed the oracles pre- dicting its eventual seizure of power in Corinth could not have been fulfilled. This Chance, the instrument of the divine will, is addressed by Pindar as the "daughter of Zeus the liberator, saving chance," and the poet Alcman called her, in an astonishing phrase, "sister of good government and Persuasion, daughter of Foreknowl- edge."

That Chance, Tyche, should be personified and deified in Oedi- pus' confident outburst and other tragic passages is nothing new; what is new is the nature of the Chance which now assumes divin- ity. It is no longer the old instrument of the divine purpose, "daughter of Foreknowledge," but an autonomous goddess who personifies the absence of causal order in the universe. She is the principle of chaos. She presides not, as the older gods did, over an ordered universe but over a disorder in which "there is no clear foresight of anything." And this goddess cannot merely coexist with the other gods. She must be either, as the daughter of Forethought, divine Chance, their servant, or, as the absence of causality, blind Chance, their mistress. The every existence of this new goddess Chance makes the existence of the old gods meaningless. That the logic of this was apparent in the fifth century is demonstrated by a passage in Euripides' satyr-play *The Cyclops*. Odysseus, preparing to put out Polyphemus' eye, appeals to Hephaestus and Sleep to help him. "Do not," he says, "destroy Odysseus and his crew, after their glorious labors at Troy, at the hands of a man who cares nothing for gods or mortals. Otherwise we must think that Chance is a divinity, and"—here follows the logical conclusion— "that the power of the other divinities is inferior to that of Chance."

This is of course exactly what was to happen in the long run; the other divinities receded before the figure of the new goddess Tyche. The pessimistic mood of the end of the fifth century deepened in the fourth as Greece, torn apart by incessant warfare, succumbed ignobly to the perseverance, intrigue, and raw aggressiveness of a half-savage Macedonian king. In this atmosphere of impotence and defeat the goddess Chance seemed to reign supreme. In spite of the efforts of the philosophers to reduce chance to a subordinate position (Plato, for example, counters the idea that "practically all human affairs are matters of chance" with a new version of the archaic relationship of "divine chance" to divine will—"All things are god, and with god chance and occasion"), the goddess Chance, who symbolized the century's "sense of drift," continued to be the obsessive refrain of the prayers and speculations of the ordinary man. In the last years of the fourth century Demetrius of Phalerum wrote a book on Chance, and the historian Polybius approvingly quotes from it a passage which identifies Chance as the governing force in human history: "Chance, which makes no contracts with this life of ours, makes everything new contrary to our calculation and displays her power in the unexpected." Though she had fewer temples, the goddess Tyche superseded the Olympians in the mind of the common man; she was the only appropriate icon of a world which persistently mocked all human calculation and the logic on which it is based.

Such was the paradoxical ending of a search for truth which began by criticizing and then proceeded to abandon the Olympian deities as inadequate representatives of a cosmic order. The quest for rational principle and appropriate religious personifications of a rational universe ended in the deification of anarchy. The movement of more than a century of brilliant and searching thought is movement not forward but back to the starting point, from gods to goddess, from the Homeric Olympians to the goddess Chance. But this circular progress is not on one plane; the point of return is on a lower level. The movement is a descending spiral.

This self-defeating advance of the search for an intelligible order in the universe is paralleled in Sophocles' tragedy by the intellectual progress of Oedipus and Jocasta. Their successive changes of attitude towards the gods and the oracles which represent the divine prescience in the play, brilliantly motivated by the initial situation and the turns of the plot and fully appropriate to the respective dramatic characters, are yet symbolic of the mental agonies of a generation which abandoned a traditional order of belief with a hopeful vision of an intelligible universe, only to find itself at last facing an incomprehensible future with a desperation thinly disguised as recklessness.

The Oedipus of the opening scenes, formally pious in action and speech but betraying in one phrase after another a confidence in man's worth as equal to that of the gods, is symbolic of the mood of imperial Athens and bears a clear resemblance to the representative figure who set the tone of the era and gave it his name, Pericles. As an official of the Athenian state Pericles performed religious acts (among which was presumably the consultation of the Delphic oracle), but if the oracle's firmly expressed support of the Spartan cause against Athens in 431 B.C. caused him any qualms, they find no reflection in the confident speeches attributed to him by Thucydides in the opening books of his *History*. In his funeral oration over those who fell in the Samian War, Pericles compared the Athenian dead to the gods, and the language he used is typical of the rationalist spirit of the age. The Athenian dead are immortal, like the gods—so the historian Stesimbrotus reports his argument—"for we do not see the gods, but infer [*tekmairometha*] their immortality from the honors which they receive and the benefits which they confer upon us." This is a statement which illustrates clearly the application of the Protagorean dictum, "Man is the measure of all things." The immortality of the gods is deducted from the fact that man honors them (in spite of their invisibility) and the fact that they confer benefits on man. And by the same tokens Pericles proves the immortality of the Athenian dead who gave their lives for the city.

The mood of the Athenian leadership at the beginning of the war was one of outer conformance and inner skepticism. The skepticism would come out into the open only if circumstances forced it; but the calamitous surprises of the war quickly achieved precisely that effect. In the inferno produced by the plague, which made no discrimination between the just and the unjust, the conviction grew that "it made no difference whether one worshiped the gods or not"; and in the frequent Euripidean attacks on the Delphic oracle (in plays produced at a religious festival in the city's name) we have some measure of the strong Athenian reaction against Delphi's enthusiastic encouragement of the Spartans at the beginning of the war.

So with Oedipus. His true feelings do not find open expression until the prophet of Apollo accuses him of the murder of Laius. Immediately the respectful, amost adulatory tone of Oedipus' first address to Tiresias (300–15) is replaced by incredulous and contemptuous fury. All the opprobrious epithets which fifth-century Athens could invent for cynical peddlers of superstition are hurled at the blind prophet's head: "intriguing quack," Oedipus calls the representative of Apollo, "deceitful huckster, with an eye for profit, and for nothing else."

That a king should attack a prophet is nothing new in Greek literature. In the first book of the *Iliad* Agamemnon threatens Chryses, the priest of Apollo, with physical violence (i. 26-8) and angrily reviles the prophet Calchas for taking the priest's part (i. 105 ff.). But Oedipus' attack on the prophet is not like Agamemnon's. Agamemnon reviles Calchas as a "prophet of evil," but he does not question the truth of the prophet's statement (though it accuses him of wrongdoing), and he proceeds to follow the prophet's advice. Oedipus not only rejects the prophet's statement but also goes on to attack the claims of prophecy itself. He contrasts the failure of Tiresias to solve the riddle of the Sphinx with his own success; his words imply a contemptuous comparison between the sources of information open to the prophet (the birds, 395, and the god, 396), and his own intelligence, which without any source of information stopped the Sphinx. Oedipus has rejected the statement of a prophet "in whom alone," according to the chorus, "truth is inborn" (299), who "sees the same things as Lord Apollo' (284–5), and in Oedipus' proud words can be seen the outline of the next step in his progress, the rejection of all prophecy, including the prophecy of a god.

But for the chorus the first step is disturbing enough. At first they "neither accept nor reject" (485–6) the prophet's words; they "can find nothing to say." But in the end they reach a formula which seems appropriate: Tiresias is after all a man, and therefore fallible—to reject his words does not necessarily mean that one rejects Apollo. "Zeus and Apollo have understanding and know the deeds of mortals. But when it comes to men—that a prophet is more right than I am, there is no true judgment of this" (498–501). So the complicated rhythm of the development is established: as Oedipus' words reveal that he is ready to take the next step towards total rejection of prophecy, the chorus draws the line where it stands—it will accept, reluctantly, the rejection of a human prophet but not of divine prophecy.

It is Jocasta who crosses this line first; and the decisive nature of the step she takes is stressed dramatically by the hesitant and complicated way in which she takes it. When she hears that the basis of Creon's supposed attack on Oedipus is neither personal knowledge of the facts nor an informant (704), but the statement of a prophet (705), she carries the argument forward to an intermediate stage. A prophet might be wrong, so ran the argument of the chorus, and one prophet might be wiser than another (502), but Jocasta claims that no one human prophet is any better than any other—they are all wrong. "Listen and learn that there is no human creature which possesses the art of prophecy" (709). This general proposition she claims that she can prove, and without much loss of time.

But the proof consists of the failure of a prophecy, not of Tiresias, but of Apollo. It is the oracle given to Laius. "An oracle came to Laius once . . ." (711); the vague formula is Herodotean, and in Herodotus it is used when the means of communication between the god and the recipient is unknown or irrelevant—an exclusive stress is placed on the content of the oracle and the reaction to it. What should follow in the formula is the place from which the oracle came, but Jocasta continues with a qualification: " . . . came . . . I will not say from Phoebus himself, but from his ministers" (*hyperetôn*, 712). The oracle said that Laius would be killed by his own son, but instead Laius was killed by brigands, and his three-day-old son, his feet skewered together, had long before been thrown out on to the barren mountainside. "In this case Apollo did not bring to fulfilment that the son should be the father's killer, nor that Laius should suffer the dreadful thing he feared at his son's hand. Such were the precise formulations [*diôrisan*, 723] of prophetic voices. Do not concern yourself with prophecies. For whatever the god seeks and needs he will easily make clear himself" (720–5).

This is an extraordinary statement. The false oracle came not from Apollo but from his "ministers." Who were they? Not, this time, Tiresias, for if so Jocasta would have named him—the case against the prophet's fallibility would be clear and sufficient. She must be referring to Apollo's "ministers" at Delphi, the priests or the priestess responsible for the delivery of the prophecy. The ministers gave voice to the prophecy, but Apollo did not bring it to fulfilment; it was not his prophecy. If he needs to say anything he will reveal it in person, not through "ministers." Here is subtle doctrine. It avoids indicting Apollo, but delivers a death blow to Apolline prophecy, which had from time immemorial been delivered through his ministers at Delphi. How is Apollo to prophesy, if not through human beings who serve him? "There is no human creature," Jocasta said, "which possesses the art of prophecy"; as she explains that statement it becomes clear that she might just as well have added "and no god either."

Before the scene is over this is precisely what she does say, fully and clearly. As was to be expected of the superlative plotting of this play, she does so in reaction to a fresh revelation. Her first attack on prophecy, which was intended to comfort Oedipus, has had the paradoxical effect of plunging him into fear that Tiresias may be right. He is unimpressed by her general argument; he can see nothing but the incidental detail; the fact that Laius was killed at the junction of three roads. To explain his fears to Jocasta he gives her an account of his life previous to his arrival at Thebes, and this account includes the prophecy given to him by Apollo at Delphi: that he would kill his father and beget children by his mother. Oedipus does not try to belittle this prophecy as the work of Apollo's "ministers." "Phoebus," he says unequivocally, "spoke and foreshadowed dreadful disasters" (788–90).

Jocasta has dismissed the prophet Tiresias and exposed the falsity of the prophecy made by the "ministers" of Apollo; if she is to be of any comfort to Oedipus now she must extend her indictment to include what Oedipus himself calls the word of Phoebus. She does not hesitate: she now makes a significant correction of her first hesitant formulation and states openly what she previously implied. The eyewitness of Laius' death, she says, may possibly go back on what he said, but he cannot demonstrate that the death of Laius was consistent with the prophecy. "Loxias plainly said that he was to die at the hands of my son." The oracle to Laius, she now says, came not from "ministers" but from the god himself. To counter the words of Tiresias all she needed was a false oracle from Apollo's human ministers; to counter the oracle given to Oedipus by Apollo she needs a false oracle delivered by Apollo himself; and by this bold correction she makes the same oracle serve both arguments. The oracle, man-given or god-given, is false and will be forever false, for the son who was to kill his father died first. When she sums up her argument with her famous defiance of prophecy— "From now on I would not, for the sake of a prophecy, look this way, or that" (857–8)—she is dismissing all the prophecies so far revealed: the accusations of Tiresias, the oracle given by Apollo's ministers, or rather by Apollo, to Laius, and the oracle given by Apollo to Oedipus. The logic of the changing situation drives her to the position that was in any case implicit in her first statement, the rejection of all prophecy, human and divine alike.

The chorus could doubt Tiresias but not Apollo. It reacts violently against Jocasta's defiance of prophecy, and its attitude is colored by other aspects of the scene it has just witnessed. Since it last expressed its unimpaired loyalty to Oedipus (691 ff.) it has learned much. It has heard that Jocasta's child by Laius was exposed on the mountainside in a particularly barbarous fashion, and that this was done to prevent the fulfilment of a Delphic oracle; that Oedipus, the savior of Thebes, came to the city stained with blood, possibly the blood of Laius; that Oedipus is a fugitive from a Delphic oracle which predicts for him the same unhallowed destiny as that foretold for Laius' son. All these dreadful revelations of pollution, actual and threatened, combined with Jocasta's proud rejection of prophecy and Oedipus' firmly expressed approval of her statement, impel the chorus to disassociate itself from the rulers of Thebes. It appeals to higher authorities and laws in terms which reject implicitly and explicitly the whole philosophical outlook on which Oedipus and Jocasta now base their hope and action.

"May destiny [*moira*, 863] be with me," the chorus sings. The word is carefully chosen; it is the word Jocasta used when she described the prophecy given to Laius, "that destiny [*moira*, 713] would come to him, to die at the hands of his son." Prophecy and destiny are linked; Jocasta explicitly rejects the first, and implicitly the second; the chorus, which will end by vindicating prophecy, begins by accepting destiny. It prays for "reverent purity of word and deed" (*hagneian*, 865). Both Oedipus and Jocasta, the one as the main actor and the other as the accomplice in the taking of human life, are "impure" and both are irreverent in word. Their deeds no one in Thebes dare question, but the chorus appeals to the "high-footed laws proclaimed, brought to birth [*teknôthentes*, 867] in the clear air of heaven, whose father is Olympus alone—no mortal nature of human kind begot [*etikten*, 870] them." The images here reflect the chorus' horror at the tainted births foretold in the oracles delivered to Oedipus; the appeal to the higher laws emphasizes the inadequacy of man-made law—the law in Thebes is Oedipus, he is *tyrannos*.

The chorus realizes that it is facing a harder choice than before; once it had to choose between Oedipus and Tiresias, now between Oedipus and Apollo. It does not hesitate: "I shall not cease to hold the god as my champion" (*prostatên*, 882). The word they use is the Athenian political term used to describe the position of the dominating personality in Athenian affairs, and its appearance here stresses the fact that this statement is a transfer of allegiance. But if Apollo is to be their champion, he must vindicate himself; the oracles must be fulfilled (902–3). The old oracles given to Laius (which Jocasta has apparently proved can never be fulfilled in any circumstances) are "dying"; Oedipus and Jocasta are "excluding" (*eksairousin*, 907) the oracles, as Protagoras did the gods. Apollo is no longer "made manifest by the honors paid him." The power of the gods is overthrown.

But the chorus is overestimating the confidence of its rulers. In spite of Jocasta's comforting demonstrations of the falsity of prophecy, Oedipus is a prey to agony and fear, and, with the pilot stricken, Jocasta herself is afraid. She appears with garlands and incense, announcing her intention to visit "the temples of the gods" (911). But every word she says shows that this is not in any sense a recantation. She has not changed her opinion of oracles, old or new (915–16); it is an erratic move, the unreasoning expression of fear. "The idea occurred to me [*doksa moi parestathê*, 911]," she says, "to come as a suppliant to the temples of the gods." The reason (*gar*, 914) is the agitation of Oedipus, which she regards as a sign that he has lost control of himself (915–16), and which she tried to overcome by advice (918). Only when her attempt to stiffen Oedipus' resolution failed did she come as a suppliant to the gods. She now addresses herself to the altar at which the priest sat in supplication at the opening of the play. "I have come in supplication, with these symbols of prayer, to you, Lycean Apollo, for you are the nearest." This is surely an unusual formula of prayer. True enough, Apollo's altar is the nearest, and it is only natural that her visit to the "temples of the gods" should begin with it, but to tell him so in the invocation of the prayer argues at least a religious insensibility.

With the electrifying news brought by the Corinthian messenger Jocasta's confidence surges back, for here is further proof of what she tried to demonstrate to Oedipus by inference: the "new" oracles given to him at Delphi are proved as false as the "old" oracles given to Laius at Thebes. "Prophecies of the gods," she cries, "where are you?" And more precisely still: "See what the awful oracles of the gods have come to" (953–4).

The proofs now seem overwhelming, and Oedipus matches Jocasta's confident scorn. "Why should one carefully observe the earth of the Pythian prophet or the birds that scream over our heads . . . ?" He dismisses the prophetic art of Tiresias and of Apollo in the same breath: "Polybus has taken the present prophecies with him to Hades where he lies hidden—they are worthless" (971–2).

This is not quite true, as he at once realizes. Polybus has taken only half the prophecies with him; there remains still the fear of the marriage with his mother. And here, as before, Jocasta is one step ahead of Oedipus, and now presents him with a philosophical basis for release from this and every other fear. "What has man to fear, whose life is governed by the operation of chance?"

This word tychê, "chance," has been used often before in the course of the play, its explosive epiphany in these lines has been well prepared. In the earlier scenes it is used in the old sense: fortune, good or bad, viewed as the expression, not the negation, of divine order. "You brought us fortune then, with auspicious bird omens" (tychên, 52), says the priest to Oedipus, associating the liberation of Thebes from the Sphinx with Tiresias' art of divination from birds, and thus placing Oedipus' great achievement in a context of meaningful relationship between god-given signs and human intelligence and action. This context Oedipus will soon deny (398), but for the moment he himself prays, when Creon returns from Delphi with the oracular response: "O Lord Apollo, may he walk in the brightness of some saving fortune" (tychêi . . . sôtêri, 80–1), thus associating tychê directly with the god and the oracle which he impatiently awaits. He later twice uses this word of the misfortunes of Laius (102, 263), the second time in a striking personification: "now Tyche has jumped on his head," a metaphor drawn from the pancration, the merciless "all-in" fighting event of the Greek athletic games. The word is used here in a different sense, for the death of Laius is not, so far as Oedipus can see, an event associated with divine plan or order: it is something terrible which simply "happened" (*etychen*). As the action unfolds further, this word is made to express the feeling of both Oedipus and Jocasta about events which they cannot comprehend; it begins to assume the meaning assigned to it by Pericles—"to chance we ascribe whatever turns out contrary to calculation." So Jocasta, when asked by the chorus to take Oedipus into the palace, replies: "Yes, I will, when I know the nature of what has chanced" (*tychê*, 680). She is referring to the apparently irrational quarrel between Oedipus and Creon. "To whom else should I confide," says Oedipus later, just before he tells his story to Jocasta, "passing through such chance as this?" (*tychês*, 773). He is referring to the chance discovery that the place where Laius was killed was the same as the scene of his own bloody action so many years ago. And a few lines later, speaking of the drunkard's taunt which set him on the road to Delphi and Thebes, he says: "a chance event [*tychê*, 776] occurred to me, surprising enough indeed, but not worth all the attention I gave it."

The transition from this use of the word *tychê* to describe unexpected events to the philosophical abstraction in Jocasta's famous speech is made through the contrast between chance and the oracle which Jocasta draws when she hears the news of the death of Polybus. "This is the man that Oedipus, in fear that he would kill him has fled from so long. And now he is dead, by chance [*pros tês tychês*, 949) and not at the hand of Oedipus." Polybus died "in the course of nature," as Jebb correctly translates this phrase, but also in defiance of the oracle; *tychê* is opposed to divine prediction. From this it is only a step to proclaim the universal dominance of chance, the absence of divine and the futility of human forethought, a world of chaos where the golden rule is "live by hit and miss, as best you can." In such a world Oedipus has nothing to fear from prophecies.

Jocasta goes on to point out to Oedipus that the prophecy about marriage with his mother, like that about killing his father, can be judged by reference to similar prophecies which have proved false. Many men have had such a prophecy about their mothers, for they have dreamed of such a consummation (and dreams, though subject to a variety of interpretation, were generally considered prophetic in the fifth century). These prophecies, too, Jocasta dismisses; "the man who values such things as nothing bears life's burden most easily" (982–3).

Oedipus is not entirely convinced. Though, as he says, Jocasta has made a good case, it is not so good a case as the one against the oracle about his father; in fact it could be as good a case only if his mother Merope were dead. As long as his mother lives he cannot banish fear. Strong as the evidence is, he cannot yet accept the universe of chance.

It is the Corinthian messenger who now delivers the convincing argument. Oedipus is not the son of Polybus and Merope. His whole life history is a striking example of the operation of chance. Found on the hillside by one shepherd (or so the Corinthian messenger believes), passed on to another, given to the childless king Polybus, brought up as the heir to a kingdom, Oedipus went to Delphi as a result of a chance remark made by a drunkard, to hear a dreadful prophecy which made him a self-banished exile from Corinth forever. He came to Thebes a homeless wanderer, answered the riddle of the Sphinx, and won the *tyrannis* of the city and the hand of a queen. Even his name he owes to chance. "You were named the man you are from this chance" (*ek tautês tychês*, 1036), the messenger reminds him. The whole story, the beginning of which is only now being brought to light, seems like a powerful demonstration that Jocasta was right. Such a fantastic series of coincidences seems expressly designed to mock the idea that human destiny is predictable; it is a paradigm of the inconsequent anarchy of the universe.

Jocasta was right, but for Oedipus in his present mood she seems to have stopped short of the full truth. He accepts the rule of chance, but it is not, for him, a blind chance which nullifies human action and condemns man to live at random. Chance is a goddess, and Oedipus is her son. She is "the good giver," and he will not be dishonored when his real identity is at last established. It is typical of Oedipus that he accepts a doctrine which is offered to him as a warrant for "living at random" and transforms it into a basis for controlled action; as the son of Tyche he will press on the search to the end—his parentage is a guarantee of success. He makes out of Jocasta's nihilizing chance a goddess who controls the universe and has selected him as her chosen vessel: he is kin to the moons that mark the months for all men and for Oedipus the ebb and rise of his own great destiny.

The implication of this magnificent speech of Oedipus is clearly that he is equated to the gods. The chorus, breath-taken at the sudden and (apparently) auspicious revelations, inspired by Oedipus' courage and infected by his enthusiasm for the unimaginable vistas that now open up before him, proceeds to make the idea explicit. Oedipus, they sing, will prove to be not a foreigner but, to their great joy, a Theban; his nurse and mother is revealed as the Theban mountain Cithaeron (1089 ff.) But his real parentage must be greater yet. Which of the mountain nymphs bore him to Pan? To Apollo? Or was his father Hermes? Or the Theban divinity Dionysus?

These exultant speculations, put forward as prophetic (*mantis*, 1086) and addressed to Apollo for his approval (1096–97), are the penultimate step in the long search for the origins of Oedipus. "My father," Oedipus told Jocasta, "was Polybus of Corinth, my mother Merope, a Dorian." But that was before the Corinthian messenger released Oedipus from fear. Since then his mother, in his mind and in that of the chorus, has appeared to the imagination in a variety of identities, which run the gamut from small to great: a third-generation slave (1063), the goddess Tyche, the mountain Cithaeron, a long-lived nymph, a nymph of Helicon. And the image of his father, once stable in the figure of Polybus of Corinth, has been tentatively identified with the Corinthian messenger, Apollo, Pan, Hermes, and Dionysus. As the last notes of the chorus' joyful song die away, Oedipus begins the final enquiry which will bring the search for the truth to an end; he will soon know his parents as Jocasta, who has already gone off into the palace to hang herself, and Laius, whom he killed at the crossroads so many years ago. He is the son not of Chance but of mischance, as the herdsman tells him (1181); the revelation of his parentage, far from raising him to the level of the gods, reduces him below the level of all normal humanity. And the vicissitudes of his astonishing career are revealed as the working not of Jocasta's blind chance nor the anarchic goddess Chance but of the old "divine chance," *theia tychê*, the expression in action of divine foreknowledge, the mode of fulfilment of Apollo's oracle.

This intellectual progress of Oedipus and Jocasta, which parallels the intellectual progress of the age of enlightenment, has been carefully set in an ironic dramatic framework where it is exposed as wrong from the start. At one point after another the words which characterize the power, decision, and action of Oedipus find a significant echo in contexts which emphatically oppose to his human greatness the power, decision, and action of the gods. The assumption of divine stature implicit in Oedipus' attitude is thus made explicit and at the same time exposed as false. The priest, for example, addresses Oedipus as "the one in power" (*all' ô kratynôn*, 14), and the chorus, much later, at the point where it transfers its allegiance from the *tyrannos* to the god, uses exactly the same words to address Zeus (*all' ô kratynôn*, 904). The priest hails Oedipus as "savior" (*sôtêra*, 48) a title which Oedipus accepts (*eksesôs'*, 443); the priest meanwhile has prayed that "Apollo will come as savior" (*sôtêrios*, 156). Oedipus claims that he has "stopped" the Sphinx (*epausa*, 397), but it is on Apollo that the priest calls to "stop" the plague (*paustêrios*, 150). Oedipus claims to "wield the power" in Thebes (*kratê . . . nemôn*, 237), but Zeus, the chorus sings, "wields the power of the lightning" (*astrapan kratê nemôn*, 201). Oedipus calls himself "great" (*megan*, 441; cf. 776), but the god, says the chorus, is "great" in his laws (*megas theos*, 872). Oedipus has "empire" (*archê*, 259, 383) but the "empire" of Zeus is immortal (*athanatan archan*, 905). Oedipus promises "strength" (*alkên*, 218; cf. 42) but it is to Athena that the chorus prays for "strength" (*alkan*, 189). Oedipus talks to the Thebans like a father to his children (*tekna*, 1; cf. 6), but the chorus finally appeals to "father Zeus" (*Zeu pater*, 202). Oedipus "destroyed" the Sphinx (*phthisas*, 1198), but it is to Zeus that the chorus appeals to "destroy" the plague (*phthison*, 202). All these echoes are like a mockery of Oedipus' pretensions, and in addition the language of the play rings with sardonic puns on his name which seem to find their way into the speech of the characters like echoes of some far-off grim laughter. *Oidipous*—"Swollen-foot"—the name emphasizes the physical blemish which scars the body of the splendid *tyrannos*, a defect he would like to forget but which remainds us of the cast-out child he once was and forshadows the outcast man he is soon to be. The second half of his name, *pous*, "foot," recurs constantly in passages which, though the speaker is usually not conscious of the force of his speech, refer to Oedipus' real identity as the murderer of Laius. "The Sphinx," says Creon, replying to Oedipus' veiled reproach that he had not exerted himself enough in the original search for the murderer of Laius, "the Sphinx forced us to look at what was at our feet" (*to pros posi skopein*, 130). Tiresias invokes the "dread-footed curse of your mother and father" (*deinopous ara*, 418). And two of the choral odes heavily emphasize this word by repeating it in strophe and antistrophe. "It is time [for the unknown murderer] to set his foot in motion in flight" (*phygai poda nôman*, 468), they sing, and in the corresponding antistrophe they describe the murderer as "a wild beast, alone, cut off," *meleos meleôi podi chêreuôn* (479)—a phrase which can be taken metaphorically, as Jebb does ("forlorn on his joyless path"), but which means literally "forlorn and miserable with miserable foot." In the next choral ode, the one in which they abandon Oedipus and pray for the fulfilment of the oracles, the chorus' words repeat the same pattern: "The laws of Zeus are high-footed" (*physipodes*, 866) is answered in the antistrophe by "pride . . . plunges into sheer necessity wherein no service of the foot can serve" (Jebb's translation of *ou podi chrêsimôi chrêtai*, 876). These words literally mean "where it uses a useless foot"; they repeat in a negative form the "miserable foot" (*meleôi podi*) of the previous ode. These phrases all point with terrible irony to the maimed foot of Oedipus which is the basis of his name and the key to his identity; two of them, *hypsipodes* and *deinopous*, are like punning forms of the name itself.

These mocking repetitions of the second half of the hero's name evoke the Oedipus who will be revealed, the hunted murderer. The equally emphatic repetitions of the first component of his name stress a dominant characteristic of the imposing *tyrannos*. *Oidi*-means "swell," but it is very close to *oida*, "I know," and this is a word that is never far from Oedipus' lips; his knowledge is what makes him the decisive and confident *tyrannos*. *Oida* recurs throughout the text of the play with the same grim persistence as *pous*, and the suggestion inherent in the name of the *tyrannos* is ironically pointed up in a group of three assonantal line-endings which in their savage punning emphasis are surely unparalleled in Greek tragedy. When the messenger from Corinth comes to tell Oedipus that his father Polybus is dead, he enquires for Oedipus, who is inside the palace, in the following terms (924–6):

> Strangers, from you might I *learn where*
> is the palace of the *tyrannos Oidipous*,
> best of all, where he himself is, if you *know where*.

Here it is in the original:

> Ar' an par' hymôn ô ksenoi mathoim' hopou
> ta tou tyrannou dômat' estin Oidipou
> malista d' auton eipat' ei katoisth' hopou.

These violent puns, suggesting a fantastic conjugation of a verb "to know where" formed from the name of the hero who, as Tiresias told him, does not know where he is—this is the ironic laughter of the gods whom Oedipus "excludes" in his search for the truth. They watch the critical intelligence work its way laboriously and courageously through to the absolutely clear vision which, once found, it cannot bear to face. Their presence is manifested in this intrusive ironic pattern in the language of the characters, which is a riddling reminder that there is a standard beyond man by which Oedipus is measured. As Oedipus finds out in the end, man is not the measure of all things; rather, as Plato was to say much later, "the measure of all things is—the god."

CEDRIC H. WHITMAN

Jocasta†

Jocasta exercises a curious charm over the reader of the play. Strictly speaking, she is unnecessary to the plot, for the actual information which she gives about the murder might have come

† From Cedric H. Whitman, *Sophocles: A Study of Heroic Humanism* (Cambridge, Mass.: Harvard University Press, 1951), pp. 132–138. Copyright 1951 by the President and Fellows of Harvard College. Reprinted by permission of the publisher.

from any source. But aside from the obvious fact that it is natural
for her to be in the play, and that she greatly increases the tragic
pathos by her presence, she occupies a special position in her relation to the hero. She completes him, and only toward the very end
of the play does he free himself from a certain emotional depend-
ency on her. Similarities appear between Antigone and Electra,
Ismene and Chrysothemis, Tecmessa and Deianeira; but Jocasta is
unique. She is queenly without being in the least heroic; womanly
and warm, but without the yielding sweetness which we find in
Deianeira. She has a suave and compliant way, but at the same
time she is highly influential with Oedipus and commands defer-
ence from all. Not merely in word is she the wife and mother of
the king; she is both and behaves like both simultaneously, with
the profoundest ease and grace. It is almost as if she knew her own
terrible secret.

Her attitude toward religion has caused considerable worry. Her
obvious skepticism about oracles of course exposes her to the suspicion that Sophocles, who supposedly believed in them, must have
shaken his head as he wrote her lines. On the other hand, when
she is frightened by Oedipus' extreme agitation, she brings an
offering to Apollo, an act which led Wilamowitz to dismiss her as
merely frivolous. To doubt the veracity of an oracle is not, however,
to be an atheist; nor does Sophocles seem really to have disap-
proved of his heroine. Indeed, it is far more likely that he shared
her view, at least to some degree. In 429 B.C., Athens was far too
full of fraudulent, beggarly oracle-mongers for any educated man to
be utterly naïve in the matter. Yet, superficially at least, Jocasta's
attitude seems to be reproved. After the great scene in which she
has successfully convinced Oedipus that Creon is guiltless of treason, Teiresias in all likelihood simply mistaken, and oracles always
open to doubt, the chorus sings an ode which has been almost universally taken for a pronouncement ex cathedra by the poet himself:

But if any man walks haughtily in deed or word, with no fear
of Justice, no reverence for the images of gods, may an evil doom
seize him for his ill-starred pride, if he will not win his vantage
fairly, nor keep him from unholy deeds, but must lay profaning
hands on sanctities.

Where such things are, what mortal shall boast any more that
he can ward the arrows of the gods from his life? Nay, if such
deeds are in honor, wherefore should we join in the sacred dance?

No more will I go reverently to earth's central and inviolate
shrine, no more to Abae's temple or Olympia, if these oracles fit
not the issue, so that all men shall point at them with the finger.

Nay, king,—if thou art rightly called,—Zeus all-ruling, may it not escape thee and thine ever-deathless power!

The old prophecies concerning Laius are fading; already men are setting them at nought, and nowhere is Apollo glorified with honours; the worship of the gods is perishing.

These lines supposedly contain Sophocles' warning against the weakening of morals in Athens during the Peloponnesian War and reveal the "psychological impulse which drove him to remonstrate with his beloved Athenians: 'Look, that is man and his luck; look, that is God and His wisdom.' " But no Athenian, faced with the plague and the other catastrophic events of the year 429, would have denied that man was weak and the gods irresponsible and mighty. The year of the plague and Pericles' death gave little evidence that the gods cared to do anything good for man. If Sophocles had wished to reawaken public religion, he could scarcely have chosen a worse way than by preaching the careless power of the gods and the nothingness of man—the very beliefs, in fact, which were themselves the concomitants of the Athenians' lawlessness and moral decay. Out of their sufferings a general irreverence did indeed arise, a suspicion that the world was utterly irrational and that human actions made little difference to Providence. But Sophocles seems to have felt the pressure of irrational evil at least as early as the *Trachiniae*, and if he did not altogether lose his faith, at least he altered it, and wrote far more bitter plays.

The ode certainly reflects the temper of the times, but it is not spoken as a reproof, either to Jocasta or to the Athenians. It should be remembered that these same choristers, in a preceding ode, had refused outright to believe Teiresias' words:

Never shall I, till I see clear proof,
Take sides with accusers:

. . . .

Therefore, in my mind,
Never shall you [Oedipus] incur the charge of villany.

Now, indeed, though themselves troubled by the doubtfulness of all "divine matters," the choristers are far from being shocked by Jocasta's complete dismissal of the art of prophecy and are inclined to agree with her, though at the same time they intersperse little prayers that the fallacies of religion may not be the whole truth. They profess no faith with fervor. They threaten Zeus and Apollo with neglect and contempt unless the oracle does come true, which is as much as to say: "I believe this prophecy is probably true, but if I see no evidence, so much for prophecies and the gods in general." Their address to Zeus is typical of an ancient kind of prayer which included not merely supplications but also threats, in the event the supplications were not heard. And at the same time, poured into the old traditional shell, is the disquieting current of real unbelief, that same agnostic despair which Thucydides says accompanied the plague, the feeling among the people that the gods who permitted the world to go as it did deserved no respect. "Wherefore should I join in the sacred dance?" The poem is a popular reflection, not a credo by the poet.

It is also a little strange that the chorus at this point should pray against Oedipus, when they cry out to the gods to make the truth of their oracles manifest. But this is only further proof that the chorus in Sophocles represents the somewhat confused morality of the bourgeoisie, who can feel that the times want stabilizing and can see well enough that Oedipus has been violent with Creon and that Jocasta has been high-handed about prophets, but who cannot see the real implications of the scene or understand the genuine intelligence that is guiding the king and queen. Sophocles could not have written the scene as he did, if he thought that all it meant was what the chorus sings. This is not to say that the ode is not one of Sophocles' finest. The popular attitude appears in a sympathetic light, but it is a confused attitude, a passive one, and not particularly noble. It praises purity in word and deed, humility and avoidance of hybris, free competition and fair dealing; it hopes that the gods will defend their prerogatives. It is all quite proper. But it omits the whole question of action, which is the business of those on the stage, in contrast to those in the orchestra. It overlooks the moral question of the play, the fall of an innocent man; more important, it overlooks the heroic inward drive of arete which motivates that fall. It reflects the atmosphere in which the play grew but it does not give the play's moral.

Aspasia's court, with its free thinking and loose morals, has been suggested as a source for the character which Sophocles gave the queen, and more particularly for her remark, "It's best to live at random." There may indeed be a touch of Aspasia about Jocasta, as there may be a touch of Pericles in Oedipus. Within the framework of the play, Jocasta qualifies as an intellectually gifted woman with powers of argumentation, clear judgment, and reason, all of which Aspasia possessed to some degree at least. But there is no evidence for thinking that Sophocles differed greatly from the ingrained skepticism of his fellow Athenians. Sophocles was no stranger to Aspasia's society, and he was a friend of Pericles. Besides, a dubious attitude toward the oracle was no new thing in the Sophistic Age. Well before the free-thinking movement, the Alcmaeonids bribed the Delphic Oracle; Peisistratus trumped up a goddess to escort him to Athens; and Themistocles, on the eve of

Salamis, manipulated a few signs and wonders to get the people out of Athens.

The general remarks of Plutarch about the religious attitude of Pericles and the little anecdote that he tells to illustrate it show clearly the "intelligent piety" of the Periclean circle, an attitude which the devout and moral Plutarch seems to approve. Signs and wonders may not be devoid of all meaning, but they must not command our minds. The refined Jocasta, like Pericles, refused the superstitions of professional divination, or *mantike,* but was prepared to believe in a real sign from a god himself. In her attitude we can see very clearly the meaning of man as the measure; the human judgment was regarded as sufficiently dignified to discriminate in divine matters, somewhat indeed as it was found to be during the Reformation. There was no impiety in such discrimination. As for the Delphic Oracle, it maintained its reputation in general, despite some well-known frauds and mistakes. It still could be right, and popular belief favored its pronouncements. But there was no creed or faith which bound one to its infallibility.

By no Athenian standards whatsoever are the king and queen godless or sinful in their religious attitude. In their "intelligent piety," the emphasis is assuredly on intelligence, but that fact only signalizes the more the inwardness of Sophocles' idea of divinity for man. If Jocasta views her religion intelligently, Oedipus surely views his intelligence religiously. At least, it builds itself within him into a daemonic drive on which he stakes all, in the conviction that it is his duty to know. It is a kind of inspiration with him; and Jocasta, though unable to match him in ultimate tenacity, is fully his match in argument. The long scene in which the two of them hold the stage alone is one of the most skillful and mighty dramatic *tours de force* in literature. It would have been easy for the secret to come out entirely, or for the scene to fall to the level of mere conversation through the narration of past events or the discussion of the value of prophecy. But Sophocles has successfully avoided this pitfall by making both characters speak every time from their whole beings; each keeps the secret dark because he does not know the secret. Each knows only what he knows. Thus the argument becomes more a revelation of character than a discussion of an idea. Both characters aim at perfect honesty. Yet each is so isolated within the limits of his own knowledge that only so much of the central secret of the story emerges as serves to pique Oedipus further and build the ever-increasing suspense.

The dilemma which Jocasta faces at the beginning of the scene is this: if Teiresias is telling the truth, Oedipus is lost; if he is lying, as Oedipus first thinks, there is likelihood of collusion between him and her brother, Creon. Jocasta must prove that neither of these possibilities is true, and she handles the problem in a masterly way. She begs Creon off for the moment, and the chorus helps her in the lyric scene which follows. Then, when Oedipus is quieter, she questions him, and when he says that Creon sent the seer to make this charge, she quietly ignores the implication of treason, and by the effective method of example, shows that seers can be wrong without being necessarily corrupt. Even Delphi had been mistaken; why should they fear Teiresias? The effect of Jocasta's argument is different from her intention, however, for the story she tells makes it look as if Teiresias may be right. At least, Oedipus begins to think so, but Jocasta, who believes the story of the six robbers, still sees no reason to put faith in prophets. She will fetch the witness, to humor Oedipus, but she is sure of what she knows. Even if he changes his tale, it will prove only that Delphi was wrong, for Laius was supposed to have been killed by his son!

Jocasta has argued very successfully. Creon is absolved and Oedipus is calmer, though—not surprisingly—still slightly confused. A course of rational action has emerged. But the queen has been more successful for herself than for Oedipus. In arguing against Teiresias, she has unwittingly brought up evidence for him, by casually mentioning the three wagon ways where Laius was killed. Oedipus remembers killing a man at a meeting of three wagon ways, and it is now his turn to begin to be clearheaded. Jocasta, however, has convinced herself fully—and why should she not?— that the prophet is wrong. In the later scene when the messenger reports the death of Polybus from natural causes, she is only the more convinced, as Oedipus is too, that all divination is inaccurate. It all fits perfectly with Jocasta's views of the matter. The genius of this famous plot lies in the fact that the evidence on which the various characters draw their various conclusions leads truly to those conclusions. There is no element of blind folly, hybris, or unwillingness to learn.

The fact that Oedipus and Jocasta are both wrong does not mean that they both are fools, or victims of a reprehensible "free-thinking" movement. They behave with thorough intelligence throughout. If the oracle comes true, that does not make the chorus wise. For the chorus would never have found out whether it were true, had not Oedipus been willing to stake everything, his very rights as a human being, on the effort to know. Intellectually Jocasta is a fitting mate for Oedipus. Consistently with the rest of the play, she is characterized almost entirely by her mental traits: she first appears interfering in a political quarrel, and her effectiveness in that scene depends not on her emotions (in contrast to Tecmessa, for instance), or on her moral will (as is the case with Antigone and Electra), but on her opinion. Throughout, we are confronted with Jocasta's intellectual gifts, her skill in argument, her views on life, religion, and the world at large. She is accustomed to dealing with men, and she deals with Oedipus well. She stands beside him throughout his ordeal, or almost, and the same tragedy which overtakes Oedipus overtakes her. Both think fast and clearly, but find truth too late and too bitter for them. Both had been careful: Jocasta had exposed her child, Oedipus had left Corinth. Both are disillusioned, first in the gods, and finally in themselves. And both can bear disillusion with the gods, but Jocasta cannot bear disillusion with herself.

RICHMOND LATTIMORE

The Chorus in the *Tyrannus*†

Oedipus Tyrannus is a tragical tragedy despite its frame of romantic comedy, and we should be slow to type Oedipus himself. He is an intellectual man, but not *the* intellectual of the time (Pericles or another). He prides himself on his insight and wit, but for a man of great intelligence he makes disastrous mistakes. Partly, it is a combination of hasty temper and a passionate reliance on quick judgments, which makes him rush to Delphi, then rush away from Delphi indignant with Apollo for not answering his question, or jump to the conclusion that Jocasta's distress is caused by snobbery and anguish for having married a man who was not, after all, a king's son. When he leaves Delphi, he is so sure of his assumptions that he does the two things he should never do: he kills a man who could well be his father, and marries a woman old enough to be his mother. Partly, he makes mistakes through the obsessions of a tyrant—that others are jealous and work through bribery and treachery to unseat him. This makes him assume, wrongly, that the outside brigands who killed Laius must have been suborned from inside Thebes, and suspect that Polybus died through conspiracy. It makes him break into the whole action against Creon and Tiresias. So far, he is the tragedy tyrant, like Creon in *Antigone* or Theseus in *Hippolytus*. But no farther. Oedipus condemns Creon without trial, but lets him off at the pleading of the Chorus, though he is sure they are wrong. And Oedipus can answer to the vague threats of Tiresias against him (443):

I do not care <what happens to me> if I save this city.

† From Richmond Lattimore, *The Poetry of Greek Tragedy* (Baltimore: The Johns Hopkins Press, 1958), pp. 91–102. Copyright © 1958 by The Johns Hopkins Press. Reprinted by permission of the publisher.

No tragedy tyrant could say that; and such a man is rewarded by the love and respect of his people (the Chorus) such as no tragedy tyrant ever earns or gets. Oedipus is a tyrant, not *the* tyrant, and unique as he is, he is unique again because he adds one more aspect: the lost child, the strange, hunted creature who came from the mountain and will go back to the mountain.

All combine in the most puzzling stasimon in *Oedipus*—the second—after all has been called into question: the honesty of Creon, the good sense of Oedipus, the official report of the murder of Laius, the identity of the murderer, the truth of oracles, the value of religion (863–910):

> May it be always given me to know
> guarded purity in all speech,
> in all action. For this, ordinances stand high
> in the bright mountain
> air where they were born. Olympus
> is their sole father. It was no
> mortal growth of men brought
> them forth: nor shall indifference
> store them away in sleep.
> Here the god stands great, ageless forever.
>
> Lust breeds the tyrant man. Lust,
> when fed and puffed with vanity
> on what disaccords with the time's advantage,
> clambering the sheer height
> goes over the drop, where nothing breaks his fall,
> where no firm foothold serves
> longer. But I pray god
> not to break that hand hold which serves
> well the community.
> I shall not loose my hold upon the god, my guide.
>
> But if one, gazing too high
> for thought and action, advances
> without fear of justice, without
> caution, where spirits live,
> may a bad fate seize him,
> his wages for ill starred lusting,
> if he gains unfairly his advantage,
> nor refrains from the forbidden,
> if he lays lewd hands on secret things.
> What man shall hold off the bolts of god
> from his life, in such action,
> or if such works go unpunished, why
> should I go through the ceremonies of worship?
>
> No longer shall I go to the earth's
> secret centerstone, religiously,

nor to the temple which is at Abae,
nor yet to Olympia,
no, unless this code is put together
to be manifest before mortals.
Then, oh Power, if Power is what you should be called,
Zeus, lord of all, oh give heed,
let your domain, ever immortal, not ignore.
For the old oracles for Laius are dying
out; men throw them aside
now, and nowhere is Apollo regarded.
God's worship is going.

To begin with the last: we are almost irresistibly forced to think that this belongs to the time, about 426, after the death of Pericles and after the plague came out of nowhere to waste Athens. Apollo had promised the Peloponnesians he would help them against Athens; the city was full of oracles; the enlightened, one supposes, ignored them. Apollo must show them. He showed them. He struck, absurdly, unpredictably. The plague came. The failure of the intellectual, as of the tyrant, is to insist on his own *gnóme*. Pericles was both intellectual and essentially tyrannical. But I go no further, for Oedipus was not Pericles. But his tragedy is the intellectual's tragedy: his tragic flaw, if you must, that his wit can not cover, foresee, account for all, and nonsensical forces can make nonsense of it; or, as Aeschylus put it, "Science is weaker than Nature is."

Now to go back. The intellectual's tragedy is the tyrant's tragedy. "Lust breeds the tyrant man." Or is it "lust"? The word is *hybris*. Should we say "violence"? We have just emerged from the scene where Oedipus is most tyrannical. In the famous debate on forms of government in the third book of Herodotus, *hybris*, "lawless violence," marks the tyrant, both the insane, bloody acts of Cambyses and the unscrupulous intrigues of Magian nobodies. *Hybris* combines with "jealousy" (*phthonos*) to make the tyrant suspicious of good men, vindictive, one who kills without due process of law, as Oedipus has just been saved from killing Creon. Oedipus is too great to refuse his Chorus, but this is a personal favor; the almost crazy, uneasy suspicion remains. But *hybris* not only characterizes the tyrant in action, it produces him; for escaping the violent tyrant, we may fall into the hands of the violent rabble or the violent nobles who by their violent disorder set up the situation for a redeemer and liberator—the tyrant again. Violence breeds the tyrant.

In a general sense. But we can get a still stricter meaning on another interpretation: the reference is to Jocasta and (it is only fair to add) Laius. The tragedy of incontinence: lust breeds (plants, begets) the tyrant. Against this, it can be argued that the citizens (the Chorus) do not know that the child of Jocasta and Laius, who lusted and must breed, is now their tyrannical tyrant; they do not even think he is alive; and they and Jocasta have been working together in complete sympathy so that it would be strange for them to turn suddenly on her.

Yet I think it does apply to Jocasta, since Sophocles fits the words to her, and the audience can pick up and follow. Like Oedipus again and again through the ironies of the play, the Chorus say more than they know. All meanings are combined: the civic violence which breeds the tyrant, the tyrant's violence which makes him tyrannical in action, with the violence of lust breeding the tyrant, the child who should never have been born and who, born in defiance, lays hands on secret places and defiles his mother, the wife who is no wife.

Along with this, we have the persistent imagery of the climber on the mountain, in high places where spirits live and the overdrop is sheer, danger natural and supernatural, where the climber must use not only feet but hands, and needs a guide—ideally a divine guide. No recorded Greek ever climbed a mountain for the sport of mountain-climbing, and the notion of finding the hardest way up a peak is peculiarly gothic or baroque for an Athenian, or, as Spengler would say, Faustian; but there were occasions, religious and military occasions at least, when mountains had to be climbed. The mountain-climb figured early, from Hesiod on, as a symbol of the slippery, punishing, dangerous quest for achievement or excellence (*aretē*) which stood at the top; just as, in this stasimon, the laws of righteousness stand in the thin, pure Olympian air.

The Greek wilderness is the mountains. All cultures have their wildernesses. The northern foundling might be a child of the great forest, but Greece is not a land of flat forests; its wilderness, whether of woods or scrubby barrens or cliff and boulder, is of the big mountains which are scarcely ever out of sight anywhere in mainland Greece. These were the domain of emptiness, spirits, wild beasts, and tough shepherds; the Athenian city man knew little of them, not that he did not lead a hardy life of military service that would seem impossibly strenuous today, but the citizen-spearman was a fighter of the plains and more at home on a warship than on a mountain top.

The mountains were the wilderness. To Athenians thinking of Thebes, *the* mountain was Cithaeron, visible from Athens; invisible in fact from Thebes, but seen from the near hills as a bold black trapezoid dominating the Asopus Valley. Parnassus is higher, steeper, and snowier, but a sacred mountain with civilized Delphi perched in its underslopes. Cithaeron is all wild.

On such mountain sides the Chorus imagine the outcast murderer (463–82):

> Who is he, whom the magic-singing
> Delphian rock proclaimed
> the bloody-handed murderer
> whose crimes were too deep to tell?
> Run, he must run now
> harder than stormy horses,
> feet flying in flight,
> for the armed god is after him, leaping
> with fire and flash, Apollo, Zeus' own,
> and the forbidding Death-
> Spirits horribly haunt him.
>
> The message shone, it showed
> even now from the snows
> of Parnassus. Manhunt the hidden
> man. After him all.
> He lurks, a wild bull
> in the wild wood, in the holes
> of the rock side
> lonely-footed, forlorn wandering,
> dodging aside from the mid-centered
> prophecies, which, things alive,
> hover to haunt him.

In the first long angry response of Tiresias, where the chief image is of a ship come home to harbor (obvious enough), the mountain, and the stalker on the mountain, project, even obtrude (412–23):

> I tell you, since you have baited me with my blindness:
> you have your eyes, and do not see where you are standing
> in evil, nor where you are living, nor whom you are living with.
> Do you know whose son you are? Unconscious enemy
> of your own people, here on earth, and under the ground,
> the double-goading curse, father's and mother's in one,
> shall stalk you on its feet of horror from this land,
> you who see straight now, but shall then see only dark.
> What harbor shall not be full of your cries,
> what Mount Cithaeron shall not echo to them soon
> when you learn what that marriage is, that awful haven
> where, after your fair voyage, you brought in your ship?

The foundling, in Greece, was the child of the mountain side. The foundling was often protected by divine wild spirits of the place, or he might have been a spirit himself, or even a great god, Dionysus, Hermes, even Zeus. The Chorus fancy Oedipus, the mountain-child, fosterling of Cithaeron, as by-blow of some mountain-walking god, Pan, Apollo, Hermes, or Dionysus, by one of the nymphs of the mountains. Oedipus, in answer to the doubts, as he thinks, of Jocasta, identifies himself with nature (1076–85):

> Let her break forth her tempers as she will, but I
> will still find out what seed made me, although it be
> humble. She being proud, perhaps, as women are,
> thinks the obscurity of my birth is some disgrace.
> I count myself the child of Fortune. While her gifts
> are good, I shall not call myself degraded. I
> am born of her. She is my mother. And the months
> my brothers marked me small, and they have marked me great.
> So born, I would not ever wish I had been born
> anything else, to keep me from learning who I am.

Tyché, Fortune or Coincidence, is here the way in which things come out or work, that is, another Greek way of saying Nature. The natural son is the child of Nature. After the catastrophe, it is to nature and the pathos of places that Oedipus chiefly appeals (1391–1403):

> Cithaeron oh Cithaeron, why did you take me? Why
> did you not kill me when you took me? Thus had I
> never made clear to men the place where I was born.
> O Polybus and Corinth and my father's house
> of old, as men then called it, what a festering sore
> you fed beneath my outward splendor, I who now
> have been found evil in myself, and evil born.
> O three roads, hidden valley,
> oak wood and narrow meeting at the threeway cross,
> who drank the blood of my own father which was spilled
> by my own hands, do you remember still
> what things I did to you, and then, when I came here,
> what things I did again?

It is as if Oedipus had been set free from ordinary city life when he was put away into the hands of the mountain Shepherd. It is natural that the child of the wilderness who lived in the city should go home to his wilderness to die—to ask to go, even though the story has not told that he did so; and thus we have come back to our beginning (1449–54):

> But let it never be thought right that I should stay
> in the city of my father, and be part of it,
> but let me go to the mountains and live there, where stands
> Cithaeron, called *my* mountain, which, when they still lived
> my mother and my father gave me, for my final tomb.
> So let them kill me at last, for they destroyed my life.

We have completed the circle but we have not resolved all the play. Never think that. We can read *Oedipus* as many times as we like, and every time find new truths and throw away old falsehoods that once seemed to be true. There is always a dimension that escapes.

While it is true that *Oedipus* is a particularly compact combination of themes, where themes of foundling, mountain-spirit, murder, manhunt, tyrant cohere because we are constantly led from one into the other, yet in this play one can, perhaps more clearly than elsewhere in Sophocles, separate the poetic from the dramatic. Or at least we can separate the "daemonic" or "barbaric," because it is not absolutely needed. There are splendid characterizing lines and rhetorical effects, without this kind of poetic material. And the daemonic is not "so." The finished play is not about any nature-child or mountain-spirit. He exists only in the imagination of the players. The Oedipus of the action is a perfectly plausible, too human man, and the closest he has ever come to being a child of Fortune or Nature, or Year Spirit with the months for brothers, is to be handed from one kindhearted Shepherd to another, in a summer of babyhood on the high pastures. The play King, with his greatnesses and his faults, does not need to be a splendid barbarian at heart, like Ajax. He is a homicide: but on the level of discourse we may see him as thinking himself so set upon, so right in his defense, that the deadly brawl at the crossroads has scarcely troubled his conscience since. He never was a hunted monster, something like a great, wild beast, fierce but scary, driven among the high rocks. That is all the imagination of old men. We can so play trenchant characters that all seems motivated, and we can forget that what first drove the action was the shape of a universal pattern story from the childhood of men.

Oedipus is acted today, often professionally, and more frequently, I believe, than any other Greek play. It is commonly given in what almost passes as an authorized version—that of Yeats—which has cut down or cut out those daemonic passages we have been considering. It is good theatre, and it is truly dramatic, but it is no longer haunted.

In a stasimon of *Antigone*, also, among the moralities we see an image of the high snows of Olympus where Zeus is forever, deathless and sleepless, with his laws; and by contrast, an image of the pit below, this time the darkness of the sea stirred to waves that batter the promontories. The gods of Sophocles are there, but remote, unattainable as the snows of Olympus; we can only see the effects, and are closer to the dark underpit. The tragedies of Sophocles concern resolute, intelligent, civilized people, determined to understand everything; they never do, because there is a dark non-sensical element in things, which eludes their comprehension and, often, destroys them; but which has its own wild beauty.

ROBERT COHEN

Oedipus and the Absurd Life†

The theatre is a living medium, and one of the aspects of the greatness of *Oedipus Tyrannus* is that it can be produced with modern actors before a modern audience with stunning dramatic results. The lapse of twenty-five hundred years has done nothing to still the anguish of Oedipus's quest, nor the magnificence of his defeat. Quite simply, *Oedipus Tyrannus* is a play which receives its force from an uncompromised, penetrating analysis of the human predicament; a play which will excite empathic response as long as our race endures.

The "stuff" of Oedipus is human identity. It must be clear by now that this is not a play about the evils of murdering strangers at crossroads, but a demonstration of a man slamming into his own self at an inopportune and unguarded moment. It is a wholly archetypal play, set in a primitive, precivilized environment, and unappeased by subplots, comedic refreshments, romance, or discursive choral reflections. Its strength is in its directness and purity; also its inevitability. As French playwright Jean Giraudoux once remarked, "*Le plus bête des hommes voit toujours assez clair pour devenir aveugle.*" Even the stupidest man will always see clearly enough to blind himself.

Oedipus is a *tyrannus*. The word cannot now be fairly translated, but it certainly does not mean "king." It is important to remember that *Oedipus* is *not* set in the sophisticated, brilliant, arty world of Sophocles. The story was sung by Homer three centuries previous to its fifth century dramatization, and was a distant legend even in Homer's time; part of the Aegean mythic history which predates Christ by more than a millennium. In reaching back into prehistory, Sophocles found an unstructured political-ethical cosmos which allowed free reign to the primitive forces he lets loose. Shakespeare did much the same in *Macbeth* and *King Lear*. Oedipus is not a "king," with all the modern legal implications of primogeniture and constitutionalism. He is simply a tribal chief; or the lead wolf in the wolfpack, who receives his position through brute power and loses it the moment he can no longer exert that power. When in the course of the play Oedipus is defeated and Creon takes his place, the chorus simply watches and attests to the changeover; there is neither formal abdication nor legal re-investi-

† Robert Cohen, "Oedipus and the Absurd Life." Reprinted by permission of the author.

ture. It is like the old wolf cowering blindly into exile while the others growl and turn their obeisance to the next in line.

As a *tyrannus* Oedipus does not overly excite our admiration. His characterization is rather flat; he is a man in a state of appalling ignorance, who lives in dread that the sky is about to fall on him and that he will be unable to do anything about it. He is a strong man, presumably (he did manage the murder at the crossroads), but not unusually bright. His ability to decipher the riddle of the Sphinx has been much misinterpreted. Riddles are for children, particularly that one, and Oedipus's ability to solve it indicates no genius; simply an uncluttered, and fairly imaginative mind. "Then I came—ignorant Oedipus—I came and smothered her," he brags to Teiresias. He is stubborn, bullheaded, frequently stupid, often rude, and admittedly and unashamedly untutored; in short, a primitive, pre-Hellenic chieftain.

Oedipus believes he is questing truth in the search for the murderer of Laius, as ordered by the oracle at Delphi. But in actuality he is following Delphi's more general imperative: "Know thyself!" There are actually two Oedipus's in the play. There is the foundling, son of Laius and Jocasta, who has his feet pierced and is left to die on Cithaeron. And there is the tyrant, son of Polybus and Merope, who destroys the Sphinx and becomes tyrannus of Thebes and husband of Jocasta. In a metaphoric sense, these are Oedipus's inner (the foundling) and outer (the tyrant) identities. They remain separate for a generation, yet they come crashing together at the play's climax, and the collision is like nuclear fusion. The synthesis of identities, a monstrous adhesion, creates a new Oedipus, one ready as neither before him to go to Colonus; one crippled by the discovery of the human predicament and yet ennobled by reaching a harmony of identities. Oedipus, at the conclusion of the play and after a terrible agony, knows himself.

It is important to stress the routine nature of this conflict. All men suffer a dual identity: the one that they inwardly feel and the one they receive from the outer world. One man to himself is a generous and Christian patriot; to his neighbors he is a bigot. Another to himself is a morally corrupt failure; yet to his colleagues he is a great scientist. Goethe's great Faust capitulates to the difference between his self-opinion and the opinions of those around him. Virtually all men suffer from their inability to unite their failures with their ambitions, and their successes with their self-doubts. *Oedipus Tyrannus* merely characterizes this divorce, this confrontation with oneself.

It goes without saying that most men end up in some sort of adjustment with themselves, or at least find a means to reconcile this confrontation. Most live within the forced dialectic between their conflicting identities, and maintain for themselves an uneasy alliance, perhaps sadly but equably. Some drown the confrontation in alcohol, some give in to it consciously (suicide) or unconsciously (schizophrenia), and some join in an alliance with it and live on what Sartre calls "the far side of despair." Most often these are peaceable and undramatic responses to the accepted human condition. Oedipus, since his moment of self-realization comes upon him so suddenly and with such gruesome details, is a figure for grand tragedy. He finds that Oedipus the tyrant has feet of clay—literally the pierced and swollen feet which gave him his name—and that in fact he is Oedipus the foundling, the parricide, the mother-lover. The moment is catastrophic. It is the fundamental question of man of any age—"Who am I?"—pursued resolutely and dogmatically to its shattering end. Whereas a wiser, better-adjusted man would simply let the dialectic ride and the questions go unanswered, Oedipus perseveres. This—his terrible persistence—determines his heroic character.

Oedipus's case is an extreme one, which makes *Oedipus Tyrannus* more than simply a credible narrative. His crime was enormous, grotesque. Even without Freud's landmark discoveries about mother-incest, we can appreciate that this was one of the most egregious sins of antiquity; had it not been, Sophocles would no doubt have chosen a different story. And Oedipus's reaction is fully commensurate to his deed. He tears out his eyes, a total repudiation of his willingness to seek truth and to merge his two warring identities. If there could ever be a moral to this play it would be this: that to find yourself is at the same time to destroy yourself.

Oedipus is a ritualized mimetic drama; a classic example of the play which is, in Aristotle's words, the imitation of an action. Structurally, it is one of the simplest plays ever written; Oedipus seeks the truth, finds it, and acts upon it. There is precious little discussion or sidetracking; and there is no thematic opposition to the main line of the play. To succeed in such a simple work, Sophocles had to create it in a scale of majestic proportions, and he did. *Oedipus* is a vertical play of towering magnitude, of great sustained power and cruelty. The action gathers force and snowballs to an inexorable conclusion, picking up speed with geometric progression, moving from pole to pole in little more than an hour. The dialogue is spare and direct, filled with questions and cross-examinations, void of reflections and rhetorical indulgences. The chorus echoes the tragedy more than it engages in it, and it thereby heightens the play's tone of incantation. *Oedipus* begins with a ceremony of lamentation and ends with the symbolic *sparagmos*, or tearing asunder of the hero, as was done to Dionysus in the ancient dithyrambs, and to Osiris in the Egyptian Passion Plays. *Oedipus* is a religious, not an intellectual drama. It is religious despite the fact that nothing in the play presumes a deistic philosophy. It is a celebration rather than an analysis of man's search for himself; a ritualization of his internal confrontation. Sophocles, having discovered the essential human duality, seeks not to explain or solve it, but merely to expose it mercilessly in a terrible rite of expiation. This ritualization of man's intrinsic anguish is the basic ingredient of the contemporary genre: the theatre of the absurd.

Most theories of tragedy insist that tragedy must be ennobling. Presumably, this is a refinement of the well-known Aristotelian concept that tragedy "purges" our pity and terror through some emotional upheaval. Tragedy, we are thereupon led to believe, enlightens us to the superior order and harmony of the cosmos. Such theories are often advanced to explain and justify the dismal fate of Oedipus which Sophocles stages for us, but we must be forgiven if we find them unacceptable. *Oedipus* concludes in an overt affirmation of man's failure and his despair. When Jocasta has destroyed herself, and Oedipus, his eye sockets gored and bloody, returns to the stage, the chorus (and audience) are profoundly shaken. Pathetically, Oedipus begs for his daughters (denied) and for some directions (also denied). Creon, aghast at the events which have led to his assumption of power, gropes for policy; we know that his reign will hardly be less wretched. As Oedipus stumbles away and Creon unsteadily attempts to salvage the city, the chorus—who after all can find not a single reason to explain all that has happened to them—merely reminds itself and us that "none of us mortals/can truly be thought of as happy/until he is granted deliverance from life/until he is dead/and must suffer no more." Man's feebleness, ruthlessly demonstrated, is crushingly and unambiguously confirmed.

What *Oedipus* gives us, positively, is not a purgation of this despair, but an enthusiasm for Oedipus's single great quality: his absurd courage. This becomes the motive force of the play. Oedipus, as he begins to see where he is going, secretly delights in it. He assumes his identity with absurd conviction. Labeled a bastard in Corinth, he rushes to Delphi to investigate. Labeled a parricide by Teiresias, he propels his questions to everyone in sight. "I have to hear!" he shouts to the panic-stricken Shepherd. Though he sees himself sinking into a vortex, he plunges deeper and faster on his own accord. Galvanized by the inevitable, he charges into the chaos of his own existence, and bears his own responsibility. He refuses to blame the gods: "It was Apollo. He brought this pain, this suffering to me. *But it was my hand that struck the blow!*" he cries. Oedipus is a man in absurd revolt against his duality. He defies the oracles at the same time he is submitting to them. He refuses to turn back his search, he refuses to accept Jocasta's proffered compromise, he refuses to alter his collision course with destiny. He becomes an absurd hero.

In *The Myth of Sisyphus*, Camus defines the absurd life as a "permanent revolution," and defines revolt as "a constant confrontation between man and his own obscurity." These concepts are, I think, applicable here; perhaps more applicable than Aristotle's pronouncements of catharsis and peripeteia. Oedipus's ennobling quality is his commitment to the impossible, his quest into the darkness of human existence. He follows this quest to its final depth—and finds himself. This is Sophocles' most shattering irony: Oedipus confronts obscurity and finds Oedipus. Oedipus foundling and Oedipus *tyrannus* are one. He has accepted the absurd, challenged it, and borne the responsibility of losing to it. Blind, proud, and with a profounder power, Oedipus stumbles on to Colonus, like Beckett's Pozzo on the way to Saint Saviour, held up by his awesome dignity. Creon is left to his own blindness.

FRANCIS FERGUSSON

Oedipus Rex: The Tragic Rhythm of Action†

> . . . quel secondo regno dove l'umano spirito si purga.
> *Purgatorio*, CANTO I

I suppose there can be little doubt that *Oedipus Rex* is a crucial instance of drama, if not *the* play which best exemplifies this art in its essential nature and its completeness. It owes its position partly to the fact that Aristotle founded his definitions upon it. But since the time of Aristotle it has been imitated, rewritten, and discussed by many different generations, not only of dramatists, but also of moralists, psychologists, historians, and other students of human nature and destiny.

Though the play is thus generally recognized as an archetype, there has been little agreement about its meaning or its form. It seems to beget, in every period, a different interpretation and a different dramaturgy. From the seventeenth century until the end of the eighteenth, a Neoclassic and rationalistic interpretation of *Oedipus*, of Greek tragedy, and of Aristotle, was generally accepted; and upon this interpretation was based the dramaturgy of Corneille and Racine. Nietzsche, under the inspiration of Wagner's *Tristan*

† From Francis Fergusson, *The Idea of a Theatre: A Study of Ten Plays, The Art of Drama in Changing Perspective* (Princeton: Princeton University Press, 1949), pp. 13–18. Copyright 1949 by Princeton University Press. Reprinted by permission of Princeton University Press.

und Isolde, developed a totally different view of it, and thence a different theory of drama. These two views of Greek tragedy, Racine's and Nietzsche's, still provide indispensable perspectives upon *Oedipus.* They show a great deal about modern principles of dramatic composition; and they show, when compared, how central and how essential Sophocles' drama is. In the two essays following, the attempt is made to develop the analogies, the similarities and the differences, between these three conceptions of drama.

In our day a conception of *Oedipus* seems to be developing which is neither that of Racine nor that of Nietzsche. This view is based upon the studies which the Cambridge School, Fraser, Cornford, Harrison, Murray, made of the ritual origins of Greek tragedy. It also owes a great deal to the current interest in myth as a way of ordering human experience. *Oedipus,* we now see, is both myth and ritual. It assumes and employs these two ancient ways of understanding and representing human experience, which are prior to the arts and sciences and philosophies of modern times. To understand it (it now appears) we must endeavor to recapture the habit of significant make-believe, of the direct perception of action, which underlies Sophocles' theater.

If *Oedipus* is to be understood in this way, then we shall have to revise our ideas of Sophocles' dramaturgy. The notion of Aristotle's theory of drama, and hence of Greek dramaturgy, which still prevails (in spite of such studies as Butcher's of the *Poetics*) is largely colored by Neoclassic taste and rationalistic habits of mind. If we are to take it that Sophocles was imitating action before theory, instead of after it, like Racine, then both the elements and the form of his composition appear in a new light.

In the present essay the attempt is made to draw the deductions, for Sophocles' theater and dramaturgy, which the present view of *Oedipus* implies. We shall find that the various traditional views of this play are not so much wrong as partial.

Oedipus, Myth and Play

When Sophocles came to write his play he had the myth of Oedipus to start with. Laius and Jocasta, King and Queen of Thebes, are told by the oracle that their son will grow up to kill his father and marry his mother. The infant, his feet pierced, is left on Mount Kitharon to die. But a shepherd finds him and takes care of him; at last gives him to another shepherd, who takes him to Corinth, and there the King and Queen bring him up as their own son. But Oedipus—"Club-foot"—is plagued in his turn by the oracle; he hears that he is fated to kill his father and marry his mother; and to escape that fate he leaves Corinth never to return. On his journey he meets an old man with his servants; gets into a dispute with him, and kills him and all his followers. He comes to Thebes at the time when the Sphinx is preying upon that City; solves the riddle which the Sphinx propounds, and saves the City. He marries the widowed Queen, Jocasta; has several children by her; rules prosperously for many years. But, when Thebes is suffering under a plague and a drought, the oracle reports that the gods are angry because Laius' slayer is unpunished. Oedipus, as King, undertakes to find him; discovers that he is himself the culprit and that Jocasta is his own mother. He blinds himself and goes into exile. From this time forth he becomes a sort of sacred relic, like the bones of a saint; perilous, but "good medicine" for the community that possesses him. He dies, at last, at Athens, in a grove sacred to the Eumenides, female spirits of fertility and night.

It is obvious, even from this sketch, that the myth, which covers several generations, has as much narrative material as *Gone with the Wind*. We do not know what versions of the story Sophocles used. It is the way of myths that they generate whole progenies of elaborations and varying versions. They are so suggestive, seem to say so much, yet so mysteriously, that the mind cannot rest content with any single form, but must add, or interpret, or simplify— reduce to terms which the reason can accept. Mr. William Troy suggests that "what is possibly most in order at the moment is a thoroughgoing refurbishment of the medieval fourfold method of interpretation, which was first developed, it will be recalled, for just such a purpose—to make at least partially available to the reason that complex of human problems which are embedded, deep and imponderable, in the Myth." It appears that Sophocles, in his play, succeeded in preserving the suggestive mystery of the Oedipus myth, while presenting it in a wonderfully unified dramatic form; and this drama has all the dimensions which the fourfold method was intended to explore.

Everyone knows that when Sophocles planned the plot of the play itself, he started almost at the end of the story, when the plague descends upon the City of Thebes which Oedipus and Jocasta had been ruling with great success for a number of years. The action of the play takes less than a day, and consists of Oedipus' quest for Laius' slayer—his consulting the Oracle of Apollo, his examination of the Prophet, Tiresias, and of a series of witnesses, ending with the old Shepherd who gave him to the King and Queen of Corinth. The play ends when Oedipus is unmistakably revealed as himself the culprit.

At this literal level, the play is intelligible as a murder mystery. Oedipus takes the role of District Attorney; and when he at last convicts himself, we have a twist, a *coup de théâtre*, of unparalleled excitement. But no one who sees or reads the play can rest content with its literal coherence. Questions as to its meaning arise at once: Is Oedipus really guilty, or simply a victim of the gods, of his famous complex, of fate, of original sin? How much did he know, all along? How much did Jocasta know? The first, and most deeply instinctive effort of the mind, when confronted with this play, is to endeavor to reduce its meanings to some set of rational categories.

The critics of the Age of Reason tried to understand it as a fable of the enlightened moral will, in accordance with the philosophy of that time. Voltaire's version of the play, following Corneille, and his comments upon it, may be taken as typical. He sees it as essentially a struggle between a strong and righteous Oedipus, and the malicious and very human gods, aided and abetted by the corrupt priest Tiresias; he makes it an antireligious tract, with an unmistakable moral to satisfy the needs of the discursive intellect. In order to make Oedipus "sympathetic" to his audience, he elides, as much as possible, the incest motif; and he adds an irrelevant love story. He was aware that his version and interpretation were not those of Sophocles but, with the complacent provinciality of his period, he attributes the difference to the darkness of the age in which Sophocles lived.

Other attempts to rationalize *Oedipus Rex* are subtler than Voltaire's, and take us further toward an understanding of the play. Freud's reduction of the play to the concepts of his psychology reveals a great deal, opens up perspectives which we are still exploring. If one reads *Oedipus* in the light of Fustel de Coulanges' *The Ancient City*, one may see it as the expression of the ancient patriarchal religion of the Greeks. And other interpretations of the play, theological, philosophical, historical, are available, none of them wrong, but all partial, all reductions of Sophocles' masterpiece to an alien set of categories. For the peculiar virtue of Sophocles' presentation of the myth is that it preserves the ulimate mystery by focusing upon the tragic human at a level beneath, or prior to any rationalization whatever. The plot is so arranged that we see the action, as it were, illumined from many sides at once.

By starting the play at the end of the story, and showing onstage only the last crucial episode in Oedipus' life, the past and present action of the protagonist are revealed together; and, in each other's light, are at last felt as one. Oedipus' quest for the slayer of Laius becomes a quest for the hidden reality of his own past; and as that slowly comes into focus, like repressed material under psychoanalysis—with sensory and emotional immediacy, yet in the light of acceptance and understanding—his immediate quest also reaches its end: he comes to see himself (the Savior of the City) and the guilty one, the plague of Thebes, at once and at one.

This presentation of the myth of Oedipus constitutes, in one sense, an "interpretation" of it. What Sophocles saw as the essence of Oedipus' nature and destiny, is not what Seneca or Dryden or Cocteau saw; and one may grant that even Sophocles did not exhaust the possibilities in the materials of the myth. But Sophocles' version of the myth does not constitute a "reduction" in the same sense as the rest.

I have said that the action which Sophocles shows is a quest, the quest for Laius' slayer; and that as Oedipus' past is unrolled before us his whole life is seen as a kind of quest for his true nature and destiny. But since the object of this quest is not clear until the end, the seeking action takes many forms, as its object appears in different lights. The object, indeed, the final perception, the "truth," looks so different at the end from what it did at the beginning that Oedipus' action itself may seem not a quest, but its opposite, a flight. Thus it would be hard to say, simply, that Oedipus either succeeds or fails. He succeeds; but his success is his undoing. He fails to find what, in one way, he sought; yet from another point of view his search is brilliantly successful. The same ambiguities surround his effort to discover who and what he is. He seems to find that he is nothing; yet thereby finds himself. And what of his relation to the gods? His quest may be regarded as a heroic attempt to escape their decrees, or as an attempt, based upon some deep natural faith, to discover what their wishes are, and what true obedience would be. In one sense Oedipus suffers forces he can neither control nor understand, the puppet of fate; yet at the same time he wills and intelligently intends his every move.

The meaning, or spiritual content of the play, is not to be sought by trying to resolve such ambiguities as these. The spiritual content of the play is the tragic action which Sophocles directly presents; and this action is in its essence *zweideutig*: triumph and destruction, darkness and enlightenment, mourning and rejoicing, at any moment we care to consider it. But this action has also a shape: a beginning, middle, and end, in time. It starts with the reasoned purpose of finding Laius' slayer. But this aim meets unforeseen difficulties, evidences which do not fit, and therefore shake the purpose as it was first understood; and so the characters suffer the piteous and terrible sense of the mystery of the human situation. From this suffering or passion, with its shifting visions, a new perception of the situation emerges; and on that basis the purpose of the action is redefined, and a new movement starts. This movement, or *tragic rhythm of action*, constitutes the shape of the play as a whole; it is also the shape of each episode, each discussion between principals with the chorus following. Mr. Kenneth Burke has studied the tragic rhythm in his *Philosophy of Literary Form*, and also in *A Grammar of Motives,* where he gives the three moments traditional designations which are very suggestive: *Poiema, Pathema, Mathema.* They may also be called, for convenience, Purpose, Passion (or Suffering) and Perception. It is this tragic rhythm of action which is the substance or spiritual content of the play, and the clue to its extraordinarily comprehensive form.

H. D. F. KITTO

Hamlet and the Oedipus†

The *Oedipus Tyrannus* begins by describing twice, once in dialogue and once in lyrics, the plague which is afflicting Thebes. The cause of the plague is the presence in the city of a man who has done two things foul and unnatural above all others: he has killed his own father, and he is living incestuously with his own mother. The details of the plague are so described that we can see how its nature is strictly proportioned to its cause: to death is added sterility; the soil of Thebes, the animals, and the human kind are all barren. The meaning is obvious—unless we make it invisible by reducing the play to the stature of Tragedy of Character: what Oedipus has done is an affront to what we should call Nature, to what Sophocles calls Dikê; and since it is the first law of Nature, or Dikê, that she cannot indefinitely tolerate what is ἄδικον, or contrary to Nature, she rises at last against these unpurged affronts. The plague of sterility is the outcome of the unnatural things which Oedipus has done to his parents.

Hamlet begins in the same way. The two soldiers Marcellus and Bernardo, and Horatio, who is both a soldier and a scholar, are almost terrified out of their wits by something so clean contrary to the natural order that

> I might not this believe
> *Without the sensible and true avouch*
> *Of mine own eyes.*

Professor Dover Wilson, learned in sixteenth-century demonology, has explained that the eschatology of Horatio and Hamlet is Protestant, that the Ghost is a Catholic ghost, and that Bernardo and Marcellus are plain untheological Elizabethans. On this it would be impertinent for an ignoramus to express an opinion, but it does seem that if the 'statists' in Shakespeare's audience, and scholars from the Inns of Court, saw and savoured theological *expertise* in

† From H. D. F. Kitto, *Form and Meaning in Drama* (London: Methuen and Company Ltd., 1956), pp. 253–256. Reprinted by permission of the publisher.

this scene, they would be in danger of missing the main point: that the repeated appearances of the Ghost are something quite outside ordinary experience. Horatio the scholar has heard of something similar, in ancient history, 'a little ere the mightiest Julius fell'. So perhaps this present unnatural terror 'bodes some strange eruption to our state'; or—a less disturbing thought—perhaps the ghost is concerned for some uphoarded treasure hidden in the womb of the Earth.

But at this point Shakespeare decides to write some poetry—and he is never so dangerous as when he is writing poetry:

> It faded on the crowing of the cock.
> Some say that ever 'gainst that season comes
> Wherein our Saviour's birth is celebrated,
> The bird of dawning singeth all night long:
> And then, they say, no spirit dare stir abroad,
> The nights are wholesome; then no planets strike,
> No fairy takes, nor witch hath power to charm,
> So hallowed and so gracious is the time.

Pretty good, for a simple soldier. The intense and solemn beauty of these verses lifts us, and was designed to lift us, high above the level of Horatio's conjectures. The night 'wherein our Savior's birth is celebrated' is holy and pure beyond all others; therefore these nights which the Ghost makes hideous by rising so incredibly from the grave, are impure beyond most. Unless Greek Tragedy has bemused me, this passage does more than 'give a religious background to the supernatural happenings' of the scene; they give the 'background', that is, the logical and dynamic centre, of the whole play. We are in the presence of evil. Hamlet's own prophetic soul recognises this as soon as he hears of the Ghost:

> Foul deeds will rise,
> Though all the earth o'erwhelm them, to men's eyes.

If we may assume that Shakespeare had not read Sophocles—and that Hamlet had not read him, at Wittenberg, behind Shakespeare's back—the parallel with the Oedipus becomes the more interesting; for when Oedipus has at last discovered the truth the Chorus observes:

> ἐφηῦρέ σ' ἄκονθ' ὁ πάνθ' ὁρῶν χρόνος,
> δικάζει τὸν ἄγαμον γάμον πάλαι
> τεκνοῦντα καὶ τεκνούμενον.

Time sees all, and it has found you out, in your own despite. It exacts Dike from you for that unnatural marriage that united mother with son. (1213–1215)

'Foul deeds will rise': there are evils so great that Nature will not allow them to lie unpurged. So, returning to the battlements with Hamlet, and enquiring with him

> *Why thy canonized bones, hearsed in death,*
> *Have burst their cerements; why the sepulchre*
> *Wherein we saw thee quietly inurned*
> *Hath o'ped his ponderous and marble jaws*
> *To cast thee up again—*

we learn the cause: fratricide, incest, 'Murder most foul, strange and unnatural'.

Here, most emphatically stated, are the very foundations and framework of the tragedy. We can, of course, neglect these, and erect a framework of our own which we find more interesting or more congenial to us. We can say, with Dr. Gregg, that the Ghost is all my eye; or, with Professor Dover Wilson, that the first act, 'a little play of itself', is 'an epitome of the ghost-lore of the age'—in which case it becomes something of a learned Prologue to the real play; or, like Dr. de Madariaga, we can neglect this encircling presence of evil, and substitute what we know of sixteenth-century Court manners; or, again without constant reference to the background which Shakespeare himself erected, we can subtly anatomise the soul and mind of Hamlet, on the assumption that Hamlet is the whole play. But if we do these things, let us not then complain that Shakespeare attempted a task too difficult for him, or conclude that the play is an ineffable mystery. Turning it into 'secular' tragedy we shall be using the wrong focus. The correct focus is one which will set the whole action against a background of Nature and Heaven; for this is the background which the dramatist himself has provided.

Essays on the Problem of Guilt

J. T. SHEPPARD

The Innocence of Oedipus[†]

My assertion that Oedipus is innocent demands, as I am aware, defence and explanation. It must be admitted that the hero, when he stands revealed as the murderer of his father and the husband of his mother, feels himself utterly vile, polluted, and the polluter of all who have dealings with him. He has done, however unwittingly, things which have made him worse than the meanest of criminals. Are we not forced to admit that Sophocles here treats his Oedipus as a sinner duly punished? Has he not failed to realise that it is the motive and the knowledge of consequences that determine moral guilt?

Without doubt, there was a time when a Greek audience would have been unable to distinguish between the guilt of the deliberate parricide and the misfortune of a man like Oedipus. Some vague minds even to-day find it impossible to realise that, for example, Tess of the D'Urbervilles was a chaste woman. And in the audience of Sophocles, though Greek literature and Greek law entitle us to claim that the work of enlightenment had gone far, there must have been many simple people who, if they had been examined by a lawyer, could not have made the distinction clear. Our question, however, concerns Sophocles, and an audience which is swayed by the emotions suggested by this play. How would ordinarily intelligent Athenians of the time of Sophocles feel, not simply think, about Oedipus?

In the first place, very few of them—Euripides and some of his friends—would realise clearly that the supposed 'pollution' and the infectious nature of that pollution were the figments of old superstition. The *Hercules Furens* allows us to say so much. They would be able easily enough to imagine the state of mind of a person who believed in the definite, material, and infectious, pollution. But, for their own part, they would feel, as would an enlightened man of our own day, that the ignorance of Oedipus absolves him from all

† From J. T. Sheppard, *The Oedipus Tyrannus of Sophocles* (Cambridge, England: Cambridge University Press, 1920), pp. xxiv–xl. Reprinted by permission of the publisher.

blame. Anyone, however clear-headed, must, of course, feel that it is natural and right for Oedipus to experience a terrible emotion, with something of remorse and disgust, an instinctive sense of shame and intolerable pain. But we have no right to suppose that this is all. Most of the audience, perhaps Sophocles himself (though the *Oedipus at Colonus* makes this doubtful), felt and recognised as right the peculiar horror expressed by Creon when he bids the citizens put out of sight 'a thing polluted so that neither Earth nor Light nor Heaven's Rain may welcome it.'

That difference between the ancient and the modern view must in fairness be admitted. To the average spectator of our play the man who had shed human blood was, until absolved by ritual purification and also, in some cases, by a judicial verdict of justification, physically unclean, infectious, and likely to be a cause of disaster to all with whom he came in contact. How strongly this superstition worked, even in the days of the 'enlightenment,' we may gather from the commonplaces which occur in a series of speeches composed by the orator and statesman Antiphon as a model for pleaders in Athenian courts. This is the kind of argument to which a jury will respond:

> It is against your own advantage that this person, so blood-stained and so foul, should have access to the sacred precincts of your gods and should pollute their purity; should sit at the same table with yourselves, and should infect the guiltless by his presence. It is this that causes barrenness in the land. It is this that brings misfortune upon men's undertakings. You must consider that it is for yourselves you are acting when you take vengeance for this murder. . . .

The notion of the potent and disastrous blood-pollution is alive in Athenian society, no mere archaistic and imaginative revival of the poet. Though the clear vision of human love enables the Theseus of Euripides to see the essential innocence and harmlessness of his friend, even he does not deny the need for purification. His contempt for the danger of infection is for the audience a revelation of generosity, a triumph of reason and of friendship over the current superstition.

But we must make yet another admission. Though there are few traces here of the crude old superstition whose vitality is attested, for example, by the words of Plato's *Laws*. 'He that has been slain by violence is angry against the doer, and pursues his murderer with shocks and terrors,' there is certainly an appeal to the tragic notion that the dead man cries for vengeance. Though Sophocles has deliberately suppressed the Aeschylean and pre-Aeschylean notion of the ancestral curse and the inherited taint, we must not forget, in estimating the probable effect of his work, the ancient feeling, to which sanction was still given even by the enlightened practice of Athenian justice, that a killing was a wrong inflicted primarily on the family, and that it imposed, upon the kinsman, in the first place the duty of requital. It is the family of a murdered man that demands the trial of his murderer. It is on a kinsman, who must claim first cousinship at least to the deceased, that the duty of prosecution falls. This fact, and the frame of mind which it induces, must be remembered when we try to realise the emotional effect of the parricide of Oedipus. It may help us if we recall another passage of the *Laws*, in which Plato, prescribing for the good government of a typical Greek city, will have the parricide slain and his body thrown out naked and unburied at a crossroad beyond the precincts of the city. All the officials shall bring stones and shall stone the corpse, thus throwing upon its head the pollution of the state. 'The Justice that stands on watch, the avenger of kindred bloodshed, follows a law . . . ordaining that if any man hath done any such deed he suffer what he has inflicted. Hath a man slain his father? He must some day die at the hands of his children. . . . When the common blood is polluted, there is no other purification. The polluted blood will not be washed out until the life that did the deed has paid a like death as penalty for the death, and so propitiated and laid to rest the wrath of the whole kinship. In our play, I know, there is nothing quite so savage as this. Yet the savage superstition is alive in Athens and we shall not appreciate the full tragedy of Oedipus unless we take that fact into account.

Of the incest I need say little. But here also we must remember that for a Greek audience there comes into play, not merely the natural feeling which we share, but also the superstitious sense of a taboo, which makes the tie of family not less but more binding, the pollution not less but more horrible, than it is for us. I will mention only the fact that an Athenian was held justified in killing an adulterer at sight if he were caught with the slayer's wife or mother or sister or daughter, or even with his concubine, if she were the mother of children whom he had acknowledged as his own. So much depended on the purity of citizen blood that a man was forbidden to take back an unfaithful wife under penalty of the loss of citizen rights.

These differences between the normal ancient view and the modern view must, in frankness, be admitted. But do they really imply the sweeping corollary, for example, of Professor Murray? Is it true, that Sophocles expects and allows his audience to adopt that further superstition of 'the terrible and romantic past' which makes incest and parricide 'not moral offences capable of being rationally judged or even excused as unintentional'? Is it true that he has allowed 'no breath of later enlightenment to disturb the primaeval gloom of his atmosphere'? That is the question we have to face.

For some of my readers, I hope, to put the question thus plainly is to answer it. Sophocles has, indeed, used all his constructive art in the invention of a plot whose minor incidents as well as its broad effects reveal the hero's piety, his respect for the natural bond of the family, and his instinctive detestation of impurity. But there are some critics who are somehow able to ignore the general impression, or to attribute it to a modern enlightenment which, they think, Sophocles did not share. Because Aristotle has remarked that the hero of a drama, if it is to produce in us the emotion proper to tragedy, must not be perfect, must have faults and make mistakes, such critics refuse to accept the broad presentation of the tragic figure of Oedipus, a hero not without faults, yet noble, involved, not because of his faults, but in spite of his virtue, in pollution. They must needs find some 'ἁμαρτία,' besides the tragic mistake, to justify the hero's fall. For such critics it is necessary to dwell for a moment on the detail which was devised by Sophocles, not to justify the catastrophe, but to make us admire the hero and realise his essential nobility.

In Aeschylus, as we have remarked, a sufferer is generally himself responsible for his calamity. The tragedy comes from the fact that a tendency to evil is too strong for the sinner to resist. It is true, therefore, that the story of Oedipus might have been so presented as to suggest the guilt of the sufferer or some mysteriously inherited tendency to evil. Of that fact the Athenian audience was aware. But the Athenian spectators would not therefore, like some modern critics, weigh and ponder every little incident of his story as it unfolded itself to see whether, in fact, Sophocles had made his hero guilty. Happily we can be certain that even had they applied that method the result would have been an acquittal. An Athenian jury would have been amused by the plea of a prosecuting critic who argued, like some modern scholars, that the hero is revealed at lines 779 ff. as a person prone to criminality because he had been brought up as a spoilt young prince; that he must have been provocative in his behaviour since one of his companions was driven to insult him by the taunt of bastardy; that he was hasty and over-inquisitive in his appeal to Apollo, and was ungrateful in his neglect to inform his supposed parents of his departure; or finally—for this plea has been urged by a critic who saw the futility of all the rest—that his ἁμαρτία consisted in the criminal negligence with which, in spite of the oracle's evasive answer, he killed an old man and married a comparatively elderly woman. He ought, we are solemnly told, to have been put upon his guard. No jury, I venture to assert, and *a fortiori* no intelligent audience, would find him guilty on such grounds and assess such punishment for such offences.

And however well the prosecuting counsel argued, the advocate for the defence would have an easy task. As Wilamowitz showed, the poet has been careful to leave no loophole for misunderstanding. It would have been so easy to make Oedipus the aggressor, as does Europides, for instance, in the *Phoenissae*. In Sophocles he is attacked in a lonely mountain pass and defends himself against an unprovoked assault. For killing thus committed as an act of self-defense Athenian justice would have pronounced him innocent. After a ceremonial purification he would have been no further troubled by the affair. Unfortunately, 'against his will'—for the whole tragedy assumes that he could not naturally have suspected the truth—the man whom he so justly slew was his own father, the woman whom he quite properly married was his mother. Thus, as an 'involuntary sinner,' he was plunged into calamities most terrible.

But indeed an Athenian of the time of Sophocles would hardly have considered the detail with such care. To him the name of Oedipus suggests, not guilt, but chiefly misfortune. The moral fervour of Aeschylus had given a new interpretation to old stories. But for most Athenians the stories must have continued to illustrate, not the profound reflections of Aeschylus, but the perfectly reasonable, though unreflective, view which most people normally do take of stories. 'Oedipus was at first a happy man, the king of Thebes, the saviour of the state, blest with children, loved by his subjects ... but afterwards he became, when he made the great discovery, of all men the most wretched.'

As for those critics who look for the ἁμαρτία in the course of the drama, not in its antecedents, it should be sufficient to answer that the plague which sets in motion the tragic events is itself the result of the pollution already incurred, and that at the outset, before ever he has insulted Teiresias or suspected Creon of disloyalty, the hero is already an incestuous parricide. Here I must insist on the clearness of the distinction made at the crisis of the tragedy between the 'involuntary' acts which have brought on the catastrophe, and the 'voluntary evils' of excessive agony and self-mutilation which are its result. The messenger who brings from the palace the news of Jocasta's death insists upon the involuntary nature of the 'sin.' He sharply distinguishes 'those many secret evils that lurk hidden in the house—so foul, not all the waters of Phasis and of Ister could wash it clean'—from those 'other evils' which in a moment shall be displayed to the light, ills *voluntary, not unpurposed,*' ἑκόντα κοὐκ ἄκοντα.

The laws of nature have been violated, and the violator has incurred pollution. Yes, but the pollution was incurred without the willing consent of the sinner, in spite of a life whose governing purpose had been to avoid the sin (793 ff., 997 ff.). Oedipus himself makes a like distinction: it was Apollo who brought these things to pass (1329 ff.), the ills which are the worst: but the blinding stroke upon the eyes was inflicted, not only by the hand, but with the full will and intent, of Oedipus.

This distinction between the voluntary and the involuntary is, of course, a commonplace of Greek tragedy. Its recognition marks an important stage in the history, not only of criminal law, but also of morality and religion. For this drama it has an importance which seems to have escaped the notice of many learned interpreters. To its significance for an Athenian audience the earlier literature will perhaps provide a key. Poets who died before the great 'enlightenment,' whose morality was the model for old-fashioned propriety, and who would certainly have felt that Oedipus was physically polluted and infectious, had yet a perfectly good conception of the difference between the intentional criminal and the unfortunate who had committed an unintentional crime. It was quite possible for a Greek to believe that certain conduct had made a man physically unfit for human society, and yet to acquit him of all blame. The thought is expressed in different language from our own. But essentially, we shall find, the normal Greek view of such a case was likely to be no less sympathetic and intelligent than our own.

For a statement of the fundamental notions we may go to Simonides, whose spirit, though he was a poet of Ceos, has been recognized as Attic. He was a favourite at Athens, and an acknowledged exponent of the higher elements of popular morality.

Scopas, a prince of Thessaly, asking, doubtless, for flattery, had suggested to Simonides as a theme for song the famous saying of a great statesman, Pittacus of Mytilene. Pittacus became sole ruler of his city at a time of civil discord, but laid down his office, not attempting to make himself a despot, because, as he said, 'It is difficult to be a man of virtue.' When Scopas, prince of Thessaly, asks his courtier poet for an opinion on that *dictum,* we have the right to think, in words like those of Herodotus concerning Croesus: 'This he asked, expecting to be told that it was indeed difficult, but that Scopas by peculiar excellence had conquered the difficulties. Had Pittacus been Scopas, he had not needed to lay aside his power.' But the poet took his harp and answered in far different fashion, courtly yet wise:

> Difficult, say you? Difficult to be a man of virtue, truly good, shaped and fashioned without flaw in the perfect figure of four-squared excellence, in body and mind, in act and thought?

That is the text. There is a gap in our tradition. Later comes this answer:

> Nor to my ears does the current phrase of Pittacus ring true—though wise was he who uttered it. He said 'twas difficult

to be a man of virtue. I answer, only a god can have that boon. For a man—if he be overtaken by a calamity against which no device availeth, needs must he be evil; there is no escape. As any man is good if fortune grant it, so if his fortune bring him evil, evil is the man: and those of us are best whom the gods love. Therefore will I not waste the lot and portion of life that is granted me in an empty aspiration, a bootless quest, the search for a perfect man among all of us that reap the harvest of the earth's wide fields in Hellas—though, if I find one, I will bring you news. No! I have praise and love for every man who does no deed of shame of his own will. Necessity not even the gods resist. ... Enough for me a man who gives not way to utter evil, utter lawlessness, a man who hath in him the sense of that fairness which profits his city, a man who hath in him the sense of that fairness which profits his city, a man whose heart is sound. No reproach shall such a man have of me—because you cannot count the generation of the children of utter folly. All deeds are good if they be free from baseness.

There is scope here for misunderstanding, and indeed Simonides has been accused of flattering the prince by extolling 'the morality of the second-best.' The truth is that he is warning his patron against self-righteousness. Pittacus was wise, for he realized the temptations and dangers of power. He is to be criticized only because his maxim did not sufficiently insist on the dangers that beset a man, as man, even if he is not a king. Let Scopas remember, however well he rules his people, that, even so, he is but a man, and therefore imperfect. The best of men can, it is true, obey their sense of right, refusing to violate Aidôs; and, therefore, of the best it may be said that they are in a sense 'good' since there is nothing 'shameful' in their intentional and purposed deed and thought. But, even so, they are not secure. Perfection, if calamity comes, is not possible. In some circumstances the best that can be attained is the avoidance of the wilful violation of justice and moderation. If calamity 'unmanageable,' not to be put off by any wit of man, engulf us, we cannot be perfect men . . . yet we may, if we are as noble as Oedipus, be worthy of praise and love, even in our shame and actually in our moral catastrophe.

Is that not true? The Stoics denied it. Virtue, and therefore happiness, they said, were possible for all men, however sick in mind and body and estate. But, in order to make good that claim, they had to narrow their definition of virtue. The good will is always possible—save in insanity. And the good will is always, in itself, virtuous. True, and no man is to be blamed if he has well striven, 'doing of his own will nothing shameful.' But is it possible for the best life to be attained without good fortune, or, as Simonides and Sophocles would say, without the gift of the gods? Simonides answers by a distinction important for the understanding of the

Oedipus, as it is for much else in Greek literature and in our own experience. *A man may be guilty through no fault of his own*[1], and no man, however excellent in intention and in act, no man, even, however blest by fortune or the gods, achieves and keeps perfection.

That this idea, essentially true, is expressed in language which misleads many of us, and shocks some, is due to the inheritance of a tradition which used epithets, now exclusively moral, in a political sense. A 'good' man has sometimes meant a brave and cunning fighter, a wise counsellor, a just judge. Elsewhere and in a different society it means a successful, respectable, and therefore probably industrious labourer, or trader, or householder. Sometimes, again, it has meant a man born of 'good family' and maintaining the standards, whatever they happen to be, of his class. In all these cases the possibility of 'goodness' must obviously depend on good fortune—and it is true enough that there is something which deserves to be called 'goodness' in the happy warrior, the substantial householder, or the aristocratic 'noble.' Simonides, though he admits the obvious, adds—he is probably not the first to add it—that there *is* a sort of goodness, limited, yet valuable, which is not dependent on the turn of luck. Thus he gives us a new interpretation, entirely free from cynicism, of the Homeric observation that men's minds are good or bad according to the kind of weather Zeus allows them. The distinction between the will to goodness and the possession of it is implied, though not quite clearly stated. There remains a danger of relapse into a vague theory of irresponsibility. But we, if we emphasize too much the Will, run another danger. We may be tempted to flatter ourselves and our prince by saying that there is no need to trouble about the poverty and misery of our people, because, forsooth, all men can have, without money and without price, the Will to Virtue which is independent of the gifts of the gods.

It may help us to judge more fairly of Simonides—and also of Sophocles—if we notice other passages, not inconsistent with our text, but complementary to it. For example, see what the poetry of

---

1. That is one of the most important principles in Greek morality. An amusing application will be found in Herodotus III 43, the story of a ruler who tried in vain to be the 'most just of men.' An application whose importance and truth we must all at this time recognise is made by Thucydides (III 82) when he says that 'War, because it puts men into a situation in which they are not free agents (ἀκουσίους ἀνάγκας), makes them like their circumstances'— worse than they are in time of peace. When Socrates enunciated his paradox that no one willingly does wrong, he was using old language for his new thought. The old proverbial moralities divided evils into 'voluntary and involuntary.' 'Ills sent by the gods, inevitable, destined, necessary,' must be borne without excessive grief and complaint. Such an evil was the pollution of Oedipus. But the self-blinding was an additional evil, self-imposed, voluntary, and therefore morally different. The comment of Socrates would have been that this act also was involuntary, since it was done with the intent of finding forgetfulness: had he known, as later he knows, that peace of mind comes only through Sophrosyne, Oedipus would not have mutilated himself.

Simonides has made of Hesiod's practical advice to the farmer who would be prosperous and respectable:

> 'Tis said [that is, we know, by Hesiod and many others] that Virtue dwells upon the inaccessible hills, attended by the chaste dancing company of Nymphs divine, not visible to the eyes of all mankind, but only to him whose heart has felt the pang of struggle and the sweat . . . to him who has won his way by manhood to the height.

There is no 'morality of the second-best' in that! But it is true, unfortunately, that a farmer, however well he works, may be foiled by weather and by soil. So, in the moral sphere, there are real limitations to man's freedom. Though he strive hard for excellence, a man needs the gift of the gods, success, if his virtue is to be the successful virtue, the perfect prize of excellence at which he aims.

> None winneth virtue without the gods, no city and no mortal man. 'Tis the god that deviseth all, and among men there is no life altogether free from calamity.

Moreover, it is from this very fact that a man, however good his intention, however brave his effort of thought and will, may always fail—falling, as the Greeks say, into involuntary evils, because the gods or his daimon or luck or circumstances will have it so—that a pious Greek refuses to call men happy till they are dead. This same Simonides may remind us:

> Since you are but a man, never presume to say what to-morrow brings—nor, when you see a man happy, how long a time he will be so.

Perhaps the noblest expression of the frame of mind suggested to a Greek by such reflections is the Spartan prayer:

> King Zeus, grant us the good for which we pray—aye, and the good we pray not for: and, though we pray for it, avert from us the evil.

Upon that lofty strain it would be pleasant to end my chapter. But I dare not stop here. Our attempt to prove the innocence of Oedipus has led us back to the problem which lies at the heart, not only of the tragedy of the Greek theatre, but also of the tragedy of human life. If the innocent suffer—and who, in these days, will deny it?—if the faults of men are visited upon their own heads and the heads of others in retribution more terrible than the faults deserve, what are we to think of the justice of the gods? That question, which remains with us, was faced and variously answered by the Greeks. The terms in which they answer it are not our own: but if we rightly understand their meaning, the answers are the answers with which the world must reckon to-day.

In the house of Zeus, said Homer, stand two jars from which he dispenses to mortals good and evil alike. That simple doctrine is not compatible with the perfect goodness of the gods. Still more incompatible is another ancient doctrine that the gods are jealous of a man's prosperity and deliberately tempt him to his own destruction. We need new explanations when philosophy or religion insists upon the goodness of the gods. We shall certainly deny the doctrine of the divine jealousy and the divine temptation. We may deny that evil comes from the gods. But we cannot escape the fact that some of our evils, at any rate, are certainly not due to man. We may say that evil is the punishment of sin, that a man must pay for his faults or for the faults of his ancestors, or we may tell ourselves that suffering is the only road to wisdom. Even so, we have not solved the problem. If we are mystics and assert that apparent evil is, in the sight of the gods or of the Absolute, good, we abandon in logic, though not, of course, in practice, our right to judge of good and evil.

Of the mystical confusion of good and evil we shall find no trace in our play. Of the truth that suffering is a school of wisdom greater use has been made, as we shall presently see, than is admitted by most interpreters. But there is no suggestion that the wisdom justifies the suffering. The theme of an inherited guilt is, we have already remarked, ignored. That the omission is deliberate becomes obvious when we remember that Sophocles was familiar with the work of Aeschylus, and when we recall how this *motif* is used in the *Antigone* (584 ff.). The tragedy ensues by normal human processes from the act of Oedipus himself. Yet the character and the life of the hero are such as to exclude, for a Greek as for a modern audience, the notion that he has deserved his fate, though his tragedy is heightened by the fact that his defects are precisely those which for a Greek are normally associated with the righteously afflicted sinner. Finally, the plague, the oracles, the prophecies of Teiresias, and the sense, in the background, of the mysterious potency of Zeus and Apollo, imply that, in some sense, the evil comes from the gods. It comes, however, not by miraculous intervention, but through the normal processes of human will and human act, of human ignorance and human failure. Sophocles justifies nothing. He accepts, for his tragic purpose, the story and the gods, simply treating them as if they were true. Whether he thought that in ancient times a real king Oedipus had actually suffered this agony is of no importance. Whether he believed in prophecies or not really matters little. His Oedipus stands for human suffering, and he neither attempts, like Aeschylus, to justify the evil, nor presumes, like Euripides, to deny its divine origin. That is because his gods—whether he believed in them, or exactly in what sense, does not matter—stand for the universe of circumstance as it is. Aeschylus and Euripides both demand for their worship a God who is good and just. Both therefore must attempt to solve the 'problem of evil.' The pagan gods of Homer and Sophocles require no such reconciliation. They are great and good, and great and bad—like things, and men, and nature. They square with the tragic facts of life, and therefore, we, who do not think that the lightning is the flash of the bolt of Zeus, who do not believe that Apollo was born of Leto in the island of Delos, can yet believe in the essential truth of the Sophoclean Apollo. There are in human life great tragedies, moving and wonderful because they flow from human action and are in some measure due to human blunders, yet tragedies for which in no full moral sense can responsibility be ascribed to man. Man is often the victim of circumstance—yes, often his own nobility demands that he shall sacrifice his own most noble qualities. Well, the 'circumstance,' which alone we can call responsible, is poetically represented by Apollo. And the tragedy, which admits this non-moral power, can appeal to all the listeners, whether like Aeschylus, they say at the end of the play: 'Ah yes, it is terrible. Yet my religion tells me that at the heart of it there is the working of a righteous God,' or whether, with the pessimist, we cry out in condemnation of such a universe, or whether we simply admit the tragic facts—and, as to their explanation, are fain to confess our ignorance.

That the language, and sometimes the thought, has an admixture of superstition I have no wish to deny. We recognise a belief which probably none of us shares, when, for example, after Oedipus has told Jocasta of the terrible pronouncement of Apollo, he cries:

> If any judge my life and find therein
> A savage Daimon's work, he hath the truth.

In my version I have ventured to translate the words ὠμοῦ δαίμονος by 'malignant stars,' a phrase which recalls to us a kindred, but more familiar, notion. We hear again, from the chorus, of the *Daimon* of Oedipus, immediately after the revelation of the truth. Finally, at the sight of the blinded and humiliated king, the chorus cry:

> What Fury (δαίμων) came on thee?
> What evil spirit from afar
> Leapt on thee to destroy?

And Oedipus himself asserts that his calamity is the work of an evil δαίμων:

> Alas! Curse of my life (δαῖμον), how far
> Thy leap hath carried thee!

Of the various meanings and applications of the word Δαίμων we need not speak, but something must be said of the popular sense of which Sophocles has here made so tragic a use. Probably none of us believes that with every man there is born and lives and dies a supernatural being, 'an individualised Fortune,' a being upon whom his prosperity and his misfortune somehow depend, his 'guardian angel' if his character and luck be good, a veritable 'demon' if he be born to wickedness or calamity. How far Sophocles himself believed in such a supernatural *Daimon* we do not know. He may, for all we know, have travelled far upon the road towards that 'rationalistic' interpretation of life which issued in the doctrine that a man's character is his fate (ἦθος ἀνθρώπῳ δαίμων). The important point for us is this: although the memory of the old superstition, and the fact that some of the audience are probably themselves superstitious, add emotional value to these allusions, yet, so far as the moral inference is concerned, no harm is done. The poet's presentation of the character of the hero, and the judgments which are implied both as to his moral responsibility and as to his innocence, are as clear and as just as if the poet had been a modern rationalist and had substituted for the vivid *Daimon* the vagueness of 'disastrous accident' or 'circumstances unforeseen and beyond control.' For moral judgment, though not for the dramatic value of the poem, it makes little difference whether you attribute the 'involuntary evils' to the gods or to the *Daimon* or to complications of circumstance.

I do not, of course, deny that there is a danger in these, as in all superstitions. My purpose is simply to suggest that the attribution of that part of human misfortune which is not due to man either to fate (Herodotus 1 19, Soph. *Phil.* 1466), or to Zeus ὁ παντ' ἀνάσσων *O.T.* 894, οὐδὲν τούτων ὅτι μὴ Ζεύς Soph. *Trach.* 1278), or to a man's *Daimon*, does not *necessarily* and *always* imply a false estimate of human moral responsibility. For morality, all depends on the particular application which is made. Some men, for example, profess to believe that war is due to the anger of God, some that it is due to the malignant activity of the devil. The result may be, and sometimes is, a criminal negligence or a fanatical barbarity. But what matters for morality is simply that such persons, whether or not they are superstitious, should be sufficiently clear-sighted to help one another in the task of abolishing all natural, human, and avoidable causes of such crime. No Athenian could possibly have inferred from the fact that the calamity of Oedipus is ascribed to his *Daimon* or to Apollo the notion that it is useless for a man to attempt to live decently and to honour his parents. Most doctrines are capable both of a higher and of a lower moral application. There were many in the audience who would have accepted without question the immoral theory, had it been suggested by the poet's treatment, that the gods tempt men to their ruin. They would have felt, like the grumbling old moralist of Megara:

> In nothing be over-zealous! The due measure in all the works of man is best. Often a man who zealously pushes towards some excellence, though he be pursuing a gain, is really being led astray by the will of some divine power which makes those things that are evil lightly seem to him good, and makes those things seem to him evil which are for his advantage.

Sophocles, as we shall see, has made his story a reminder of the fallibility of human endeavour and of the importance of moderation: But he has not treated Apollo or the *Daimon* of the hero as a devilish tempter luring him into sin. His moral is more nearly, though not quite exactly, expressed in another pronouncement of Theognis:

> No man, O Kyrnus, is the cause of his own ruin or his own advantage. The gods are the givers of both; nor hath any man, as he works, the knowledge in his heart whether the end of his labour be good or evil. Often he thinks to make the issue evil, and lo! he hath made it good, or thinking to make it good, he hath made it evil. To no man also cometh all that he desires. The limits of a cruel helplessness restrict us. We are but men, and so our thoughts are vain; no certain knowledge have we; and it is the gods that bring all ends to pass according to their mind.

No one, I suppose, has insisted more strongly than the poet Pindar on the need for personal effort if success or virtue is to be won: but no one, also, has insisted more strongly on the doctrine that both good and evil come from 'the gods' or from a man's *Daimon*. Pindar's athletes and princes stand at the height of human fortune. They need to be reminded, first, that success has come, not only by their own effort, but also as the gift of the gods, and, secondly, that no mortal is exempt from those reverses of fortune which come also from the gods. Just as a man must strive if he is to succeed, yet may fail in spite of noblest endeavour, so, if he fail, he may or may not be guiltless, yet his failure will be due to causes greater than himself. 'It is according to the *Daimon* of their lives that men are born wise and good' (*Ol.* ix 29), and 'the flower of wisdom grows in a man as the gift of a god' (*Ol.* xi 10): 'it is the fate which is born with a man that decides the issue of all his doing' (*Nem.* v 40), and 'we are not all born for a like fortune, but are set on different roads by the different apportionment of fate which is given to each' (*Nem.* vii 5). 'It is the goddess Theia who gives the athlete his glory,' though 'men's valour differs according to their Daimones . . . and Zeus himself, who is master of all things, give us our good and our evil' (*Isth.* v 7, 11, 52). Pindar, it is true, lays more stress on the aristocrat's inheritance of virtue and good fortune than would a democratic Athenian. But the essential notions persist. On the one hand, no virtue comes without the virtuous endeavour. On the other hand, in spite of all endeavour, 'in a little while the pleasantness of the life of mortals grows, and in a little while it falls to earth, shaken down by the turn of the purpose of the gods. Creatures of a day, what is to be? What is it to be nothing? A man is a dream of a shadow. Yet when there comes to a man the gleam of happiness that is given by Zeus, bright is the light that is upon him, though it be but the light of mortality, and all his life is blest' (*Pyth.* VIII 92 ff.).

Such is the spirit which the tragedy of Oedipus is intended to inspire. The name of the spirit is *Sophrosyne.* The *motifs* which the poet has used might have been so treated as to produce a very different impression. Had Sophocles chosen he might have treated Oedipus as a willing sinner justly punished. But that method would have made the tragedy less tragic. The poet and his audience would not have faced the deepest and the greatest tragedy of human life. Or, had he chosen, he could have used the theme of Apollo's oracular guidance in a spirit which insisted on the devilish relentlessness of the god. The audience would have responded, though the more enlightened of them would have been shocked. The mind of the spectators is attuned to the influences both of a higher and of a lower appeal. The reader will judge whether I am justified in suggesting that it is to the higher morality that the poet has addressed himself. He neither justifies the gods by making Oedipus a criminal nor condemns the gods because the agony of Oedipus is undeserved. He bids his audience face the facts.

To the question whether beyond the grave there is reconciliation and peace, poets, philosophers, and divines have their various answers. Tragedy, which concerns this life and the undoubted sufferings of this life, is noble still, even if the poets, philosophers, and divines can find a happy answer. Sometimes Sophocles writes as if he has the intuition of a happy solution. But his work as a tragedian is to face the facts of life. Whatever be our own interpretation of those facts, we shall be moved by their presentment in this drama.

LASZLO VERSÉNYI

[The Flaw of Oedipus]†

What motivates Oedipus' action is his own nature. 'Such being my nature, I cannot become something else, I cannot give up the search into my origin, I will know who I am.' (1084–1085). What

† From Laszlo Versényi, "Oedipus: (Autumn 1962), 25–27. Reprinted by Tragedy of Self-Knowledge," *Arion*, 1:3 permission of the publisher.

he fulfills and saves, by not deviating from it, is his own nature. But that is also what destroys him, his own nature—*daimōn*, fate portion or need, the need for self-knowledge. If so, 'know thyself' is here, no longer the pious, safe and sound precept of the Delphic oracle meaning 'know your limit and stay within it,' 'do not transgress,' 'nothing in excess.' Rather, it is a demonic obsession that leads to a fateful 'excess': that of a man exceeding, transcending and turning upon himself—in order to become what he is. While the Delphic motto reminded man of his weakness and mortality, of the gulf between him and the gods, in short, of his finitude, the new *gnōthi sauton* delivers man (from others, men and gods), makes him independent (for he deals with nothing but himself) and self-sufficient (even to the extent of being his own henchman). *Gnōthi sauton*, as the fundamental nature of man, turns him into his own battlefield on which he assumes the roles of all antagonists himself, is simultaneously savior and destroyer, victorious and defeated, and thereby attains to a new heroism and a new greatness, that of a man abandoned to the most difficult fate, the fate of overcoming himself. If Oedipus is a paradigm for all men, the Antigonean ode, 'Many are the wonders,' has indeed turned into its opposite in *Oedipus Rex*: 'Many are the terrors, yet none more terrible than man.'

What has man done to deserve such fate? What is Oedipus' *hamartia*? In a sense, this last question has already been answered. If all the action in the drama is impelled by nothing but Oedipus' nature, and if this nature can be expressed by the now transformed demand, 'know thyself,' then it is this demand for self-knowledge, man's possession by the demand, that is the 'tragic flaw' that leads to Oedipus' downfall. *Hamartēma* means not 'sin' or 'guilt' but, literally, 'error': erring in the darkness of life, full of ignorance yet having to know. In contrast to late Sophistry's self-confident pride in *polumathia* and to its expression in the optimistic appraisal of 'man the knower' in the first ode of the *Antigone*, the *Oedipus* demonstrates that the urge to know might in itself be an 'awful' (*deinon*) thing, a terrible gift of man's which can lead to pain rather than joy, defeat rather than victory. Self-destruction might be the natural outcome of self-assertion through self-knowledge. Indeed, owing to the nature of human knowing, self-destruction might be merely another name for, another aspect of, self-assertion.

Knowledge necessarily leads to negative results and to the opposite of what the knower intends if the subject of knowledge is by its nature not amenable to rational enquiry. If the world is, by its nature, not open to man's limited insight and if man himself must always remain essentially hidden to himself, intelligence is man's doom rather than his salvation. Given man's *daimōn*—that he must know—and the irrationality that lies at the heart of things, it is not any particular human act but human existence itself that is tragic, and the fault lies not in Oedipus as this particular man but in Oedipus as Man living in a world which is, ultimately, not made for man the knower.

Oedipus' *hamartia* is thus not sin, guilt or personal (and avoidable) failing but a flaw inherent in life and in man as a being not attuned to his world or, what is the same thing, a flaw in the world in which man is abandoned to his failing, limited and utterly inadequate devices. Man fails, and his life is tragic because he is insufficient unto himself. This is evident in the *Oedipus*. Throughout the play, first unconsciously then consciously, Oedipus tries to know himself, equate himself (what he knows himself to be) with himself (what he essentially is), but the final result is merely the revelation that there is something basically wrong with the equation: Oedipus revealed to, and equated with, himself finds himself essentially unequal to the equation, unequal to the task, unequal to being what he is and what he now knows himself to be. Man the knower cannot live without knowing (himself), yet he cannot live having found out. Neither blindness nor sight are conducive to life: not knowing what he is, man cannot be what he is; knowing what he is, man cannot bear to exist. Life is *hamartia*, an erring, for to live is to be out of balance, and every effort of the knower to right this balance merely tips the scale toward his doom.

That does not mean that there is no order, pattern, law to life, for it is precisely this not-to-be-resolved tension between what a man is and what he knows himself to be, between what a man has accomplished and what he has yet to become, and the resolution of this tension in death (the final 'righting' of the human imbalance) that is the rhythm, order, and way of things, the unbreakable balance of human existence. That such order may be called, in our terms, unjust, cruel and meaningless, may be quite true, but it is also irrelevant once our terms, our knowledge and our insight have been found inadequate. If man's intelligence does not measure up to the world, it can hardly be used for measuring, weighing and judging it. Given his tragic vision, the poet can justly affirm that 'all is well.'

'All is well,' however, is not a one-sided statement in Sophocles. It is not, at least in *Oedipus Rex*, an affirmation of divine *diké* versus human justice, and exaltation of *physis* as the whole of things, over against man as an insignificant, unbalanced-perishable, and therefore almost negligible, detail. Man is, rather, included, with all his failing and inadequacy, in the affirmation, and the 'all is well' refers to human existence as it is as well as to the more than human order.

P. H. VELLACOTT

The Guilt of Oedipus†

In this paper I propose to deal with some difficulties in Sophocles' *Oedipus Tyrannus*, of which some have been noticed before, others I think have not. I am going to propose an unorthodox explanation, not through any love of unorthodoxy, but in the spirit of Oedipus himself, who when faced with a puzzle could not resist following a fact to its logical conclusion. The Sphinx's riddle was not, after all, a very hard one; and Oedipus doubtless grew tired of being praised for ingenuity. My thesis too disclaims that dubious quality. Ingenuity is what many of us have been using all our lives to explain difficulties in this play which may after all be insoluble.

The story, as it existed in Sophocles' time, before he wrote his play, seems to have been as follows: Laios king of Thebes was told by the Delphic oracle that if he married Iocasta his son would kill him. He ignored the oracle and married Iocasta. When the child was born Laios pierced and bound his ankles and exposed him on Kithairon, where he was found by a shepherd who took him to Corinth; there he was brought up as the son of King Polybos. The Delphic oracle later told Oedipus that he was fated to kill his father and marry his mother. He set out towards Thebes, and on the way killed Laios, not knowing who he was. Arrived at Thebes, he vanquished the Sphinx by guessing her riddle, and for reward became king of Thebes and married Iocasta. Sixteen or more years later, when Thebes was visited by plague, Oedipus investigated the murder of Laios and discovered his own double guilt; whereupon Iocasta hanged herself and Oedipus blinded himself.

Now this story, in its elaboration of detail and in the vividness of its characters, compares with the greatest of the Greek legend-cycles—with those of Herakles, Theseus, the war at Troy; in particular, because of the way it shows a family curse descending through three generations, it invites comparison with the myth of the House of Atreus. It has the same splendour of setting, the same extremes of emotion, the same concern with both sexual relationship and dynastic power, the same close link with the supernatural

† P. H. Vellacott, "The Guilt of Oedipus," *Greece and Rome*, Vol. XI (October 1964), 137–148. Reprinted by permission of the author and The Clarendon Press, Oxford.

[This article was written five years ago and contains some emphases which I have since modified, particularly the emphasis on the moral aspect of the myth; this, I feel, in part justified the comment it drew from Professor E. R. Dodds. My general thesis remains, and will shortly be published in the form of a book called *Sophocles and Oedipus*.— *Author's Note*] as evidenced in the Delphic oracle and the utterances of prophets, the same sense of inescapable Fate. Yet there is one point of difference between the two myths; and it is a central point.

The story of the House of Atreus shows from beginning to end the actions of men and women as being carried out under the eye of gods in a universe where cause and effect have a moral significance. The central figure, Agamemnon, is shown faced with a desperate dilemma, but there is no doubt that the decision he made was the wrong one, and that his sin incurred the retribution which followed. The central figure of the Theban legend, Oedipus, is by contrast apparently innocent. The worst he is usually accused of by students of Sophocles' play is hasty temper—and this itself is Sophocles' own invention rather than part of the basic myth. As a result the whole sequence of events is barren of any significant moral or religious content. There is an inherited curse, but no real sin to justify it; so that the only lesson to be drawn is one of total pessimism, and the only attitude encouraged is that of uncomprehending resignation. What is more disturbing, the story appears to show two crimes of the most heinous and polluting kind actually brought about by divine guidance—a circumstance which can only be regarded as a direct blow at the concept of a coherent world in which Zeus upholds a moral standard.

Let us try to picture Sophocles, with the example of the *Oresteia* to challenge his consciousness of his own poetic power, contemplating the Oedipus-myth as dramatic material. When a dramatist begins to write a play about characters whose story is already fixed in outline, before he can compose any dialogue, he must collect all the material he intends either to use or to assume as part of the story, and in imagination live it all through, dramatizing in his own mind many scenes which will never find a place in his play, but which will clarify for him a character's state of mind at a given moment, or fill in decorative or poetic background. There is a great deal of this in *Agamemnon*, where Aeschylus pictures for us such inessential details as the distress of the forsaken Menelaus, the scene in Troy on Helen's arrival; besides the essential details given in the long sequence about Iphigenia in the first great Ode. In Sophocles' *Oedipus*, however, the unfolding of the plot depends closely on a long string of events stretching back thirty-five years, all narrated at various points in the dialogue, and beginning the story at the time when Laios consulted Apollo as to whether he should marry Iocasta, and was told that, if he did, his son would kill him. The birth of Oedipus, the maiming of his feet, the exposure, the deception, the childhood in Corinth, the visit to Delphi, the encounter by the road-junction, the Sphinx and her riddle, the deliverance of Thebes from the first plague—all these events Sophocles pieces together, every one of them necessary to his story. Yet in none of these do we find what we are looking for—what Sophocles must surely have looked for—some sin, some fault in Oedipus' character which would justify to men the seemingly cruel and immoral ways of Zeus or of Apollo or of Fate. There is no question here of an individual god being arraigned, as Euripides arraigns Aphrodite or Apollo, while the concept of justice itself remains secure in the hand of Zeus. The terrible destiny of Oedipus is shown as one put upon him by supernatural powers in general, by that comprehensive Fate which governs every man's life.

We do, however, glean from these narratives which Sophocles gives us one detail which makes moral as well as dramatic sense. Laios, after receiving divine warning that if he married Iocasta his son would kill him, clearly committed two sins: he ignored the warning and married Iocasta; and then, having begotten a son, he was morally guilty of that son's death; though the formula of exposure on the mountain, being designed to give the infant a one per cent chance of survival, cleared Laios from ritual pollution. Here, then, is a sin in the previous generation; but when we look for its repetition in Oedipus (as Agamemnon repeated his father's guilt) we find nothing. How can there be a true tragedy without a sin? Where is the dignity, the awe, of *nemesis* without *hybris*? True, in line 873 the Chorus seem to rebuke Oedipus for *hybris*, alluding apparently to his extraordinary and groundless accusations against Teiresias and Kreon; but this bad behaviour of Oedipus, besides being inexplicable in view of the character established for him in the opening scene, does not belong to the main stream of the story at all. Usually the best that can be said for it is that Sophocles inserted it to provide Oedipus with a sin to justify his downfall; and to some this explanation will seem unworthy of Sophocles.

I have given above a list of the past events in the story which Sophocles has included as narrative in his dialogue in order to provide us with the essential background of his drama—the birth of Oedipus, the journey to Delphi, and so on. Perhaps you observed that I omitted from my list one detail; one which is more significant than any other. The details I mentioned are all essential to the usual version of the story; but Sophocles added one detail which is *not* essential to the usual version: the incident of the man who got drunk at a banquet and told Oedipus he was not the son of Polybos. Sophocles could have invented a dozen reasons why Oedipus should visit Delphi; but he used this one. Now see how Oedipus continues his story to Iocasta: 'At Delphi I was not given the knowledge which I came to seek, but was told that I was fated to marry my mother and kill my father. When I heard this, I turned my back on Corinth, to go towards any place where I might never see the fulfilment of this shameful oracle.'

That statement would make sense, if Oedipus had gone to Delphi on some state mission for King Polybos. But Oedipus went to Delphi, says Sophocles, because he had been led to doubt that Polybos was his father. It has generally been assumed that the horror of the new prophecy drove clean out of Oedipus' mind the question about his parentage which he had come to ask. That might have been so, had the question and the prophecy been unconnected. In fact they were so obviously and frighteningly connected that I do not believe Sophocles could imagine that Oedipus would fail to connect them. The doubt about his parentage doubled the menace of the prophecy. He would have been thankful indeed, could he have believed that by turning his back on Corinth he could face the rest of the world without apprehension. That was now impossible: he knew that he might meet his true father or his true mother anywhere in Greece; no place was safe.

We must leave for the moment the question why Oedipus apparently expected Iocasta to accept this curious *non sequitur*; and turn instead to ask, what did Sophocles intend us to picture as Oedipus' state of mind when he left the Delphic oracle? He had come there convinced that there was a mystery connected with his birth; the oracle plainly confirmed this. So now, if he was to avoid heinous pollution, he must make for himself two unbreakable rules: never to kill an older man; and never to marry an older woman. The incident at the banquet makes it clear that these two rules, and not the resolve to keep away from Corinth, would be the probable preoccupation of Oedipus' thoughts as he left Delphi. Then, twenty-four hours later, in the midst of an angry scuffle, his head singing from a vicious blow, he looks up and sees before his eyes a furious middle-aged face with greying hair. For a fraction of a second comes the thought of the oracle's warning—this is the man I must not strike. But his blood is boiling; the man has struck him first. The grey hair lies in the dust, near four other bodies. Oedipus has, at the first opportunity, ignored a divine warning. That this man could be his father would be a coincidence so incredible as to be impossible; but this was the risk he ought not to have taken. He is guilty. Sophocles, by inventing and introducing the incident at the banquet, has entirely changed the moral situation of Oedipus in the story. He is no longer the innocent victim of malevolent powers. *Dike*, Justice, daughter of Zeus, a goddess forgotten in the version of the myth which had been current for centuries, reappears, resuscitated by a single subtle creation of the poet.

We shall soon need to look again at the long central scene where Oedipus tells his story to Iocasta. But this scene can only be understood if first we are clearly aware of what happened in the previous scene, where Oedipus confronts Teiresias. Here is a summary of the information which Teiresias gives Oedipus (1) line 337, a hint: 'You have not seen that your own kinswoman is living with you.' (2) line 353, a plain statement: 'You are the defiler of the land.' (3) this is repeated in line 362: 'You killed Laios.' (4) line 366: 'You are living in shameful union with your nearest kin, and do not know it.' (5) line 373: 'You call me blind, deaf, and dull-witted—soon everyone will hurl those reproaches at you.' (6) line 414: 'You do not see what a terrible situation you are in, or whom you are living with.' (7) line 415: 'Do you know whose son you are? And you are an enemy to your own kin both dead and living.' (8) line 420: 'You will shrick aloud when you learn the truth about your marriage—a truth which shall make you level with yourself and with your children.' (9) lines 437-9: 'The mystery of your birth shall be revealed today.' (10) lines 450 ff.: 'The killer of Laios is here, passing as a foreigner, but in truth a Theban; brother and father of his children, son and husband of his mother.'

Now look at the man to whom all this is said. First, he is a famous solver of riddles. Second, he had been told at Delphi that he would kill his father and marry his mother. Third, even before that he had doubted if he was the son of Polybos. Fourth, he remembered only too well killing a man—an older man—on the road from Thebes to Delphi, at a time and place corresponding with the murder of Laios, as Kreon has just reminded him. Fifth, Kreon has also told him that only one man escaped—another point which Oedipus can hardly have forgotten. Sixth, if Oedipus had misgivings about having killed an older man, he must certainly have had more misgivings about having married an older woman. Now, how could a man bearing all that in his memory listen to the repeated and repeated words of Teiresias and not recognize the truth?

One more point before we move on to the central scene. Let us look at our hero's name. He announces it himself in line 8: ὁ πᾶσι κλεινὸς Οἰδίπους καλούμενος. 'Called by all men Oedipus.' 'Oedipus' means 'swollen-footed'. Let us look into a later scene, that with the Messenger from Corinth, lines 1031 ff.

OED. What pain had I when you took me in your arms?
MESS. Your ankles could bear witness to that.
OED. *Oimoi*, why do you mention that ancient injury?
MESS. Your feet were pierced, and I'm the man who freed you.
OED. That terrible disgrace (δεινὸν ὄνειδος) I bore from the cradle.

Nothing could show more clearly that Sophocles thought of the maimed feet as something of which Oedipus was bitterly and constantly conscious.

Now we are ready for the central scene, where everything becomes even more astonishing. Here is Oedipus, remembering the oracle, remembering his encounter by the cross-roads; and a few minutes ago he was told by Teiresias again and again, 'You killed Laios; Laios was your father: Iocasta is your mother.' To him Iocasta now says, 'Laios was once told by an oracle of Apollo that his son and mine would kill him. So as soon as the child was born Laios pinned its ankles together and exposed it on a mountain. Subsequently Laios was killed by robbers near a road-junction.'

Each of these statements connects at once with a thought seething on the surface of Oedipus' mind. The oracle given to Laios corresponds with the oracle given to Oedipus. Iocasta's mention of the road-junction reminds Oedipus of his encounter at that spot. But the third is by far the most significant: the maimed ankles, added to everything that has been said already, *must* identify Oedipus, to his own perception, as Iocasta's son. Yet Oedipus in his reply passes over the unique clue of the maimed ankles, and takes up the commonplace clue of the road-junction—though Iocasta has not even said that it was the road to Delphi. What was Sophocles' purpose in making Iocasta mention the maimed ankles at this point? It was quite unnecessary. Are we to say he didn't know what he was doing? We must also remember another point. The close connexion of so many strands of evidence might well be missed by a modern English theatre-audience; but Sophocles wrote this play for an audience whose minds were trained by constant practice in law-courts to follow arguments and weave evidence together. What then was he trying to do in this play?

So far I have drawn your attention to certain facts of the text. When we come to draw inferences, perhaps the only indisputable one is, that Sophocles' intention in this play is something beyond what we have hitherto understood. A second inference, which may be called probable rather than certain, is that Sophocles intended, by the incident at the banquet, to present Oedipus to us as consciously guilty. This idea is strengthened by the fact that it makes the sin of Oedipus the same as that of Laios, and so gives poetic as well as moral meaning to the hereditary curse. The next step in our inquiry, then, is to follow up the implications of this idea.

Let us assume that Sophocles, steeping his imagination in the story, and pondering its characters and their experiences as a dramatist inevitably does, finds himself examining the possibility that Oedipus really was guilty. He has killed this man—an older man; he had been warned that he was fated to kill his father; and he is far from certain that his father is Polybos. That this dead man should be his father would be an incredible coincidence; nevertheless Oedipus, conscious that he had acted rashly, can hardly fail to look at the dead man's face to see if it bears any resemblance to his own. Also, knowing that one servant escaped back to Thebes, Oedipus, on entering Thebes himself, can hardly fail to keep his ears open for any talk of a man lately murdered on the Delphi road. Indeed he could not fail, even if he had been innocent, to be told by every Theban he met that the king had been murdered, with the time, the place, and details of the carriage, horses, and servants. Greeks talk all the time about everything. If we are speaking factually about the myth, rather than critically about the play, it is certain that within an hour of entering Thebes Oedipus knew that he had killed Laios. Then he volunteered to interview the Sphinx, knowing that the prize was Laios' widow. Therefore—again speaking factually—it is certain that Oedipus said to himself: 'If the man I killed was my father, and if I overcome the Sphinx and marry the queen, the oracle will be exactly fulfilled, and I shall have only myself to blame.' A horrible thought. What could he do to reassure himself? He could try to clear his mind of the suspicion of a likeness between himself and the dead man. He could inquire how old the queen was, and if she had had a son eighteen years ago. Suppose he was told she had? Then the risk was too appalling, and he must give up all idea of becoming king of Thebes. And yet, *why* was he now forced into this frustrating position? Because a drunkard had shouted 'Bastard' at him. The thing was ridiculous; but for that one drunken word, his course and his conscience would have been clear. Was a drunkard's shout to rob him of a throne? Finally, is it surprising that Iocasta, whose adolescent beauty had inspired the cautious Laios to defy Apollo, should in her maturity, at thirty-five, prove irresistible to Laios' son?

If Sophocles, in order to add moral and religious content to this marvellous story which so curiously lacked it, ever conceived and explored the possibility that Oedipus was in fact guilty, he could hardly fail to reason as I have reasoned, and so to see just how it came about that a good man like Oedipus could, in extraordinary circumstances, make this fatal decision to run a ninety-nine per cent risk, and stake his life on a one per cent possibility that he was after all the son of Polybos. He still had two more bridges to cross: first, the moment when he would meet the queen and scan her face to tell how old she was, and to discern any possible likeness to his own; second—and here we come to the central feature of the whole story, embodied in the name—the moment when his wife would see the scars on his feet. It was clear that if Iocasta was in fact a mother who eighteen years ago had lost a son with scarred feet, she would not be likely to forget his eighteenth birthday. The news that her husband had been killed by an unknown assailant would certainly suggest to her that the Delphic oracle nineteen years ago had told Laios the truth, and that her son was perhaps not far off; so that now, meeting a wandering foreigner aged eighteen she would look in his face for a likeness to her late husband, and at his feet for the scars.

The final stage of this course of reasoning presents us with the picture of Oedipus and Iocasta living together in mutual love, each having chosen to believe as truth the one per cent possibility that their marriage was lawful; building up for themselves a version of past events which was satisfactory and painless, even if it involved some dangerous corners; and pushing the terrible probability further and further into the recesses of forgetfulness—which in busy lives can be very deep; while his guilt retains for Oedipus just enough reality to act as a constant spur to make amends for the frightful wrong he may have inflicted on Iocasta and on Thebes, by devoting himself tirelessly to the tasks of a loving father of his family and of his people. This is the character so emphatically established for him in the opening scene of the play. Then at last, after sixteen or seventeen years, came the return of the plague; and Oedipus knew that the gods, who neither forget nor forgive, were at work, his respite was at an end and his ordeal before him. If Sophocles once set foot on the path of reasoning which supposes the gods to be just and Oedipus to be guilty, I see no point at which he could have turned aside before reaching the situation I have just described.

Take the words of the Priest of Zeus in lines 31 ff. 'We regard you, Oedipus, as the first of men, both in the ordinary chances of life and in dealings with the gods. Now help us, either by some utterance you have heard from a god, or perhaps a word from some man has given you knowledge. For with men of experience I observe this, that the results of their decisions live. You brought us good fortune before: now be the same as you were then.' 'Be the same' . . . Oedipus, resolute to be now utterly different from the man he was then, replies: 'There is not one of you whose sickness is as grievous as mine. I assure you, I have shed many tears, and paced many paths in the wanderings of anxious thought.'

The outcome of those pacing thoughts was now clear in his mind. There were three points. First, he must submit himself to public exposure of the two facts that he killed his father Laios and that Iocasta is his mother. Second: after the exposure, the choice would appear to be suicide or banishment—but suicide would admit defeat at the hands of Fate, and Oedipus would not admit defeat. He had sinned, and he would pay; but he had a right, even though guilty, to live. Third: there was one thing which was his own private concern, which Thebes—which even his children—need never know; and that was, the fact that his guilt had been knowingly incurred, that he had been aware of his own pollution from the beginning. That was between himself and Iocasta, and the gods. The city could be delivered, and that ultimate truth could remain his secret and hers, to carry silent to the grave.

Now, supposing Sophocles to have perceived—and I believe he did perceive it—that the story was capable of being developed along these lines, what did he in fact do with this potential material? To begin with, it was obvious that the story, so developed, acquired a moral and religious seriousness which it did not have before. On the other hand, to present such a story on the Attic stage involved insuperable difficulties. The whole drama now took place within one man's consciousness; Oedipus could speak no unveiled word to Iocasta, nor she to him, nor either to anyone else; so how could the true situation be conveyed to an audience? In fact, my own guess would be that the story as I have outlined it was something like what actually happened to Oedipus, but that the central truth of the matter dropped out after one generation of popular telling, and never reappeared until the dramatic imagination of Sophocles looked below the surface of the folk-tale and found it. But having found it he saw that such a conception was impossible to express in the conventional forms of tragedy, and even if the attempt were made it would be missed or rejected by most of the audience. Yet this conception was so exciting as drama, and morally and theologically so moving, that to abandon it entirely in favour of the popular, and morally nihilistic, version seemed like an abdication from the poet's prophetic task. Then this possibility is to be considered: that Sophocles in the end decided to write his play on the basis of the popular concept of an innocent Oedipus lured by Fate into a disastrous trap; but that, in order to record for ever his own deeper perception, he embodied in the play certain features, notably the incident at the banquet, which, if rationally examined, would suggest what the real story of Oedipus was. The play, of course, on a prima-facie interpretation makes good enough sense—almost good enough, though there are anomalies and contradictions which may prove disturbing even in a good performance. The dramatic power of a gradual revelation conceals the moral poverty of the theme. But all the serious difficulties of the plot vanish once they are seen as subtle contributions towards this other view of the character and situation of Oedipus.

First, the statement that he had believed that in avoiding Corinth he was avoiding parricide and incest now appears as an essential element in the make-believe world which Oedipus had to construct to protect his own sanity, and in which he lived safely for sixteen years. (This statement appears again in lines 990–7.) Secondly, his ignoring of Iocasta's reference to the maimed ankles is also explained: the disclosure must be carried out one stage at a time, and the killer of Laios revealed before the son of Iocasta was identified. The third point, which I have already mentioned briefly, is more important. It is the behaviour of Oedipus to Teiresias and Kreon, which evinces a lack of stability and common sense excusable perhaps in an adolescent, but entirely destructive of the godlike character given to Oedipus in the first scene. But Oedipus' wild and angry accusations make sense if Sophocles had in mind the situation I have suggested. On this view Oedipus, being willing himself to give his life for Thebes ('The king must die' was a familiar formula), and hoping for the help of the omniscient Teiresias in his desperately difficult task, is met with a blank refusal. As his own anger swells, he realizes that anger is the one thing which will make Teiresias speak. So he goads Teiresias with extravagant charges, whereupon Teiresias utters the whole truth. Even then the Chorus appear hardly to have heard it—the truth is not only incredible but inaudible to respectable old men. Then if they will not listen to Teiresias, perhaps Kreon will help—he may well have guessed who Oedipus is, he knew Laios, and is likely to have seen the scars. So Oedipus attacks him too. But Kreon gives nothing away. His scene, however, serves to give another dimension to Iocasta, as well as to prepare the audience for his important role in the last scene.

The play *Oedipus Tyrannus*, then, was written to tell the simple story which is familiar to us and was familiar to the contemporaries of Sophocles; that was the only story which he could expect to be understood and accepted. But I believe, on the evidence I have put before you, that as he wrote it the poet had also in mind another story, which may even have been the true story of Oedipus; and that his consciousness of this story and of its importance made him include certain elements which cannot be properly accounted for on the basis of the popular version; and made him, moreover, at numerous points in the dialogue use a double irony whose significance only appears when the possibility is considered that Oedipus at the beginning of the action has known for sixteen years in what a terrible position he is, and is now engaged in an act of voluntary atonement which will save his city at the price of destroying his own life.

This view makes the final scene, if possible, even more poignant. Iocasta, who has suppressed knowledge of the truth more completely than Oedipus, sees the end coming as early as line 765, where Oedipus asks for the old slave to be sent for; Iocasta knows, though Oedipus does not yet know, that this is the same man who took her infant son to the mountain and did not kill him. From that point on, Oedipus knows that both he and Iocasta know where they are going; but he must lead, and she must follow, without a word. When she has finally rushed out in despair, Oedipus, aware that he has sent her to her death, finds the only refuge from his anguish in taunting Iocasta with pride of birth. He cannot afford to weaken yet with tears, for he has still the last lap to run—the interview with the Theban shepherd. When that is over, he will no longer need to hold back anything.

From the old shepherd Oedipus forces the last drop of truth. Only then does he stand at the point where he had so often imagined himself standing—but imagination was feeble and useless and had given him barely a faint taste of the agony and horror into which his instinctive honour and courage had now led him. He suddenly sees the utmost depth. 'I should never have been born. What I am is now brought to light; and this light shall be my last.' He goes in, finds Iocasta as he knew he would find her; and reaches his own terrible fulfilment.

Much has been written about the pessimism of the ancient Greeks; and this play is usually included in the evidence—a play which shows a man guilty of hasty temper and a woman guilty of disparaging remarks about prophecy (both very common faults) but otherwise innocent—shows them both subjected to the most dreadful agony and humiliation by blind Chance or cruel Fate. There were, of course, many Greeks who would have called that a fair picture of human life. But such a picture implies a universe in which there is no place for *Dike*, Justice, as a divinity. I believe that Sophocles saw the myth of Oedipus as containing a deeper message, as illustrating a universe where *Dike* is the daughter of Zeus. He suggests that the sin of Oedipus was not a mere matter of hasty temper, but an obstinate neglect of divine warning in the pursuit of his passions and his ambitions; the taking of a risk he had no right to take, one which put a whole city in peril. Therefore his punishment is not a blind cruelty of Fate, but one more assurance that the world is ruled by *Dike*, that cause produces effect, that Nature pays every debt. Furthermore, the central figure of this drama now appears potentially in a different light, as being no longer a pitiful, helpless plaything of circumstance, a broken man acknowledging transcendent Powers whose purpose is at best mysterious, at worst gratuitously malevolent. He is a man capable both of evil and of good, a man conscious of *Dike* as a force in the universe which he honours, and which, in its operation against himself, he will obey with dedicated courage, acknowledging his own debt. That is a picture which defies pessimism, and gives both to man and to the gods an honourable part in the development even of the most painful and terrible events.

The question which I have raised in this paper may well have other aspects; but it is the dramatic aspect which opens the inquiry;

and I think it likely, having stuck my spade into the well-raked flower-bed of Sophoclean Tragedy, that it will be found I am not so much sowing a seed of uneasiness and doubt, as watering a well-rooted plant which conscientious gardeners have for many years guiltily regarded as a weed.

E. R. DODDS

On Misunderstanding the Oedipus Rex†

On the last occasion when I had the misfortune to examine in Honour Moderations at Oxford I set a question on the *Oedipus Rex*, which was among the books prescribed for general reading. My question was 'In what sense, if in any, does the *Oedipus Rex* attempt to justify the ways of God to man?' It was an optional question; there were plenty of alternatives. But the candidates evidently considered it a gift: nearly all of them attempted it. When I came to sort out the answers I found that they fell into three groups.

The first and biggest group held that the play justifies the gods by showing—or, as many of them said, 'proving'—that we get what we deserve. The arguments of this group turned upon the character of Oedipus. Some considered that Oedipus was a bad man: look how he treated Creon—naturally the gods punished him. Others said 'No, not altogether bad, even in some ways rather noble; but he had one of those fatal ἁμαρτίαι that all tragic heroes have, as we know from Aristotle. And since he had a ἁμαρτία he could of course expect no mercy: the gods had read the *Poetics*.' Well over half the candidates held views of this general type.

A second substantial group held that the *Oedipus Rex* is 'a tragedy of destiny'. What the play 'proves', they said, is that man has no free will but is a puppet in the hands of the gods who pull the strings that make him dance. Whether Sophocles thought the gods justified in treating their puppet as they did was not always clear from their answers. Most of those who took this view evidently disliked the play; some of them were honest enough to say so.

The third group was much smaller, but included some of the more thoughtful candidates. In their opinion Sophocles was 'a pure artist' and was therefore not interested in justifying the gods. He took the story of Oedipus as he found it, and used it to make an exciting play. The gods are simply part of the machinery of the plot.

† E. R. Dodds. "On Misunderstanding the *Oedipus Rex*," *Greece and Rome*, Vol. XIII (1966), 37–49. Reprinted by permission of The Clarendon Press, Oxford.

Ninety per cent of the answers fell into one or the other of these three groups. The remaining ten per cent had either failed to make up their minds or failed to express themselves intelligibly.

It was a shock to me to discover that all these young persons, supposedly trained in the study of classical literature, could read this great and moving play and so completely miss the point. For all the views I have just summarized are in fact demonstrably false (though some of them, and some ways of stating them, are more crudely and vulgarly false than others). It is true that each of them has been defended by some scholars in the past, but I had hoped that all of them were by now dead and buried. Wilamowitz thought he had killed the lot in an article published in *Hermes* (34 [1899], 55 ff.) more than half a century ago; and they have repeatedly been killed since. Yet their unquiet ghosts still haunt the examination-rooms of universities—and also, I would add, the pages of popular handbooks on the history of European drama. Surely that means that we have somehow failed in our duty as teachers?

It was this sense of failure which prompted me to attempt once more to clear up some of these ancient confusions. If the reader feels—as he very well may—that in this paper I am flogging a dead horse, I can only reply that on the evidence I have quoted the animal is unaccountably still alive.

I

I shall take Aristotle as my starting point, since he is claimed as the primary witness for the first of the views I have described. From the thirteenth chapter of the *Poetics* we learn that the best sort of tragic hero is a man highly esteemed and prosperous who falls into misfortune because of some serious (μεγάλη) ἁμαρτία: examples, Oedipus and Thyestes. In Aristotle's view, then, Oedipus' misfortune was directly occasioned by some serious ἁμαρτία; and since Aristotle was known to be infallible, Victorian critics proceeded at once to look for this ἁμαρτία, And so, it appears, do the majority of present-day undergraduates.

What do they find? It depends on what they expect to find. As we all know, the word ἁμαρτία is ambiguous: in ordinary usage it is sometimes applied to false moral judgements, sometimes to purely intellectual error—the average Greek did not make our sharp distinction between the two. Since *Poetics* 13 is in general concerned with the moral character of the tragic hero, many scholars have thought in the past (and many undergraduates still think) that the ἁμαρτία of Oedipus must in Aristotle's view be a moral fault. They have accordingly gone over the play with a microscope looking for moral faults in Oedipus, and have duly found them—for neither here nor anywhere else did Sophocles portray that insipid and unlikely character, the man of perfect virtue. Oedipus, they point out, is proud and over-confident; he harbours unjustified suspicions against Teiresias and Creon; in one place (lines 964 ff.) he goes so far as to express some uncertainty about the truth of oracles. One may doubt whether this adds up to what Aristotle would consider μεγάλη ἁμαρτία. But even if it did, it would have no direct relevance to the question at issue. Years before the action of the play begins, Oedipus was already an incestuous parricide; if that was a punishment for his unkind treatment of Creon, then the punishment preceded the crime—which is surely an odd kind of justice.

'Ah,' says the traditionalist critic, 'but Oedipus' behaviour on the stage reveals the man he always was: he was punished for his basically unsound character.' In that case, however, someone on the stage ought to tell us so: Oedipus should repent, as Creon repents in the *Antigone*; or else another speaker should draw the moral. To ask about a character in fiction 'Was he a good man?' is to ask a strictly meaningless question: since Oedipus never lived we can answer neither 'Yes' nor 'No'. The legitimate question is 'Did Sophocles intend us to think of Oedipus as a good man?' This *can* be answered—not by applying some ethical yardstick of our own, but by looking at what the characters in the play say about him. And by that test the answer is 'Yes'. In the eyes of the Priest in the opening scene he is the greatest and noblest of men, the saviour of Thebes who with divine aid rescued the city from the Sphinx. The Chorus has the same view of him: he has proved his wisdom, he is the darling of the city, and never will they believe ill of him (504 ff.). And when the catastrophe comes, no one turns round and remarks 'Well, but it was your own fault: it must have been; Aristotle says so.'

In my opinion, and in that of nearly all Aristotelian scholars since Bywater, Aristotle does *not* say so; it is only the perversity of moralizing critics that has misrepresented him as saying so. It is almost certain that Aristotle was using ἁμαρτία here as he uses ἁμάρτημα in the *Nicomachean Ethics* (1135ᵇ 12) and in the *Rhetoric* (1374ᵇ 6), to mean an offence committed in ignorance of some material fact and therefore free from πονηρία or κακία. These parallels seem decisive; and they are confirmed by Aristotle's second example—Thyestes, the man who ate the flesh of his own children in the belief that it was butcher's meat, and who subsequently begat a child on his own daughter, not knowing who she was. His story has clearly much in common with that of Oedipus, and Plato as well as Aristotle couples the two names as examples of the gravest ἁμαρτία (*Laws* 838 c). Thyestes and Oedipus are both of them men who violated the most sacred of Nature's laws and thus incurred the most horrible of all pollutions; but they both did so without πονηρία, for they knew not what they did—in Aristotle's quasi-legal terminology, it was a ἁμάρτημα, not an ἀδίκημα. That is why they were in his view especially suitable subjects for tragedy. Had they acted knowingly, they would have been inhuman monsters, and we could not have felt for them that pity which tragedy ought to produce. As it is, we feel both pity, for the fragile estate of man, and terror, for a world whose laws we do not understand. The ἁμαρτία of Oedipus did not lie in losing his temper with Teiresias; it lay quite simply in parricide and incest—a μεγάλη ἁμαρτία indeed, the greatest a man can commit.

The theory that the tragic hero must have a grave moral flaw, and its mistaken ascription to Aristotle, has had a long and disastrous history. It was gratifying to Victorian critics, since it appeared to fit certain plays of Shakespeare. But it goes back much further, to the seventeenth-century French critic Dacier, who influenced the practice of the French classical dramatists, especially Corneille, and was himself influenced by the still older nonsense about 'poetic justice'—the notion that the poet has a moral duty to represent the world as a place where the good are always rewarded and the bad are always punished. I need not say that this puerile idea is completely foreign to Aristotle and to the practice of the Greek dramatists; I only mention it because on the evidence of those Honour Mods. papers it would appear that it still lingers on in some youthful minds like a cobweb in an unswept room.

To return to the *Oedipus Rex*, the moralist has still one last card to play. Could not Oedipus, he asks, have escaped his doom if he had been more careful? Knowing that he was in danger of committing parricide and incest, would not a really prudent man have avoided quarrelling, even in self-defence, with men older than himself, and also love-relations with women older than himself? Would he not, in Waldock's ironic phrase, have compiled a handlist of all the things he must not do? In real life I suppose he might. But we are not entitled to blame Oedipus either for carelessness in failing to compile a handlist or for lack of self-control in failing to obey its injunctions. For no such possibilities are mentioned in the play, or even hinted at; and it is an essential critical principle that *what is not mentioned in the play does not exist*. These considerations would be in place if we were examining the conduct of a real person. But we are not: we are examining the intentions of a dramatist, and we are not entitled to ask questions that the dramatist did not intend us to ask. There is only one branch of literature where we are entitled to ask such questions about τὰ ἐκτὸς, τοῦ δράματος, namely the modern detective story. And despite certain similarities the *Oedipus Rex* is not a detective story but a dramatized folktale. If we insist on reading it as if it were a law report we must expect to miss the point.[1]

In any case, Sophocles has provided a conclusive answer to those who suggest that Oedipus could, and therefore should, have avoided his fate. The oracle was *unconditional* (line 790): it did not say 'If you do so-and-so you will kill your father'; it simply said 'You will kill your father, you will sleep with your mother.' And what an oracle predicts is bound to happen. Oedipus does what he can to evade his destiny: he resolves never to see his supposed parents again. But it is quite certain from the first that his best efforts will be unavailing. Equally unconditional was the original oracle given to Laius (711 ff.): Apollo said that he *must* ($\chi\rho\tilde{\eta}\nu\alpha\iota$) die at the hand of Jocasta's child; there is no saving clause. Here there is a significant difference between Sophocles and Aeschylus. Of Aeschylus' trilogy on the House of Laius only the last play, the *Septem*, survives. Little is known of the others, but we do know, from *Septem* 742 ff., that according to Aeschylus the oracle given to Laius *was* conditional: 'Do not beget a child; for *if* you do, that child will kill you.' In Aeschylus the disaster *could* have been avoided, but Laius sinfully disobeyed and his sin brought ruin to his descendants. In Aeschylus the story was, like the *Oresteia*, a tale of crime and punishment; but Sophocles chose otherwise—that is why he altered the form of the oracle. There is no suggestion in the *Oedipus Rex* that Laius sinned or that Oedipus was the victim of an hereditary curse, and the critic must not assume what the poet has abstained from suggesting. Nor should we leap to the conclusion that Sophocles left out the hereditary curse because he thought the doctrine immoral; apparently he did not think so, since he used it both in the *Antigone* (585 ff.) and in the *Oedipus at Colonus* (964 ff.). What his motive may have been for ignoring it in the *Oedipus Rex* we shall see in a moment.

I hope I have now disposed of the moralizing interpretation, which has been rightly abandoned by the great majority of contemporary scholars. To mention only recent works in English, the books of Whitman, Waldock, Letters, Ehrenberg, Knox, and Kirk-

1. The danger is exemplified by Mr. P. H. Vellacott's article, 'The Guilt of Oedipus', which appeared shortly after my talk. was delivered. By treating Oedipus as an historical personage and examining his career from the 'common-sense' standpoint of a prosecuting counsel Mr. Vellacott has no difficulty in showing that Oedipus must have guessed the true story of his birth long before the point at which the play opens—and guiltily done nothing about it. Sophocles, according to Mr. Vella-cott, realized this, but unfortunately could not present the situation in these terms because 'such a conception was impossible to express in the conventional forms of tragedy'; so for most of the time he reluctantly fell back on 'the popular concept of an innocent Oedipus lured by Fate into a disastrous trap'. We are left to conclude either that the play is a botched compromise or else that the common sense of the law-courts is not after all the best yardstick by which to measure myth.

wood, however much they differ on other points, all agree about
the essential moral innocence of Oedipus.

II

But what is the alternative? If Oedipus is the innocent victim of
a doom which he cannot avoid, does this not reduce him to a mere
puppet? Is not the whole play a 'tragedy of destiny' which denies
human freedom? This is the second of the heresies which I set out
to refute. Many readers have fallen into it, Sigmund Freud among
them; and you can find it confidently asserted in various popular
handbooks, some of which even extend the assertion to Greek tragedy in general—thus providing themselves with a convenient label
for distinguishing Greek from 'Christian' tragedy. But the whole
notion is in fact anachronistic. The modern reader slips into it
easily because we think of two clear-cut alternative views—either
we believe in free will or else we are determinists. But fifth-century
Greeks did not think in these terms any more than Homer did: the
debate about determinism is a creation of Hellenistic thought.
Homeric heroes have their predetermined 'portion of life'
($\mu o \hat{\iota} \rho \alpha$), they must die on their 'appointed day' ($\alpha \H{\iota} \sigma \iota \mu o \nu \, \hat{\eta} \mu \alpha \rho,$)
but it never occurs to the poet or his audience that this pre-
vents them from being free agents. Nor did Sophocles intend
that it should occur to readers of the Oedipus Rex. Neither
in Homer nor in Sophocles does divine foreknowledge of certain
events imply that all human actions are predetermined. If explicit
confirmation of this is required, we have only to turn to lines
1230 ff., where the Messenger emphatically distinguishes Oedipus' self-blinding as 'voluntary' and 'self-chosen' from the 'involuntary' parricide and incest. Certain of Oedipus' past actions were
fate-bound; but everything that he does on the stage from first to
last he does as a free agent.

Even in calling the parricide and the incest 'fate-bound' I have
perhaps implied more than the average Athenian of Sophocles' day
would have recognized. As A. W. Gomme put it, 'the gods know
the future, but they do not order it: they know who will win the
next Scotland and England football match, but that does not alter
the fact that the victory will depend on the skill, the determination, the fitness of the players, and a little on luck'. That may not
satisfy the analytical philosopher, but it seems to have satisfied the
ordinary man at all periods. Bernard Knox aptly quotes the prophecy of Jesus to St. Peter, 'Before the cock crow, thou shalt deny
me thrice.' The Evangelists clearly did not intend to imply that
Peter's subsequent action was 'fate-bound' in the sense that he

could not have chosen otherwise; Peter fulfilled the prediction, but he did so by an act of free choice.

In any case I cannot understand Sir Maurice Bowra's idea that the gods *force* on Oedipus the knowledge of what he has done. They do nothing of the kind; on the contrary, what fascinates us is the spectacle of a man freely choosing, from the highest motives, a series of actions which lead to his own ruin. Oedipus might have left the plague to take its course; but pity for the sufferings of his people compelled him to consult Delphi. When Apollo's word came back, he might still have left the murder of Laius uninvestigated; but piety and justice required him to act. He need not have forced the truth from the reluctant Theban herdsman; but because he cannot rest content with a lie, he must tear away the last veil from the illusion in which he has lived so long. Teiresias, Jocasta, the herdsman, each in turn tries to stop him, but in vain: he must read the last riddle, the riddle of his own life. The immediate cause of Oedipus' ruin is not 'Fate' or 'the gods'—no oracle said that he must discover the truth—and still less does it lie in his own weakness; what causes his ruin is his own strength and courage, his loyalty to Thebes, and his loyalty to the truth. In all this we are to see him as a free agent: hence the suppression of the hereditary curse. And his self-mutilation and self-banishment are equally free acts of choice.

Why does Oedipus blind himself? He tells us the reason (1369 ff.): he has done it in order to cut himself off from all contact with humanity; if he could choke the channels of his other senses he would do so. Suicide would not serve his purpose: in the next world he would have to meet his dead parents. Oedipus mutilates himself because he can face neither the living nor the dead. But why, if he is morally innocent? Once again, we must look at the play through Greek eyes. The doctrine that nothing matters except the agent's intention is a peculiarity of Christian and especially of post-Kantian thought. It is true that the Athenian law courts took account of intention: they distinguished as ours do between murder and accidental homicide or homicide committed in the course of self-defence. If Oedipus had been tried before an Athenian court he would have been acquitted—of murdering his father. But no human court could acquit him of pollution; for pollution inhered in the act itself, irrespective of motive. Of that burden Thebes could not acquit Oedipus, and least of all could its bearer acquit himself.

The nearest parallel to the situation of Oedipus is in the tale which Herodotus tells about Adrastus, son of Gordies. Adrastus was the involuntary slayer of his own brother, and then of Atys, the son of his benefactor Croesus; the latter act, like the killing of Laius, fulfilled an oracle. Croesus forgave Adrastus because the killing was unintended (ἀέκων), and because the oracle showed that it was the will of 'some god'. But Adrastus did not forgive himself: he committed suicide, 'conscious' says Herodotus, 'that of all men known to him he bore the heaviest burden of disaster'. It is for the same reason that Oedipus blinds himself. Morally innocent though he is and knows himself to be, the objective horror of his actions remains with him and he feels that he has no longer any place in human society. Is that simply archaic superstition? I think it is something more. Suppose a motorist runs down a man and kills him, I think he *ought* to feel that he has done a terrible thing, even if the accident is no fault of his: he has destroyed a human life, which nothing can restore. In the objective order it is acts that count, not intentions. A man who has violated that order may well feel a sense of guilt, however blameless his driving.

But my analogy is very imperfect, and even the case of Adrastus is not fully comparable. Oedipus is no ordinary homicide: he has committed the two crimes which above all others fill us with instinctive horror. Sophocles had not read Freud, but he knew how people *feel* about these things—better than some of his critics appear to do. And in the strongly patriarchal society of ancient Greece the revulsion would be even more intense than it is in our own. We have only to read Plato's prescription for the treatment to be given to parricides (*Laws* 872 c ff.). For this deed, he says, there can be no purification: the parricide shall be killed, his body shall be laid naked at a cross-roads outside the city, each officer of the State shall cast a stone upon it, and then the bloody remnant shall be flung outside the city's territory and left unburied. In all this he is probably following actual Greek practice. And if that is how Greek justice treated parricides, is it surprising that Oedipus treats himself as he does, when the great king, 'the first of men', the man whose intuitive genius had saved Thebes, is suddenly revealed to himself as a thing so unclean that 'neither the earth can receive it, nor the holy rain nor the sunshine endure its presence' (1426)?

III

At this point I am brought back to the original question I asked the undergraduates: does Sophocles in this play attempt to justify the ways of God to man? If 'to justify' means 'to explain in terms of *human* justice', the answer is surely 'No'. If human justice is the standard, then, as Waldock bluntly expressed it, 'Nothing can excuse the gods, and Sophocles knew it perfectly well.' Waldock does not, however, suggest that the poet intended any attack on the gods. He goes on to say that it is futile to look for any 'message' or 'meaning' in this play: 'there is no meaning', he tells us, 'in the *Oedipus Rex*; there is merely the terror of coincidence'. Kirkwood seems to take a rather similar line: 'Sophocles', he says, 'has no theological pronouncements to make and no points of criticism to score.' These opinions come rather close to, if they do not actually involve, the view adopted by my third and last group of undergraduates—the view that the gods are merely agents in a traditional story which Sophocles, a 'pure artist', exploits for dramatic purposes without raising the religious issue or drawing any moral whatever.

This account seems to me insufficient; but I have more sympathy with it than I have with either of the other heresies. It reflects a healthy reaction against the old moralizing school of critics; and the text of the play appears at first sight to support it. It is a striking fact that after the catastrophe no one on the stage says a word either in justification of the gods or in criticism of them. Oedipus says 'These things were Apollo'—and that is all. If the poet has charged him with a 'message' about divine justice or injustice, he fails to deliver it. And I fully agree that there is no reason at all why we should require a dramatist—even a Greek dramatist—to be for ever running about delivering banal 'messages'. It is true that when a Greek dramatic poet had something he passionately wanted to say to his fellow citizens he felt entitled to say it. Aeschylus in the *Oresteia*, Aristophanes in the *Frogs*, had something to say to their people and used the opportunity of saying it on the stage. But these are exceptional cases—both these works were produced at a time of grave crisis in public affairs—and even here the 'message' appears to me to be incidental to the true function of the artist, which I should be disposed to define, with Dr. Johnson, as 'the enlargement of our sensibility'. It is unwise to generalize from special cases. (And, incidentally, I wish undergraduates would stop writing essays which begin with the words 'This play *proves* that . . .'. Surely no work of art can ever 'prove' anything: what value could there be in a 'proof' whose premises are manufactured by the artist?)

Nevertheless, I cannot accept the view that the *Oedipus Rex* conveys *no* intelligible meaning and that Sophocles' plays tell us nothing of his opinions concerning the gods. Certainly it is always dangerous to use dramatic works as evidence of their author's opinions, and especially of their religious convictions: we can legitimately discuss religion *in* Shakespeare, but do we know anything at all about the religion *of* Shakespeare? Still, I think I should venture to assert two things about Sophocles' opinions:

First, he did not believe (or did not always believe) that the gods are in any human sense 'just';

Secondly, he did always believe that the gods exist and that man should revere them.

The first of these propositions is supported not only by the implicit evidence of the *Oedipus Rex* but by the explicit evidence of another play which is generally thought to be close in date to it. The closing lines of the *Trachiniae* contain a denunciation in violent terms of divine injustice. No one answers it. I can only suppose that the poet had no answer to give.

For the second of my two propositions we have quite strong *external* evidence—which is important, since it is independent of our subjective impressions. We know that Sophocles held various priesthoods; that when the cult of Asclepius was introduced to Athens he acted as the god's host and wrote a hymn in his honour; and that he was himself worshipped as a 'hero' after his death, which seems to imply that he accepted the religion of the State and was accepted by it. But the external evidence does not stand alone: it is strongly supported by at least one passage in the *Oedipus Rex*. The celebrated choral ode about the decline of prophecy and the threat to religion (lines 863–910) was of course suggested by the scene with Creon which precedes it; but it contains generalizations which have little apparent relevance either to Oedipus or to Creon. Is the piety of this ode purely conventional, as Whitman maintained in a vigorous but sometimes perverse book? One phrase in particular seems to forbid this interpretation. If men are to lose all respect for the gods, in that case, the Chorus asks, τί δεῖ με χορεύειν; (895). If by this they mean merely 'Why should I, Theban elder, dance?', the question is irrelevant and even slightly ludicrous; the meaning is surely 'Why should I, an Athenian citizen, continue to serve in a chorus?' In speaking of themselves as a chorus they step out of the play into the contemporary world, as Aristophanes' choruses do in the *parabasis*. And in effect the question they are asking seems to be this: 'If Athens loses faith in religion, if the views of the Enlightenment prevail, what significance is there in tragic drama, which exists as part of the service of the gods?' To that question the rapid decay of tragedy in the fourth century may be said to have provided an answer.

In saying this, I am not suggesting with Ehrenberg that the character of Oedipus reflects that of Pericles, or with Knox that he is intended to be a symbol of Athens: allegory of that sort seems to me wholly alien to Greek tragedy. I am only claiming that at one point in this play Sophocles took occasion to say to his fellow citizens something which he felt to be important. And it *was* important, particularly in the period of the Archidamian War, to which the *Oedipus Rex* probably belongs. Delphi was known to be pro-Spartan: that is why Euripides was given a free hand to criticize Apollo. But if Delphi could not be trusted, the whole fabric of traditional belief was threatened with collapse. In our society religious faith is no longer tied up with belief in prophecy; but for the

ancient world, both pagan and Christian, it was. And in the years
of the Archidamian War belief in prophecy was at a low ebb; Thucydides is our witness to that.

I take it, then, as reasonably certain that while Sophocles did not
pretend that the gods are in any human sense just he nevertheless
held that they are entitled to our worship. Are those two opinions
incompatible? Here once more we cannot hope to understand
Greek literature if we persist in looking at it through Christian
spectacles. To the Christian it is a necessary part of piety to believe
that God is just. And so it was to Plato and to the Stoics. But the
older world saw no such necessity. If you doubt this, take down the
Iliad and read Achilles' opinion of what divine justice amounts to
(xxiv. 525–33); or take down the Bible and read the Book of Job.
Disbelief in divine justice as measured by human yardsticks can
perfectly well be associated with deep religious feeling. 'Men', said
Heraclitus, 'find some things unjust, other things just; but in the
eyes of God all things are beautiful and good and just.' I think that
Sophocles would have agreed. For him, as for Heraclitus, there is
an objective world-order which man must respect, but which he
cannot hope fully to understand.

IV

Some readers of the *Oedipus Rex* have told me that they find its
atmosphere stifling and oppressive: they miss the tragic exaltation
that one gets from the *Antigone* or the *Prometheus Vinctus*. And I
fear that what I have said here has done nothing to remove that
feeling. Yet it is not a feeling which I share myself. Certainly the
Oedipus Rex is a play about the blindness of man and the desperate insecurity of the human condition: in a sense every man must
grope in the dark as Oedipus gropes, not knowing who he is or
what he has to suffer; we all live in a world of appearance which
hides from us who-knows-what dreadful reality. But surely the *Oedipus Rex* is also a play about human greatness. Oedipus is great,
not in virtue of a great worldly position—for his worldly position is
an illusion which will vanish like a dream—but in virtue of his
inner strength: strength to pursue the truth at whatever personal
cost, and strength to accept and endure it when found. 'This horror
is mine,' he cries, 'and none but I is *strong* enough to bear it'
(1414). Oedipus is great because he accepts the responsibility for
all his acts, including those which are objectively most horrible,
though subjectively innocent.

To me personally Oedipus is a kind of symbol of the human
intelligence which cannot rest until it has solved all the riddles—
even the last riddle, to which the answer is that human happiness
is built on an illusion. I do not know how far Sophocles intended

that. But certainly in the last lines of the play (which I firmly believe to be genuine) he does generalize the case, does appear to suggest that in some sense Oedipus is every man and every man is potentially Oedipus. Freud felt this (he was not insensitive to poetry), but as we all know he understood it in a specific psychological sense. 'Oedipus' fate', he says, 'moves us only because it might have been our own, because the oracle laid upon us before birth the very curse which rested upon him. It may be that we were all destined to direct our first sexual impulses towards our mothers, and our first impulses of hatred and violence towards our fathers; our dreams convince us that we were.' Perhaps they do; but Freud did not ascribe his interpretation of the myth to Sophocles, and it is not the interpretation I have in mind. Is there not in the poet's view a much wider sense in which every man is Oedipus? If every man could tear away the last veils of illusion, if he could see human life as time and the gods see it, would he not see that against that tremendous background all the generations of men are as if they had not been, ἴσα καὶ τὸ μηδὲν ζώσας (1187)? That was how Odysseus saw it when he had conversed with Athena, the embodiment of divine wisdom. 'In Ajax' condition', he says. 'I recognize my own: I perceive that all men living are but appearance or unsubstantial shadow.'

ὁρῶ γὰρ ἡμᾶς οὐδὲν ὄντας ἄλλο πλὴν
εἴδωλ,' ὅσοιπερ ζῶμεν, ἢ κούφην σκιάν.

So far as I can judge, on this matter Sophocles' deepest feelings did not change. The same view of the human condition which is made explicit in his earliest extant play is implicit not only in the *Oedipus Rex* but in the *Oedipus Coloneus*, in the great speech where Oedipus draws the bitter conclusion from his life's experience and in the famous ode on old age. Whether this vision of man's estate is true or false I do not know, but it ought to be comprehensible to a generation which relishes the plays of Samuel Beckett. I do not wish to describe it as a 'message'. But I find in it an enlargement of sensibility. And that is all I ask of any dramatist.

P. H. VELLACOTT

The Chorus in *Oedipus Tyrannus*†

I recently saw a film of Sophocles' *Oedipus Tyrannus* containing some fine performances and some sensitive direction. One scene I

† P. H. Vellacott, "The Chorus in *Oedipus Tyrannus*," *Greece and Rome*, Vol. XIV (October 1967), 109–125.

Reprinted by permission of the author and The Clarendon Press, Oxford.

particularly remember because it made clear a point which has usually been either shirked or muddled through both in production and in scholarly comment. When Oedipus was listening to Iocasta's speech about the oracle given to Laius, he followed her with close attention as far as the phrase 'a place where three roads meet'. Then he started, turned away from her, and walked past her towards the camera with a brooding face. Behind him we saw Iocasta continuing the speech which Oedipus obviously was not hearing. The two lines 718–19 which Oedipus did not hear contain some scope for emotion on Iocasta's part (ἔρριψεν, and the rare tribrach in the fifth foot), but Oedipus was unaware of it, thinking about the road to Daulia, and heard nothing to remind him of what he knew very well, that he was standing on two scarred feet.

That is easy in a film; the screen showed only the two figures and faces. It is also feasible in a modern theatre, with a reduced Chorus tucked away at the sides of the stage. What happens at Epidaurus, where there are fifteen listening Elders possibly closer to the audience than the two actors? I once asked a distinguished writer on Greek tragedy what he thought of this; he replied with some hesitancy that he had always assumed that Oedipus was meant either not to hear, or not to grasp, what Iocasta said; but he admitted that this was unsound criticism.

It is unsound from the point of view of the reader or student. An audience in a theatre can accept what it is looking at, which is Oedipus engrossed in recollection and deaf to the words which, had he heard them, would have stopped the play then and there. For the words are: 'When the child was two days old, Laius bound together the joints of its feet, and threw it out . . .' But the people sitting in the theatre were not the poet's only audience; both reason and evidence—not least the whole of Aristophanes' *Frogs* —show that tragedians wrote also for readers, reciters, and listeners who could study and evaluate what they had to say line by line and word by word. In real life it might well happen that a man in a critical moment would accidentally fail to hear just those words which could have told him the truth he was seeking; but this is not real life, it is art; a play written by a man who chose every word he wrote. Now let us study this speech of Iocasta's.

Here is a summary of it: Laius received an oracle that his son would kill him; twenty years later Laius was killed by robbers; twenty years earlier he had exposed his infant son. This is an odd way for Iocasta to tell her story. Its unnaturalness is skilfully concealed; but why did Sophocles compose it so?—unless it was to make possible exactly that handling of the scene which I have described; so that Oedipus could be seen to start at the mention of the road-junction, and move away, not listening to the more significant words which followed, alluding to the pierced feet. In that case, why did Sophocles write those significant words at all? For Oedipus to ignore, and the audience to forget? Iocasta had no need to mention this detail. Sophocles, beyond question, put the words there to be heard and understood by someone. By whom? There is only one answer: by the Chorus. Let us concede, for the time being, that it is conceivable for such significant words to be spoken, and to be ignored by the character to whom they are spoken, and to whom they are vitally relevant. Though the situation is, I believe, without parallel in extant Greek tragedy, this may be an instance where a character is forced by emotion to break convention. But the Chorus are not a character in the story; they are there as a reliable point of reference; they are there to hear, to see, and to comment. Iocasta's reference to the maimed feet is only one of many things that they hear and put together with the rest; yet it alone would ensure that by line 1032 ('the joints of your feet could witness') they know the whole truth; and so put out of court the usual interpretation of the Third Stasimon. So, without more anticipation, let us examine the character and function of the Chorus in this play.

The Theban Elders on their first entrance claim an actual and personal part in the dramatic situation. The feeling uppermost in their minds is apprehension: 'I am taut with suspense, my trembling heart pulses with fear.' They come because they have heard that Creon has returned with a message from Delphi; but their opening question seems to imply that they do not yet know what the message is: 'O sweetly speaking message of Zeus, with what import have you come?' They are afraid because they, their families and friends, and the life of the whole city are under hourly threat from the plague. They identify themselves with Thebes: 'As you have put me on oath, so I will speak. I did not kill Laius. . . .' They are closely associated in government with Oedipus, and offer advice without waiting to be asked for it; Iocasta calls them ἄνακτες, princes. We may consider the Elders, then, as men fully involved in the situation in Thebes, but outside the particular personal emotions which concern Oedipus and Iocasta.

The Elders regard Oedipus with devotion born of gratitude for his services. Towards Iocasta and Creon they feel the loyalty due to the royal family. In Teiresias they have unreserved faith, identifying his powers of prophecy with those of Phoebus (284–5); while in the first phrase they utter (151) they identify the word of Phoebus with that of Zeus. While we are waiting for Teiresias a curious passage occurs, showing an equivocal attitude to the unknown killer of Laius. Information about him, they say, is a matter of 'obscure and ancient reports' (290); 'he was said to have been killed by certain travellers'. Creon told us (122) more confidently and more specifically that a servant of Laius had escaped, and had reported that the king was killed by a gang of bandits. Perhaps we should not press the point that Iocasta (850) says that all Thebes knew the story of the bandits; or the further point, that the Chorus later on (1051) reveal that they know of the surviving eyewitness to Laius' death, and know too that he was the man to whom had been entrusted the disposal of Iocasta's child. Leaving these points aside, we may still wonder why neither the Elders nor the king, until line 765, suggest sending for the servant who reported the killing. Oedipus in fact (293) refers to him as 'the eye-witness', τὸν ἰδόντα. The next remark of the Chorus (294–5) is curiously ambiguous. 'If he is capable of fear, he will not stay when he hears of your dreadful curse.' Who will not stay? Do they mean the eye-witness or the murderer? Oedipus' reply assumes that they mean the murderer.[1] In any case the Elders, though offering cooperation, show as little readiness as Oedipus does to grasp the one obvious clue which Sophocles has mentioned for us several times. However, Teiresias has now arrived, 'the one man of all men in whom the truth lives'. Not only Oedipus, but fifteen other shrewd, responsible men, who like him are in personal danger and looking for a way out, listen to every word the prophet speaks. They know that he knows the truth and will tell it.

At first Teiresias will tell nothing. Naturally the king is put out; but since Oedipus himself had just reminded them (280–1) that prophecy cannot be forced, it is surely with uneasiness and astonishment that the Elders watch the king suddenly lose his temper, and hear his outrageous accusations against the prophet. Then the prophet speaks to the king: 'You are the cursed polluter of the land.' What do the Elders think now?

Oedipus has been their king for seventeen years; but some of these Elders are old enough to be his father; he is a comparative newcomer—and a foreigner; and, as they know very well, he first appeared in Thebes shortly after the death of Laius, when they were distracted with fear of the Sphinx. The king dares Teiresias to say it again. The Elders hear him say again: 'You are the killer of the man whose killer you seek.' This plain statement has the authority of Apollo: could it be true? The Elders know—Sophocles has made this clear—that it could indeed be true. More unforgivable insults follow from the king; and Teiresias has more to say: 'You have been living in secret shame with your nearest of kin.' Could even this be true? Oedipus makes no direct answer; instead, he suddenly accuses Teiresias of being in Creon's pay. Teiresias

1. Another ambiguity: does οὐ μενεῖ mean 'he will not stay in hiding, but will give himself up', or 'he will not stay to be caught, but will flee the country'?

denies it, and mentions 'your parents'. Oedipus, as if caught off his guard quickly asks, 'Who were my parents?' Teiresias replies: 'You will learn today.' This is the only statement of Teiresias that could be called veiled or ambiguous; and even it says clearly enough: 'You are not the son of Polybus.' His other statements are not only clear but repeated two, three, or four times. During these exchanges the Elders are not expected to say anything; they have all the time they need for listening, remembering, calculating.[2] How old was Oedipus when he came? About eighteen. How long was it then since Laius and Iocasta were married? The Elders know; it was about nineteen years. Whether or not they had known about the royal birth and exposure (line 1051 says they had; but since that comes later in the play it should not be pressed), this calculation must surely have shaken them. Teiresias repeats once more everything he has said, and departs. Oedipus goes into the palace; and the Chorus take position for the First Stasimon.

They were frightened men before Teiresias arrived. What do they say now? 'Who is the man,' they ask, 'of whom the prophetic voice from Delphi has spoken?' ('Let's go back to the last subject but one', said Humpty Dumpty.) Recall that, a long way back in the play, Creon brought a message from Delphi telling the Thebans to find the killer of Laius. 'Who is this man?' the Elders now ask. Teiresias has just told them plainly that it is Oedipus. Then why don't they ask instead: 'Surely Teiresias can't be right?' Because if they ask that, the answer is inevitable: 'He can be right; he always is.' This the Elders cannot yet face; naturally they need time to absorb such a shock. So they try to forget for the moment what they have heard—but do not quite succeed. 'Who is the man of whom Delphi spoke, as having committed with bloody hands the most unspeakable of unspeakable crimes?' This last phrase may be meant to refer merely to the killing of Laius; but its superlative intensity suggests an involuntary revelation that what they are thinking of is the last words of Teiresias, which were of parricide and incest. Quickly they revert to the innocuous question, 'Who is the man?', assuming an academic interest in the bold robber of seventeen years ago for whom now the hunt is afoot. Apollo and the Fates are after him; he is at this moment wandering, alone and afraid, among forest and caves, like a rogue bull. With this vivid picture they resist the statement of Teiresias, that he is not alone in the forests, but living in the royal palace in Thebes, surrounded by obedient servants and a loving family; thus they reassure themselves (and who can blame them?) that they did not hear what they heard.

[2] Professor Bernard Knox, in *Oedipus at Thebes* (Yale, 1957), ch. 3, par. 4, and especially p. 150, shows the importance of the constant recurrence in this play of such words as ἐξισοῦν, συμμετρεῖν. Measurement, calculation of time—these are of the essence of the plot, as of the imagery.

After their first strophe and antistrophe, feeling a little steadier, they risk a reference to the prophet's words. 'What Teiresias said is disturbing, most disturbing. We can't accept it, we can't refute it; we don't know what to say. All is wild surmise, whether we look to the present or to the past.' Then they find a way of escape, in the form of a question which can be made to sound intelligent: 'Was there any feud between the house of Labdacus and the son of Polybus? I never heard of any.' The question is disingenuous; but again, who is to blame them? They are anxious to find a face-saving formula to offer as a comment on the shattering scene they have had to witness. Unfortunately for their peace of mind, they heard the plain words which Teiresias spoke. Convention allows a Chorus to be slow, or timid, or foolish, or all three: it does not allow them to be either stone deaf or imbecile. They have heard and understood; now they must make a decision. They decide to ignore, for the present, what they have heard, the challenge is too severe, too sudden for them. They conclude by asserting, first, their piety—'The whole truth is known to Zeus and Apollo'; then, their common sense—'We should not place too much trust in human prophets'; and finally their loyalty—'Oedipus won his throne by his services to Thebes; I will never think evil of him.' And there they leave it for the present.

But the Elders are not to be spared anything. They next have to listen while their revered king heaps outrageous insults on the innocent Creon and demands his death. This will set them on edge; for their loyalty was to Creon before ever Oedipus set foot in Thebes. When Iocasta enters, they watch the king's relapse into gloomy passiveness. Creon goes. The Chorus-Leader looks at Oedipus and Iocasta; and he speaks—to Iocasta: 'Madam, why don't you take him into the palace without delay?' An extraordinary thing to say, unless Oedipus is visibly in no state either to go unaided or to resist being 'taken' by his wife. The line can only mean that he is trembling and out of control. This is hardly surprising—if we accept that Oedipus heard and understood what Teiresias said, and knew that the Chorus had heard and understood it too; if we realize how possible it must now seem to him and to them that every word of Teiresias was true.

Let us look at the part which the Elders play in the Kommos, lines 649 ff. Their position is embarrassing; for the king's behaviour has plainly been inexcusable, and his excited rage (ὦ πόλις πόλις, 629) has been so effectually rebuked and punctured by Iocasta. Line 650 sounds like an exhausted capitulation: 'Well, then, what do you want me to do?' They reply: 'When a friend has laid himself under a curse, you should never, on unproved report, bring a dishonourable accusation against him.' This is a pointed

remark; both Creon (644–5) and Oedipus (249 ff.) had laid themselves under a curse; Creon's position in the eyes of the king is the
king's position in the eyes of the Elders. They have heard Teiresias
accuse Oedipus: there is much to make the charges seem probable;
but they are not proved, and the Elders have rightly refused to lay
Oedipus under such an accusation. They ask that the same fairness
be shown to Creon. Oedipus, however, is still choked with emotion, and does not see the comparison. He tells the Chorus that
what they are asking means his death or banishment. In saying this
Oedipus clearly implies: 'If you won't let me get rid of this traitor
Creon, he will get rid of me.' The Chorus answer with an emotional 'No!' and call as witness the Sun, 'the god who is foremost
of gods.' Why the Sun? Compare line 1426, where Creon protests
that the polluted Oedipus must not be let outdoors for the sun to
behold. Surely the Elders by this phrase suggest that the one
thought in their minds is not at all the unproved charge against
Creon, but the unproved charge against Oedipus, of incest and parricide. It is this which makes them continue with desperate
emphasis: 'May I die an outcast from gods and from men, if I have
any such thought. It is the suffering of Thebes', they say, 'which
makes us beg for peace at any cost between our rulers.' Oedipus
acknowledges their genuine feeling, and sullenly yields.

Iocasta, instead of taking Oedipus indoors, insists on his staying
where he is and recovering himself; and when she asks him
directly: 'What was your quarrel about?' he replies: 'Creon says
that I killed Laius.' An oblique and dubious statement, carrying its
own psychological interest; and it leads at once to Iocasta's speech
of revelation. This speech the Elders listen to, not with blank and
empty minds, but with everything Teiresias told them, everything
they remember about the death of Laius and the coming of Oedipus, everything they have witnessed in the last ten minutes, clear
and ready in their minds. They hear Iocasta say: 'An oracle of
Phoebus came to Laius, that he would be killed by his son and
mine.' The Elders know, if Iocasta does not, that Teiresias has said
that this oracle has already been fulfilled. Iocasta tells of the killing
of Laius. The Chorus hear Oedipus himself recognize one detail in
her account, ask for others, recognize them all, and exclaim: 'Alas,
all this is now utterly clear.' The details he acknowledges include
the personal appearance of Laius, his mode of travel, and the
number of his attendants. For the third time, there is mention of
the servant who escaped; and now at last Oedipus asks for him to
be brought. Then this very request gives the Chorus yet further
confirmation of Teiresias' words. Iocasta says: 'When this eye-
witness came from the scene of the murder, and saw you the king of
Thebes in place of the dead Laius, he begged me to let him go

away to the country, as far as possible from this city.' Can the Elders have missed the inference that the servant had recognized Oedipus? If that inference was not intended, why did Sophocles write lines 758–62 in that particular form? Or at all?

Next the Elders hear Oedipus' story of his journey to Delphi, and the reason for it. They learn, first, that even while Oedipus still lived in Corinth there was doubt about his parentage. Next they hear the oracle that was given to Oedipus, not only confirming the oracle given nineteen years earlier to Laius, but tallying with everything that Tieresias has said today. They hear Oedipus describe the killing of Laius—possibly noting that he says he killed 'every man' in the party. All this they listen to, and fit together. Because they are the Chorus, and not a character in the story, they may not, either by hazard or by temperament, hear one part and not hear another. When Oedipus speaks of his last hope, that the man who escaped told of 'robbers', not of 'a robber', can the Elders have thought this pathetic straw worth a moment's attention? Would any servant in such circumstances be likely to admit that he and four companions had allowed the king to be killed by a single assailant? To the Elders this argument of the king's must seem as futile as Iocasta's speech, lines 848–58, which is meant to sound like comfort but contains no comfort at all. Oedipus accepts it for its good intention: 'You are quite right', he says; but all that she has asserted is that prophets are sometimes wrong; and this is quite irrelevant to the present situation, in which Oedipus is evidently banished by his own curse laid on the killer of Laius. The king and queen go in together, leaving the Chorus to recite the Second Stasimon.

During the scene that has passed it has become clear beyond reasonable doubt that Oedipus killed Laius. Teiresias' second charge, that Oedipus was Laius' son, and therefore Iocasta's, has now received in the Second Episode confirmation from (1) the oracle given thirty-five years ago to Laius, and (2) the oracle given seventeen years ago to Oedipus—coupled with the fact that Oedipus is married to the widow of the man he killed. Finally there are the simple calculations of time, which fit the prophecies exactly. For all these reasons we must assume that by the end of the Second Episode the Elders see Oedipus' double guilt staring them in the face. If Oedipus is guilty, then for the last seventeen years he has, whether intentionally or not, deceived them, and polluted Thebes; he is the cause of the plague. The Elders begin with a prayer.

> May the destiny that follows me through life be one that wins the name of pious purity in all words and deeds; purity from all words and deeds against which are established those laws of lofty range, laws brought into being in the clear regions of the sky,

whose father is Olympus alone; laws begotten by no mortal human nature, nor shall oblivion ever lay them to sleep; divinity is powerful in them, and never grows old.

The Elders are in the presence of the king who has absolute authority over them; it is natural they should shrink from speaking openly. But the prayer for purity is, as plainly as they dare utter, a protestation to the gods that they wish to dissociate themselves from the polluted man who has broken the holiest laws of the universe. What, in fact, are the laws which the Elders refer to in phrases of such sublimity? This Ode, following so eventful a scene, must surely bear some reference to events of the play; the Elders are not just singing a hymn chosen at random out of the book. What laws have been broken in the play so far? Two: one which says, Thou shalt not fly into a rage against thy kinsman, nor accuse him unjustly; and another which says, Thou shalt not express scepticism about the words of prophets. The first of these is an excellent rule, but one of ethical expediency rather than of fundamental morality. As for the second, the Chorus themselves came near to breaking it in line 500: 'It is not proved that any mortal prophet knows more about the future than I do.' To suggest that these two faults fittingly introduce the theme of *hybris* in the next stanza is stretching the argument somewhat; as offences against heaven, they are simply not commensurate with the lofty splendour of these lines about the Olympian laws.

Professor R. P. Winnington-Ingram, in a recently published essay,[3] says: 'Few odes of Sophocles have led to more perplexed discussion.' Why has there been this perplexity? A clue may well be found in Jebb's note on line 216, introducing the First Episode. He summarizes the Teiresias-scene thus: 'Teiresias declares that the murderer is Oedipus.' In other words, Jebb ignored the second and more horrifying part of what Teiresias said—like the Elders, but without their reasons. He similarly ignored the fact that the Chorus listen to, and understand, what they hear in the Second Episode, and add it to what they learnt in the First. This curious attitude which Jebb adopted had a far-reaching effect on his view of the play; and how far-reaching its effect was on other people's view of the play may be judged from the programme-note to the 1965 Cambridge performance of *Oedipus Tyrannus*, which repeats (eighty-two years after) exactly the same omission. If the whole text of the play is looked at and listened to, it is evident that the Elders at the beginning of the Second Stasimon are aware that Oedipus is polluted by two acts which are not less terrible for being—as they believe—unwitting. Their awe-inspiring phrases must refer, then,

3. 'Tragedy and Greek Archaic   *Influence* (London, 1965).
Thought', in *Classical Drama and Its*

to two laws based in the very being of man: Thou shalt not shed thy father's blood; Thou shalt not enter thy mother's bed.

The second stanza begins: 'Hybris begets the tyrant.' They do not yet dare to accuse Oedipus openly; they satisfy their feelings with general statements; but these general statements will be found to correspond, with remarkable exactness, to what the Elders now know to be true of Oedipus. Why do they feel that he is guilty of *hybris*? First, the killing of Laius, even though Oedipus could not know who he was (the presence of a herald, by the way, showed that he was a king), appears by Oedipus' own account as something of a massacre, and out of proportion to the occasion. Secondly, a man who has received the oracle Oedipus received shows a singular disregard for divine warning if he first kills a man whose grey hair shows him to be twenty years older, and then marries a widow who married her first husband about a year before he himself was born. These considerations, so far from being 'outside the play', are circumstantially placed in the play by the author in many detailed allusions. Finally, the Chorus realize that Oedipus, whether intentionally or not, has for seventeen years been revered as the saviour of Thebes and is now revealed as the city's polluter and the cause of the plague. They are angry, and are not asking whether they are being just or injust. Their word for Oedipus' conduct is ὕβρις, and most Greeks would have agreed with them. Their veneration has changed to abhorrence; and with this feeling comes added fear; for they are the king's close associates, and when gods punish the guilty, the innocent are likely to fall too.

'Hybris begets the tyrant.' The *hybris* which slaughtered Laius and his men, and risked marrying his widow for the sake of ambition, begot the tyrant who now demands the death of a tried friend, and a brother-in-law, on ill-founded surmise. They continue: '*Hybris*, if in its folly it becomes surfeited with improper and unprofitable possessions, first climbs to the topmost pinnacles, then takes a sheer plunge to its helpless fate, where no firm foothold is to be found. There is, however, a kind of ambition that benefits the State, and this I pray Heaven may never bring to an end. Heaven I shall not cease to regard as our protector.' They have written Oedipus off; his guilt being so evident, his fall can scarcely be an hour behind. And in the last two lines the Elders make it clear (for the heavenly record) that while they approve Oedipus' exploit in defeating the Sphinx, it is God, and no mortal, that they now look to for deliverance.

The mounting confidence of the Elders' denunciation reaches its climax in the second strophe. 'If any man pursues an arrogant path in deed or word, showing no fear of Justice, and paying no heed to temples of the gods, may an evil fate destroy him because of his perverse wantonness, if he will not gain his advantage righteously, nor keep himself from impious deeds, but in his folly will touch things untouchable. Where such deeds have been done, what man after that shall boast that he can ward off from his life the arrows of the gods? If deeds like this are held in honour, what is the point of any religious observance?'

Every line of this is packed with significance.[4] Oedipus showed 'arrogance of deed' when he killed Laius, 'arrogance of word' when he demanded Creon's death and called Teiresias a liar. He showed himself Δίκας ἀφόβητος, 'without fear of Justice,' and lacking 'reverence for temples of the gods', when only a day or two after receiving Apollo's warning in the temple at Delphi, he gave rein to his rage and killed a grey-haired man. Therefore the Elders now pray, not in general terms, but with clear and particular intent, that Oedipus may be destroyed (κακά νιν ἕλοιτο μοῖρα) because of his δυσπότμου χλιδᾶς. χλιδή is exactly the word for a euphemistic reference to the incestuous marriage. Next, 'If he will not gain his advantage righteously'. Oedipus came to Thebes a deprived man, seeking a city, a home, and a throne; these κέρδη he gained by killing Laius. The Elders already have ample reason to presume the truth of what Teiresias said; but perhaps we should also give them credit for realizing that Oedipus, according to his own story, could hardly have been in Thebes an hour, much less several days, without knowing that the man he had killed on the road was the king; then, since the prize for defeating the Sphinx was this man's widow, and since these two facts tallied exactly with what had been prophesied in Delphi, nothing could be clearer than the necessity for caution. If in killing Laius he had already failed to 'keep himself from impious deeds' (890), at least he now had the chance to avoid 'touching things untouchable.' This crime too he had committed 'in his folly' (891). After this, how can he hope to escape? If he should escape, religion would be a mockery.

The Elders have now fully and specifically convicted Oedipus, and prayed for his destruction. They conclude their Ode by reverting to their opening theme, which was their own safety, their own piety and purity. They add a subtle emphasis to the contrast between themselves and Oedipus by using (897–8) the two words

---

4. I cannot agree with Professor Winnington-Ingram's remarks on this Ode in the essay alluded to earlier. He says that in the second stanza the Chorus 'appear to shoot off at a tangent'; whereas my present argument indicates an inevitable progression of thought. He speaks of the 'conventional catalogue of sins' in the third stanza, and later says: 'Oedipus was not guilty of these offences.' He takes the character of Oedipus as necessarily fixed by the closing lines of the First Stasimon, and does not allow that the revelations of the Second Episode can alter the judgement of the Chorus.

ἄθικτον and σέβων, which have just used of the guilty king (ἀσέπτων, ἀθίκτων, 890-1).

I will make no more pious pilgrimages to the pure [literally, 'untouchable'] navel of the earth, nor to the temple at Abae, nor to Olympia, if these things shall not fit one to the other, so that all men point to them. Therefore, Zeus Almighty—if thou art truly so named—let not this situation escape the notice of thee and of thy immortal rule! For the ancient prophecies about Laius are fading, and men now ignore them. Nowhere is Apollo honoured as infallible. Religion is vanishing.

The central point of this stanza is the repetition of the prayer that Oedipus may be destroyed. If he is not, the Elders say, the gods need expect no more worship from them; religion is in a bad way anyhow. Anger carries them to the point where they mention *with regret* that hitherto it has never been proved that Laius' unknown killer was in fact his son. They want to feel that Apollo's prophecies are infallible, even at the cost of open pollution; they want the various pieces of evidence that have come to light during the past hour, and which 'fit together' so convincingly in their eyes, to carry equal conviction with all men, so that they shall 'point at' Oedipus as the cause of the plague, and get rid of him.

When Iocasta enters at line 911, we can only guess how much she knows. What we see is that she who scoffed at Apollo's prophecies now comes with prayers to Apollo. The Chorus-Leader's answer to the Messenger from Corinth (γυνὴ δὲ μήτηρ ἥδε τῶν κείνου τέκνων, 928) is usually called 'dramatic irony'; but after the outspoken recital of the Second Stasimon it is hard not to see these words as chosen by the Leader with deliberate condemnatory intent. The same interpretation fits equally their next remarks (1051-3): 'The man who gave the child to the Corinthian shepherd is, I think, that same servant who escaped when Laius was killed; but Iocasta is the best person to tell you that.' And the third intervention of the Chorus in this scene has the same sinister undertone: 'Why has the queen rushed away in a passion? I fear that from her silence may burst forth some disaster.' They are not asking for enlightenment; they know what Iocasta has gone indoors to do, and it is the beginning of the answer to their prayer.

To the Chorus's question Oedipus replies—and his reply is a *tour-de-force* of desperate, theatrical, last-ditch defiance of the known truth—'I am the child of Chance; *she* is my mother who bore me.' The Third Choral Ode is an answer to this claim. It is to be noted, however, that though Oedipus remains on stage for the next scene, the Elders do not at first address him, but allude to him in the third person as if he were not there. They recall saying (500) 'It has yet to be proved that any prophet can outdo me.' That was their argument then for believing in the innocence of Oedipus; it now becomes their argument for believing in his guilt. What Sophocles is delineating is the self-centredness and self-assurance of ordinary men even in the face of tragedy.

If I am a prophet or have any skill in judgement, I swear by Olympus that tomorrow's full moon shall not come without your knowing, Cithaeron, that it is you that Oedipus honours as his fatherland, and his nurse, and his mother; and you shall be celebrated by us as the bringer of good gifts to our king. Phoebus, Healer, may this be pleasing to you!

Who was it, son—which of the long-lived nymphs was it who lay with Pan of the mountains and then gave birth to you? Or perhaps your mother was one whom Apollo, the giver of oracles, loved? The highland pastures are all dear to him. Or perhaps Hermes of Cyllene, or perhaps the divine Bacchus who lives on the mountain-ridges, received you as a gift from one of the nymphs of Helicon, with whom he often sports!

The Chorus begin this statement by backing it with an appeal to Olympus, the father (867) of those eternal laws which are now to be vindicated by the downfall of the man who has broken them. They then address Cithaeron, whose function as the 'nurse' of Oedipus is today leading to the discovery of his parents. Oedipus had claimed to be the son of Chance, thus endorsing Iocasta's principle that it is best 'to live at random' (979). When he says, 'Chance is the mother who bore me, and through my life the changing moons have marked the depth or height of my fortune', he is in a sense disclaiming personal guilt (whether this is his real feeling, or an attitude taken in defiance of the increasingly antagonistic Elders), protesting that he has taken life and its offers as he found them, acting on the guidance of the moment. In reply the Elders say, by inference: We know who his mother is—Cithaeron, which was also his nurse and his *father*land. Cithaeron gave him good gifts, first saving his life, later revealing his parentage. Oedipus will honour Cithaeron for this.' The whole tone is bitterly and triumphantly ironical. The last line of the first stanza ('Apollo, may this be pleasing to you!') recalls the penultimate line of the Second Stasimon: 'Nowhere is Apollo honoured as infallible' (909), and implies: 'May the disclosure of Oedipus' crimes vindicate your prophecies, destroy the man who has defied you, and persuade you to bring the plague to an end.'

The irony continues into the antistrophe. If the Elders had dared to be a little more outspoken, instead of τίς they would have said ποία; Oedipus' fanciful naming of Τύχη as his mother is thrown back at him with scorn. 'Your mother one of the long-lived ones?' The particle ἄρα after μακραιώνων points the sarcasm; so does the suggestion of *four* possible fathers; so do the two conventional clauses in lines 1103 and 1109, explaining how very likely it is that such a thing might happen. The irony of the Elders is not overt; here, as in the previous Ode, decorum is preserved and the words can bear an innocent interpretation. It is possible that many in the original audience took this Ode at its face value, as an expression of 'joyous excitement' (so Jebb puts it), 'delight in the prospect that Oedipus will prove to be a native of the land'. The less naïve, who followed the dawning of truth in the minds of the Chorus, must also have been led—some of them at least—to ask at what point all became clear to Oedipus himself. This is outside the scope of the present essay; but the understanding of the Chorus is relevant at every point to that more central question.

The Fourth Episode runs its inevitable and foreseen course, without any comment from the Elders. What is being disclosed is what they know already. With the departure of Oedipus their prayer has been answered, their victory is won. Unaware that a surprise is still in store for them, they drop their ironical tone. They have felt anger and scorn and have expressed their feelings; now the cause is removed; and first reflection returns, then pity follows. The pitifulness of death is their first theme. They guess that Iocasta has already found the only escape; they presume that Oedipus will follow her lead; they themselves are old, and every year brings them nearer to the end.

> Alas for you, generations of mortal men! How insignificant seem to me all the number of your years! Who is there, what man is there that gains more of happiness than the mere seeming, and then even the seeming vanishes! From you I learn, from your terrible, pitiable fate, Oedipus, I learn to call no earthly creature happy. . . .
> Time that sees everything has dragged you reluctant into the light; Time judges that unholy marriage where you have long been both begetter and begotten. Alas, son of Laius, if only—if only I had never seen you! I mourn like one who pours from his lips a funeral song. It is true to say that you once brought us back to life, and now you have closed our eyes in death.

They are sure that he has paid his debt with suicide. They forget their resentment, and remember the qualities which won their love. Above all they see themselves and Oedipus side by side as mortal men whose best years are gone before they have had time to learn wisdom, whose common inheritance is capacity for suffering, and weakness amidst the forces of Fate.

Then comes the Messenger from inside the palace. In reply to him, and on the appearance of the blinded Oedipus, the Elders make several remarks of astonishment, sympathy, or horror. There is no doubt that they pity him; but it would have been so much easier if he had done the expected thing and killed himself. Presently Oedipus becomes aware of them, and speaks to the Leader (1321 ff.): 'Ah, my friend, you are still there—my faithful subject; in spite of everything, blind as I am, you still care for me. I know you—I can't see you, but I recognize your voice.' Does the Elder come forward and say: 'Here I am, Oedipus; though you are fallen, I am still your friend; though you cannot see me, I touch your hand'? No. The sympathy drops away; the horror remains. 'Whatever made you blind yourself?' 'There was nothing I could take pleasure in seeing', says Oedipus; and the Leader replies: 'That is perfectly true.' Oedipus begs them to lead him out of Thebes; the Leader replies: 'I wish I had never known you.' Oedipus says: 'I wish I had died as an infant'; and the Leader answers: 'So do I.' Oedipus says: 'Instead, I lived to suffer all the agony that life can inflict'; and the Leader tells him: 'It was foolish to blind yourself; you would be better dead.' Oedipus answers this in a speech of passionate anguish, at the end of which he begs all the Elders, not the Leader only, to come near and just touch him, to break for a moment his awful isolation. Not one of them says: 'Here is my hand.' The Leader replies for them all: 'Fortunately, here comes Creon; he is the man to deal with your requests.'

If the scene I have just described is produced in fidelity to Sophocles' text, it should show Oedipus surrounded by emptiness, trying always to establish contact, and finding nothing either animate or inanimate that he can touch. The sympathy of the Chorus is perfunctory; their concern is for themselves. Oedipus has ascended out of their reach on to the heroic plane; and this the ordinary man mistrusts. The one comfort in this harrowing spectacle is that Oedipus cannot see their hard faces, that he still believes the Leader to be his faithful friend (1322); and after Creon's arrival he can forget the Elders. They have only one more speech, and that is the brief postscript to the play, addressed to the audience. Whether these lines are genuine or not, thy add nothing further to Sophocles' picture of the Elders of Thebes.

It is interesting to compare Sophocles' Chorus in the last scene of this play with Aeschylus' Chorus at the close of *The Cheophori*. Orestes had been given by Apollo not a warning but a command; yet he was as free to neglect the command as Oedipus was to ignore the warning; and Orestes' polluting act was committed not unwittingly but deliberately. The women of Aeschylus' Chorus recognize Orestes' guilt, but give him their fervent blessing as he departs to seek purification in Athens. It is easier for them, since

they, being slaves, have no responsibilities; but in fact Aeschylus'
Chorus express on their author's behalf a deep concern with the
question, 'What can be done to deal with guilt?' This is a philosophical question; and Sophocles here is not concerned with that
sort of philosophy. He is picturing human life against its background of the unalterable universe, and showing what happens
when guilt is revealed. His Elders represent the harsh, timid world
where sympathy dare not compromise conformity; they remember
their position in society and in the State, a position they will have
to go on occupying when the heroic catastrophe is over and voices
are no longer hushed with the sense of tragedy. The Elders do not
ask what the gods think of all this, only what is expedient for them
and the city to do. Theirs is not a moral problem, but a social or
political one. The moral problem they leave with Oedipus himself,
who recognizes that this is right: 'No one', he says, 'can carry my
guilt but myself.' Euripides brings his Heracles, in the play of that
name, to a similar conclusion; Heracles, like Oedipus, decides to
live, and deal with his own guilt, fitting it into a new pattern of life.
This is the heroic road, to be followed by the few; the many must
join the Elders and busy themselves with ritual purification and the
return to normal life.

In this article I have stuck closely to my title, and studied only
the part taken by the Elders in this play. I have tried to show that
the author meant his audience to understand that from the beginning of the Second Stasimon the Chorus are convinced of Oedipus'
double guilt. This does not necessarily imply that the truth is
equally clear to Oedipus at the same stage; but my earlier article
('The Guilt of Oedipus', *Greece & Rome* xi (1964), 137 ff.)
showed reasons for believing that Sophocles intended to suggest, to
those prepared to reason, that Oedipus had known the probable
truth even before his marriage.

To contemplate so radical a change in our understanding of so
familiar and notable a work is indeed disturbing; and I am not sur-
prised that Professor E. R. Dodds (see his article, 'On Misunderstanding the *Oedipus Rex*', *Greece & Rome* xiii (1966), 37 ff.),
noting what my conclusions were (though not very exactly), knew at
once that they were wrong, classed me with the 'moralists' who
mistake what Aristotle meant by ἁμαρτία, and dismissed my argument in an after-dinner footnote. The three sections of Professor
Dodds's article make three valuable statements about the play. The
first section, which includes his reference to my article, is about the
meaning of ἁμαρτία. My article, however, was concerned not with
what Aristotle wrote about Sophocles, but with what Sophocles
wrote about Oedipus. It is true that ἁμαρτία, as Aristotle uses it in

connexion with the 'tragic hero', is not a moral concept; but the text of *Oedipus Tyrannus* contains nothing about ἁμαρτία, and does contain emphatic references to ὕβρις, which is always a moral concept.

Professor Dodds says: 'By treating Oedipus as an historical personage and examining his career from the 'common-sense' standpoint of a prosecuting counsel Mr. Vellacott has no difficulty in showing that Oedipus must have guessed the true story of his birth long before the point at which the play opens—and guiltily done nothing about it.' To 'treat Oedipus as an historical personage' ought to mean to gather mythological information about him from all possible sources, as Velikovsky did in *Oedipus and Akhnaton*. My article dealt only with the information selected and presented by Sophocles: I 'examined his career' only in the text of the play. It is not surprising that I 'had no difficulty' in reaching my conclusion, since Sophocles was not composing a cross-word puzzle but intended his meaning to be seen. And since at the opening of the play Oedipus institutes an inquiry into a crime, and almost the whole action of the play consists in sending for witnesses and hearing evidence, until at last the killer is revealed—since that is the play, why should 'the standpoint of a prosecuting counsel' be an unsuitable standpoint for its interpretation?

Professor Dodds rightly insists on the critical principle that 'what is not mentioned in the play does not exist'. I asked at one point, 'What were Oedipus' reflections as he left Delphi?' Is this question 'outside the play'? No. Sophocles makes Oedipus tell us specifically what he was thinking at that time: he was preoccupied with the problem, How shall I avoid fulfilling this shameful oracle? This is natural (and it disposes incidentally of what Professor Dodds says about the prophecy being unconditional—whether unconditional or not, no one would expect any man to do anything but try to avoid it). Sophocles, however, invites us to ask this very question by making Oedipus give a quite unacceptable account of the way he proposed to avoid it, namely by keeping as far away from Corinth as possible. In the speed of performance this absurdity can be forgotten; in the study of the text it demands attention.

If a tragic poet has presented a well-known story to a popular audience on a national occasion, and has not only provided what was publicly expected of him in the form of a swift and gripping drama, but has also woven into its fabric the ever-present suggestion of another, more startling, more searching, religious and moral interpretation, skilfully concealed from those who would be shocked, clear to those who are ready to see what they find; if this was Sophocles' achievement in *Oedipus Tyrannus*, why should it be called a 'botched compromise'?

THOMAS GOULD

The Innocence of Oedipus†

Some modern readers take comfort from the fact that what the gods made Oedipus do—kill his father and take his father's place with his mother—happened years before the action of the play begins; these fated incidents are "outside" the play, therefore, as Aristotle says all illogicalities should be. The plot that grips us, it is felt, concerns these horrible memories incidentally only. The essential plot is one of wilful self-discovery. Here is how Dodds sums it up, for instance:

> Oedipus might have left the plague to take its course; but pity for the suffering of his people compelled him to consult Delphi. When Apollo's word came back, he might still have left the murder of Laius uninvestigated; but pity and justice require him to act. He need not have forced the truth from the reluctant Theban herdsman; but because he cannot rest content with a lie, he must tear away the last veil from the illusion in which he has lived so long. Teiresias, Jocasta, the herdsman, each in turn tries to stop him, but in vain: he must read the last riddle, the riddle of his own life. The immediate cause of Oedipus' ruin is not "Fate" or "the gods"—no oracle said that he must discover the truth—and still less does it lie in his own weakness; what causes his ruin is his own strength and courage, his loyalty to Thebes, and his loyalty to the truth. In all this we are to see him as a free agent, hence the suppression of the hereditary curse.

There are two things that make this theory attractive in the eyes of many readers. First, by declaring the patricide and incest to be incidental to the action, we can avoid the most distressing consequences of the Freudian and Platonic suggestion according to which our excitement at a play must be explained in terms of our own secret involvement. (It is much nicer to think of ourselves as bravely hunting for our true identities than as trying to cope with ancient sexual troubles.) And second, of course, the theory seems to solve the problem raised by our conviction that a play about a man who was not a "free agent" could not move us.

There is an essential distinction, then, according to this theory, between what Oedipus did those many years ago when he committed patricide, then incest, and the things he does within the course of the plot itself. The former may have been fated; but in each

† From Thomas Gould, "The Innocence of Oedipus: The Philosophers on Oedipus the King," part 3, *Arion*, 5 (Winter 1966), 502–506. Reprinted by permission.

move that we see him make on stage he has a choice, there is a decision he must come to. Here is Bernard Knox's version:

> The hero is faced with a choice between possible (or certain) disaster and a compromise which if *accepted* would betray the hero's own conception of himself, his rights, his duties. The hero *decides* against compromise, and that *decision* is then assailed, by friendly advice, by threats, by actual force. But he *refuses* to yield; he *remains true to himself*, to his physis, that "nature" which he inherited from his parents and which is his identity. From this *resolution* stems the dramatic tension . . . from the *stubborn insistence* of Oedipus at Thebes on knowing the full truth, first about Laius' murder and then about himself, and from old Oedipus' *resolve* to be buried in Attic soil. In each play the hero is subjected to pressure from all sides . . . Oedipus tyrannos runs into Tiresias' majestic refusal to speak, the compromising advice of Jocasta and her final desperate appeal, the agonized supplication of the herdsman at the last moment. Later at Colonus he faces the strong disapproval of Theseus, the revulsion of the chorus, the arguments, threats, and violence of Creon, and the appeal of his son . . . The Sophoclean hero and his situation are best described in that marvelous image which in the last play of all compares the blind old man to "some sea cape in the North, with storm waves beating against it from every quarter" . . . *O.C.* 1240–1. Like the cape, the hero *rides out the buffeting* of the storm and *remains unmoved*.

Nobody would want to deny that there is much truth in this manner of summing up what is stirring and admirable about the typical Sophoclean hero. It can surely be overdone, however. The refusal to yield or compromise is also a characteristic of a number of non-heroc figures in Sophocles' plays, most spectacularly Creon in the *Antigone*. (Creon does yield in the end, of course, after the gods make clear where they stand; but the same is true of Philoctetes too, after all.) Refusing to take the prudent course in order to remain true to one's nature is admirable only if one's nature is itself admirable.

What we usually mean when we say that one man remained true to his nature, whereas another did not, is that the first man, unlike the second, eschewed mere survival or security, or perhaps a short-lived or wicked power or pleasure, because he was motivated by a remoter and nobler vision of what is truly worth preserving or pursuing. Thus Knox speaks of Oedipus' remaining "true to himself, to his *physis*, that 'nature' which he inherited from his parents and which is his identity." (Notice that there is no room here for the Stoic and Christian theory of a decision as an original surge of energy. A "decision" is taken to be a move toward one alternative because that appears to the agent to fit better than other possible courses do with his vision of how he would like things to be. This is still the most practical assumption unless we are wrestling with problems of evil and the concept of a god who is invariably benign.) But good men and bad men alike can act according to their characters, their essential natures, if they are given an opportunity—that is, if they are put in a situation where at least one course open to them has calculable consequences that fit with the thing they value most. If there were no such moments, we would never be sure what a man's character was. And the admirableness or despicableness of his character is most clearly seen when the price for taking the right path is very high. The real difference between the "decisions" that resulted in Oedipus' committing patricide and incest and the "decisions" that led him to discover what he had done is that the latter, unlike the former, are so set up that we can see by the alternative to which he was attracted that his character was admirable. And even that should not be overstressed: which of us in his place would have let Thebes languish in the plague or have failed to pursue the hunt for the killer of Laius or for the identity of his parents in response to Tiresias' absurd-sounding accusations or Jocasta's sudden, inexplicable plea? Even at the last moment, when Oedipus knows in his heart what he will hear in a minute from the reluctant herdsman, is Oedipus' persistence really a feat that none of us would be capable of?

It would seem to take two things to make a dilemma "tragic": a protagonist who is an excellent man—one whose vision of life makes him act well even when compromise or prudence would have prolonged his existence (or his power or comfort or reputation); and a universe in which a good action can sometimes lead to bitter unhappiness, whereas less good actions would have been rewarded with things rightly prized as worth pursuing. If you have the former only, a man who chooses rightly, then you can conclude, like Socrates, that the things this good man gives up were not really worth the having. In that case an unjust death, for instance, will be like the execution of Socrates, no occasion for tears at all if it is correctly understood. On the other hand, the introduction of the second factor, a world where the most worth-while things can only be got by being the kind of man whom we should not admire, brings with it a fresh problem. The goodness of the good man who, in order to be true to his nature, turns down these truly worth-while things, needs some explanation, some further justification; otherwise he will appear quixotic or just foolish. That is, as Socrates and Plato were not slow to point out, tragedians tend to imply that the reason why one ought to be good is apparently *not* that being good brings us the most rewarding experiences possible in human life. But that thesis can be maintained, the philosophers argued, only if we assume that the gods do not in fact ensure that good men get good things, bad men bad things. If you are a humanist through and through, if, in other words, you believe that you can defend your notion of human excellence on rational grounds, introducing no irrational or inscrutable divinities—or no divinities who act otherwise than to reinforce the "humane" conduct of affairs—then Sophoclean tragedy is absurd. And so it would seem that fate and divine causation are a necessity for a play like the *Oedipus*: if it were not for the presence of this supernatural and essentially incomprehensible force we should have to conclude either 1) that it was all just a very sad accident, and Oedipus ought not to feel too badly, or 2) that Oedipus should not be so sure that his suffering was not a payment for some genuine fault, or 3) that Oedipus was undoubtedly rewarded in the end if he was truly good.

It is often presented as self-evident, indeed blazingly clear, that Sophocles chose to dramatize Oedipus' discovery of his old crimes, not the actual commission of those crimes, because the former are self-willed, whereas the latter were not. Only in this way, it is asserted, could he play down the traditional role of fate in the legend and make of it a moving play, one about a free agent acting on his own. But it is just as possible to explain his choice with the observation that at the time when Oedipus was actually committing the crimes he *thought* he was the master of his own life—he thought that gods merely reinforced the law that men of good intention tended to be rewarded for their efforts—whereas on that terrible day when he was made to see what he had done, he could see how wrong he had been, how horrible and unpredictable the hand of fate had been all along. "Let my lot move where it will," he concludes (*O.T.* 1458).

ἀλλ᾽ ἡ μὲν ἡμῶν μοῖρ᾽, ὅποιπερ εἶσ᾽, ἴτω.

And even the self-revelation is not really self-caused. The god sent the plague, then directed Oedipus to find the killer of Laius; and perhaps the god sent the messenger from Corinth as well—at least that is the feeling we are given when the Corinthian arrives with his fateful information just as Jocasta sacrifices to Apollo, "because you are the nearest *daimōn*" (919). Oedipus accepts the title "perpetrator" (1331) only for the self-blinding. That alone strikes the others on stage as something that Oedipus should be held responsible for. But Oedipus points out that he had been reduced to so wretched a position by the gods that, horrible as the consequences of the blinding were, they were nevertheless less horrible than the alternatives—to kill himself and so look on his parents, or live seeing and so look on his children.

PHILIP WHEELWRIGHT

The Guilt of Oedipus†

If we compare the best Hellenic studies of the last two or three decades with those of the half-century preceding, three new emphases become apparent: anthropological, psychological, and semantic. The change has been gradual, of course; and it might be objected that anthropology, in particular, is no new arrival, having been a factor in the critical consciousness of western Europe almost since the founding of the Royal Anthropological Institute in the early 1870's. But although that is true, and although scattered anthropological references can be found in the books and textual annotations of the older classicists, there are two reasons, I think, why the influence of anthropology did not become a substantial factor in classical scholarship until somewhat recently. One reason was the natural intellectual lag between any large discovery and the full realization of its pertinence. Partly the ingrained conservatism of many (by no means all) classical scholars, and partly the magnitude of the field newly opened up, made the process of reinterpretation a gradual one. The other reason lay in the uncertainty and lively disagreement among anthropologists themselves regarding the theoretical substructure of their researches. Until the turn of the century the animism of Tylor and Spencer exercised strong influence, especially in England; and such theories offered little to classical scholars that would change the tenor of their thinking or the direction of their researches. Belief in ghosts, in dreams, and in magic had always been a popular disposition, exploited by every teller of tales, without need of gloss.

But another anthropological theory began to find expression in the first decade of our century, which was to affect classical procedures a great deal. This was the theory variously called animatism, pre-animatism, and theory of mana—*protopsychism* might denote it best—associated particularly with the names of T. K. Preuss in Germany, R. R. Marett in England, and (as has been mentioned in another context), Lucien Lévy-Bruhl in France: that the primary religious phenomenon, the primordial stage in religious evolution (if we choose to think chronologically), is something vaguer and more fluid than either gods or human or ancestral souls; that it is an undefined sense of *presence*, stirring awe and perhaps dread in

† From Philip Wheelwright, *The Burning Fountain* (Bloomington: Indiana University Press, 1954), Chapter XI, pp. 218–231. Copyright © 1954 by Indiana University Press. Reprinted by permission of the publisher.

the beholder, capable on the one hand of developing at length into an object of reverence, and on the other of inviting attempts at magical control. Such is declared to have been the primitive belief-matrix from which religion, myth, and magic gradually, and sometimes divergently, evolved. The clearest indication of the power of the new theory to affect classical scholarship appears in Gilbert Murray's emphasis on the "error of treating Homer as primitive, and more generally in our unconscious insistence on starting with the notion of 'gods.' " Although Murray's specific evidences were drawn from within his own field of study, the new anthropological emphasis on intangibles was creating a climate of opinion and an openness of intellectual sensibility most favorable to his view.

The psychological element in classical modernism owes most, I suspect, to Nietzsche. The Nietzschean symbols of Apollo and Dionysus, although they oversimplified the many-sided phenomena of the Greek mind, provided a schema of interpretation which, so far as it went, was relevant. Moreover it set limits to the over-intellectualization of the Greek achievement of which traditional scholarship has often been guilty; and in doing so it invited attention to a rich field of evidence and allusion which the older scholars had not adequately explored. The effective presence of dark, vague chthonic forces, lacking the clear bright outlines and specious personality of the Olympian gods, was an aspect of the Greek thinkers' world which in the heyday of classical scholarship could be, if not quite neglected, at least explained away as atavisms. The Nietzschean rehabilitation of Dionysus, backed by such related German theories as Schopenhauer's philosophy of the will and von Hartmann's of the unconscious, and subsequently by the experimental approach to unconscious phenomena associated largely with the name of Freud, encouraged a disposition to look for non-rational mental factors in the interpretation of human phenomena. When this trend of psychological voluntarism (largely German, since the analogous work of de Biran, Ravaisson, and Fouillée in France exercised no comparable influence) began to unite early in the present century with the new protopsychic anthropology emanating largely from England, the result was to provoke the more forward-looking classicists—Jane Harrison and Gilbert Murray, for instance—to reëxamine their postulates of method and interpretation. Sometimes enthusiasm pushed them too far, as in Miss Harrison's celebrated cry, "There, I *knew* Zeus was only that old snake!" But a revised equilibrium was sought, and, in such admirable scholars as Werner Jaeger, Georges Méautis, and the late Francis M. Cornford, eventually found.

Of course the outstanding, or at any rate the most vociferated example of psychological method applied to classical problems has been Freud's Oedipus theory. Whatever the clinical uses of that provocative idea (and I suspect they have been overplayed) its interpretive value for an understanding either of the ancient legend or of Sophocles' two plays is sharply limited. For it is a commonplace among classical scholars that Oedipus himself never exhibits the well-known complex that bears his name. His marriage to Jocasta was a matter of civic duty: having rid the Thebans of the baleful Sphinx by answering her riddle correctly, he received the throne of Thebes and the widowed queen to wife as his due reward. There is no indication in Sophocles' play or in any of the surviving records of the ancient myth, that Oedipus and Jocasta were drawn to each other erotically. But clearly Freud's interpretation of the Oedipus pattern could hold good of the ancient story only if there were an erotic attraction, whether conscious or repressed, between Oedipus and Jocasta, and moreover only if they felt, or if at least one of them felt, some conflict, however dimly, between the two relationships of son-mother and husband-wife.

Freud, to be sure, foresaw and met the objection after a fashion. The fact that Oedipus performed both acts, the slaying of his father and the bedding of his mother, without suspecting the true relationships, is in Freud's view "a deviation from the analytical subject matter which is easily intelligible and indeed inevitable." Inevitable, he explains, because of the need for "a poetic handling of the material"; for Freud's idea of poetry and the poetic seems to be pretty much limited to its alleged psychic function as a ritualized substitution for ideas which in their native form are suppressed. Intelligible, he goes on to explain, because "the ignorance of Oedipus is a legitimate representation of the unconsciousness into which, for adults, the whole experience has fallen; and the doom of the oracle, which makes or should make the hero innocent, is a recognition of the inevitability of the fate which has condemned every son to live through the Oedipus complex." Thus in interpreting the Greek myth of Oedipus as an embodiment of that psychotic pattern which he has named the Oedipus complex Freud is not insisting on the motivations of the characters in Sophocles' play but on the general unconscious acceptance of that pattern, by reason of which the myth took strong hold of the Greek popular imagination, finally causing Sophocles to recognize its unparalleled dramatic possibilities.

The first palpable expression of incestuous and patricidal elements in Oedipus' own psyche occurs, so far as I know, in Dryden and Lee's late seventeenth century version of the tragedy. In the opening scene of their *Oedipus*, Jocasta addresses her husband as though haunted by some dark intuition of her true relationship with him:

When you chid, methought
A mother's love start [*sic*] up in your defence,
And bad me not be angry. Be not you;
For I love Laius still, as wives should love,
But you more tenderly, as part of me.

So much was Dryden's work. Nathaniel Lee, who wrote the second act, becomes tediously explicit:

. . . This horrid sleep
Dash'd my sick fancy with an act of incest:
I dreamt, Jocasta, that thou wert my mother;
Which, though impossible, so damps my spirits,
That I could do a mischief on myself,
Lest I should sleep, and dream the like again.

And Dryden, back on the job again in Act III, has Oedipus tell of an omen which struck him like "a pestilential blast":

A young stork
That bore his aged parent on his back;
Till weary with the weight, he shook him off,
And peck'd out both his eyes.

It would seem to have been Dryden and his collaborator then, not Sophocles, who introduced the Oedipus complex into literature. But the Dryden-Lee *Oedipus* is an inferior play, and the Oedipus story as they develop it is a hothouse growth, so artificial as to have lost most of its properly *mythic* character. Let us therefore look back to Sophocles' great play, the *Oedipus Tyrannus*, and inquire what its depth-meaning really is. For if we are to understand an archetype rightly, we must study it in its mature and artistically finished expressions even more painstakingly than in its cruder psychological and anthropological embodiments.

Erich Fromm, in *The Forgotten Language*, raises just this question of the depth-meaning of the play. Rejecting Freud's interpretation as inconsistent with the play's premises, he offers an alternative hypothesis of his own: namely that the Oedipus myth is "a symbol not of the incestuous love between mother and son but the rebellion of the son against the authority of the father in the patriarchal family; that the marriage of Oedipus and Jocasta is only a secondary element, only one of the symbols of the victory of the son, who takes his father's place and with it all his privileges." The dramatic conflict presented by Sophocles recapitulates, in Fromm's view, the prehistoric struggle between the matriarchal and the patriarchal forms of social organization. To substantiate this interpretation he appeals to Bachofen's theory that the earliest human sexual relations were promiscuous, and therefore, since only the mother's parenthood could be known, the inheritance of blood and hence of authority had to descend through her. Woman, therefore, Bachofen deduces, must have been the earliest lawgiver, and since the character of divinity in any period tends to reflect certain basic characteristics of human society, he draws the corollary that the religion of the Olympian gods was predated by a religion in which mother archetypes, dire and awful goddesses of which the Furies are the best known classical survival, were the supreme powers. Then in subsequent history (so the theory runs) man revolted against his servile role, and gradually succeeded in subduing woman, in establishing a patriarchal order on earth and the dynasty of the Olympian gods in heaven.

On the basis of Bachofen's provocative but tenuous theory Fromm amplifies his hypothesis, suggesting "that the hostility between father and son, which is the theme running through Sophocles' trilogy, is to be understood as an attack against the victorious patriarchal order by the representatives of the defeated matriarchal system." Notice his word "attack." Fromm interprets Sophocles as taking sides, as presenting a thesis. He sees the Theban dramas as intended to put across an idea—"the idea that the patriarchal world was triumphant, but that it would be defeated unless it adopted the humanistic principles of the older matriarchal order." The dramas, in short, (if we accept this interpretation) are didactic in intent; they are not primarily dramas, but dramatic vehicles for Sophocles' attack on the too brittle and too authoritarian principles of patriarchal rule, dramatic extrapolations of his nostalgia for the good old days of matriarchy.

In all interpretations let's keep our focus clear. The primary evidence of what a work of art means is always the work itself. Hints and clues may legitimately be sought outside, but their relevance and validity must always be appraised internally. Even if the theory of a primitive matriarchy should happen to be true, it does not follow that every ancient play must serve as a record of the prehistoric struggle. The *Oresteia* may indeed do so; the conflict between Apollo's command to Orestes to slay his mother and the wrath of the Furies as avengers of Clytemnestra's maternal rights lends a good deal of color to that view. But if we make any such judgment of the depth-meaning of the *Oresteia*, or for that matter if we dispute such a judgment, it must be primarily on the basis of evidence found within the play, rather than by undue reliance on sociological or psychological hypotheses. Can we find, then, in the *Oedipus Tyrannus*, any internal evidence of a conflict between the matriarchal and patriarchal principles?

The answer is plainly no, as any reader can see for himself; and even Mr. Fromm does not claim otherwise. He bases his interpretation of *Oedipus Tyrannus* partly upon the sociological theory just cited and partly upon an incident in each of Sophocles' other two Theban plays. In *Oedipus at Colonus* the now aged Oedipus expresses hatred and resentment against his two sons Polyneices and Eteocles. In the *Antigone*, where the dramatic action takes place after Oedipus' death, there is a violent flare-up of antipathy between Creon and his son Haemon. Fromm concludes: "If we interpret *King Oedipus* in the light of the whole trilogy, the assumption seems plausible that the real issue in *King Oedipus*, too, is the conflict between father and son . . ." Note the three main assumptions of his argument: (1) that the father-son antagonism in the other two Theban plays is of primary, not incidental, dramatic importance; (2) that the three Theban plays are closely enough related to justify a deduction of the meaning of one of them from the supposed meaning of the others; (3) that granted the legitimacy of such a deduction in general, it is reasonable to argue a father-son antagonism between Laius and Oedipus (for which there is no independent evidence) from the acknowledged father-son antagonism between Oedipus and his sons, and even from the existence of such a relationship between Creon and Haemon. The last assumption is so inherently weak as a principle of dramatic interpretation, and moreover is so logically dependent upon the validity of Assumption 2, that I shall not do more than cite it as a curious sample of circumambulatory reasoning. What, then, of the two remaining assumptions?

The *Antigone* is the one Theban play to which Fromm's theory of a patriarchal-vs.-matriarchal conflict might conceivably apply. Creon and Antigone in that play do seem to stand, as Fromm maintains, for the principle of order and authority, obedience and hierarchy on the one side, and on the other for the principle of blood relationship as the fundamental and indestructible tie. But this is only one aspect of their relationship to each other and to the total dramatic pattern. To overstress the dramatic conflict in these terms is to convert the *Antigone* into a sociological tract. Robert F. Goheen in his recent study of the play's dominant imagery adopts a more promising approach, examining (as Fromm never bothers to do) the specific language and imagery that constitute the play's symbolic action. "The imagery employed by Sophocles," Goheen writes, "is a functional means of communication in his dramas. It is aesthetic not simply in the sense of the decorative, but in the true sense of being a means of perception (*aisthêsis*) offered to the reader by the poet to take him into the meaning of the work." The recurrence of sight imagery, especially in the Haemon scene, throws the Creon-Antigone conflict into another perspective than the sociological. The drama becomes internalized: the emphasis is not merely on the question of domination by one sex or the other, nor even on the preferability of one or the other way of life; it is also, and far more subtly, upon the nature of human awareness. The conflict is primarily between two ways of grasping truth: Antigone's, the way of direct intuition, vs. Creon's, the way of sound sense and reason, or reliance on "right thinking" (*phronêsis*), on the linear, the measured, the plainly ordered. Each way of knowing has both its special reward and its special limitation of partial blindness. Fromm, to be sure, admits this spiritual antithesis as an aspect and derivative of the matriarchal-patriarchal conflict. But he errs, I believe, in two respects. He underrates Sophocles' artistic objectivity by assuming him to be taking sides. And he ignores the rich pattern of associated imagery—Goheen stresses in particular the images drawn from money and merchandising, from warfare, from animal life, and from seafaring—in which the characters of the two protagonists are caught up and given both fullness and concretion of meaning.

In any case, whatever our interpretation of the *Antigone*, there is no ground for drawing deductions from its supposed meaning to the meaning of the *Oedipus Tyrannus*. Fromm distorts the evidence by speaking repeatedly of the three Theban plays as a "trilogy"—despite his footnoted acknowledgment that they were not composed in the same order as the dramatic action represents. As a matter of fact they were written long intervals apart. The *Antigone* is generally accepted as having been written in or about 441 B.C., the *Oedipus Tyrannus* in 430 or later, and the *Oedipus at Colonus* shortly before Sophocles' death in 406. Moreover, each play was originally produced with two other Sophoclean tragedies, of which no record remains. Not in any sense, then, do the three extant Theban plays constitute a trilogy, and it is by no means permissible to deduce the purpose of the *Oedipus Tyrannus* from the purpose (if we know it) of the *Antiogne*.

In the *Antigone* Creon is something of a melodramatic villain. In the plays written later his character becomes more ambivalent. Fromm, since he mistakenly treats the *Antigone* as if it had been written after the two other plays, misses the significance of the character change. He describes the figure of Creon as "indistinct" in the two Oedipus plays and as "becoming" colorful and definite in the *Antigone*. Since the *Antigone* was actually written first of the three, our critical problem is the reverse of the one he raises. Why does Sophocles blur the moral outlines of his Creon figure in the later plays? The likeliest answer surely is that with advancing maturity he no longer saw the moral issue in the relatively simple black-and-white terms of the *Antigone*; he had come to accept his characters as irresolvably ambivalent—no plain heroes and villains but multi-dimensional men steeped, like all of us, in moral ambiguities, which, though we see them in shifting perspectives, we must carry with us to the grave.

How, then, may a critical reader discover proper clues to the depth-meaning of *Oedipus Tyrannus?*

The first evidence is found in the title. You cannot perfectly rely on a writer to give you a major clue in the title of his work, but it is likely enough that he may want to do so, and the possibility should be explored. What is the meaning of the title *Oedipus Tyrannus?* Not, as in so many translations, "Oedipus Rex" or "King Oedipus." And of course not "Oedipus the Tyrant" either. Liddell and Scott's unabridged Greek lexicon declares that in classical Greek the word *tyrannos* was never applied to a hereditary monarch, for whom the word was *basileus*; it was restricted to those who had received the royal power by some means other than direct succession. Not even force or trickery was necssarily involved. Oedipus used none; he was offered the throne by the grateful Theban people. No matter: he was still a *tyrannos*, or usurper, within the accepted meaning of the word. The closest translation we can give for the play's title, then, is *Oedipus the Usurper.* And we must try to see a little further what *tyrannia* or "usurpation" connoted, and especially what its moral involvements were, to the mind of a fifth-century Greek.

To usurp is to overstep the measure, to erupt the proper limits of one's station in life, or of what is morally fitting, or (it may be) of the area of human as distinguished from divine prerogative. It is the vice or guilt or "tragic flaw" (*hamartia*) of arrogance (*hybris*). Cornford's alluring hypothesis that the rise of the idea may have been connected with the agricultural arrangements in prehistoric Greece has been mentioned in Chapter X. At all events, whatever its early history the idea of overstepping the boundary soon developed cosmic, moral, and political analogies. Just as (in the fragment quoted from Heraclitus) the sun dare not overstep his appointed path, lest the Furies, in their role of the handmaidens of Justice, find him out and punish him, so likewise a man dare not step beyond the path which Destiny has appointed him. Specifically he dare not emulate the gods, for divine indignation and vengeance (*nemesis*) will crash down upon him if he does. The primary *hamartia*, from this standpoint, is usurpation.

Oedipus was a usurper not only with respect to his father's throne and his mother's bed. That aspect is present in the play to be sure, and to a Greek audience Oedipus' ignorance of the relationships would not absolve him of guilt, nor does Oedipus ever expect that it will do so. Usurpation is still a half-physical, half-mythical thing; it happens and produces its terrible consequences regardless of motive. In this respect, therefore, so far as it goes, Freud would seem to have made a valid point after all. But there is another respect in which Oedipus was a usurper more consciously. His victory over the Sphinx was almost godlike, and for man to become too nearly godlike in any way at all (recall Hippolytus' tragic excess of chastity) is a display of *hybris*, arrogance, which by the inherent laws of destiny must be stricken down. The half-articulate usurpation imagery, then, together with the accusations of usurpation which the characters directly or obliquely hurl at one another, represents one depth-theme of the drama.

Next, there is the blight, afflicting the Theban countryside as the play opens. And here we meet with a quite different conception of moral law from the one involved in usurpation. The earlier idea is primarily an Olympian conception—an affair of clear boundary lines marked off in the bright vault of space. Blight and sickness, together with their opposite, which is health, are elements in the chthonic conception, appropriate to Mother Earth and the flora and fauna that grow out of her womb. Evil doing, from this standpoint, is felt as a kind of sickness, a malady in the individual, the commonwealth, and environing nature alike, and with terrible powers of contagion. When the blood of a murdered man seeps into the earth all vegetation sickens. And the same infection creeps into the human commonwealth, the *polis*, the city. What to do save lop off the offending member as one would lop off the diseased branch of a tree? The penalty of sin is at once a withering away in some sense of the individual and his exile from the commonwealth —not by arbitrary decree but by the sheer logic of the chthonic idea.

It is worth noting with what thematic effectiveness Sophocles introduces the word *polis* again and again at the beginnings and ends of lines, where it will have greatest prominence. Finally, after numerous such echoings Oedipus caps his emotional attack on Creon with the cry, "*O polis polis!*" ("O city city!") The contrasting word *xenos* (alien) is first used by Oedipus with unconscious irony when, in explaining why he did not know the details of King Laius' murder, he says "I'm just an alien here." The irony is a double one: he is not an alien in the way he thinks, since he is actually a son of the Theban royal house; but he is presently to be an alien in a more terrible sense, namely an exile.

The third and most central set of thematic images has to do with the blindness-vs.-vision antithesis and the solving of riddles. As the usurpation theme epitomizes Olympian morality and as the blight theme epitomizes chthonic morality, so I might venture the proposition that the blindness-riddle-vision theme epitomizes the morality of the mystery cults of Greece, and in a broader way one aspect of mystical religion generally. In the higher forms of Greek mystery cults, such as the worship of Demeter at Eleusis, the rebirth cycle of crops and seasons develop into the idea of spiritual rebirth. And when that happens the agency of rebirth is no longer magic, nor is it mere orgiastic ecstasy; it involves both inward purification and the imparting of a secret. The initiates at Eleusis performed a symbolic act of entering into darkness; in the inner shrine of the Eleusinian temple a new light was lit, and the sacred mysteries were revealed through such symbols as the sacred ear of grain. Oedipus, who solved the Sphinx's riddle and now would open up the dark mystery of his own origin, is inwardly blind, as the blind visionary Tiresias tries to tell him; and in putting out his eyes after his dreadful self-discovery he completes the symbolic pattern.

What can be concluded, then, as to the depth-meaning of *Oedipus Tyrannus*? Nothing in plain expository terms; of that I am sure. Sophocles was not at all the didactic and partisan writer that Fromm would have him. Francis Fergusson remarks in *The Idea of a Theatre* that "the peculiar virtue of Sophocles' presentation of the myth is that it preserves the ultimate mystery by focusing upon the tragic human at a level beneath, or prior to any rationalization whatever." I fully concur, and at the same time I think we can penetrate a little farther into the mystery—never to its heart—by awareness of the "concrete universals" that reside in the most characteristic uses of imagery. Our analyses are at best propaedeutic They explain nothing essential, but do their work if they steer us to a fresh reading of the play with our visual and auditory imagination newly alerted.

Selected Bibliography

Sophocles' *Oedipus Tyrannus* has probably attracted more analytical, interpretive, and critical writing than any other play in the history of the western theater. For this reason, it would be neither feasible nor possible to cite every book and article known to Sophoclean scholars. The list below is confined to the more important and more interesting English works of criticism, with no attempt to cite the numerous adaptations and translations of the *Tyrannus*. For comparative purposes, however, the student may wish to consult the versions of Seneca (ca. A.D. 50), Thomas Evans (1615), Corneille (1657), Dryden (1678), Voltaire (1718), Hofmannsthal (1906), Gide (1931), and Cocteau (1934). In addition, there are countless English translations of the play, e.g., those of Jebb (1904), Yeats (1928), Grene (1942), Watling (1947), Fitts (1948), Roche (1958), Knox (1959), Yurka (1964), and Cavander (1965). The best Greek editions are still those of Jebb (1904), Sheppard (1920), and Pearson (1928). Also, the excellent and exhaustive commentary of J. C. Kamerbeek (Leiden, 1967) should not be overlooked.

Adams, Sinclair M. *Sophocles the Playwright*. Toronto, 1957.
Aristotle's *Poetics*, trans. James Hutton. New York, 1970.
Bowra, C. M. *Sophoclean Tragedy*. Oxford, 1944.
Brooks, Cleanth, and Heilman, R. *Understanding Drama*. New York, 1948.
Campbell, Lewis. *Sophocles, Plays and Fragments*. Vol. I, Oxford, 1879. Vol. II, 1881.
Carroll, J. P. "Some Remarks on the Questions in the Oedipus Tyrannus." *Classical Journal*, XXXII, No. 7 (April 1937).
Cohen, Robert S. "Oedipus and the Absurd Life" (1968).
Dodds, E. R. "On Misunderstanding the Oedipus Rex." *Greece and Rome*, Series 2, Vol. 13 (1966).
Dodds, E. R. *The Greeks and the Irrational*. Berkeley, 1951. Sather Classical Lectures, Vol. XXV.
Driver, Tom F. *The Sense of History in Greek and Shakespearean Drama*. New York, 1960.
Earle, M. L. *The Oedipus Tyrannus*. New York, 1901.
Ehrenberg, Victor. *Sophocles and Pericles*. Oxford, 1954.
Farnell, L. R. *Greek Hero Cults*. Oxford, 1921.
Farnell, L. R. *The Higher Aspects of Greek Religion*. London, 1912.
Feder, Lillian. " 'The Unwary Egotist': A Study of the Oedipus Tyrannus." *The Centennial Review*, V (1961).
Feldman. Thalia Phillies [Howe]. "Taboo in the Oedipus Theme." *TAPA*, 93 (1962).
Fergusson, Francis. *The Idea of a Theatre*. Princeton, 1949.
Fortes, Meyer. "Analysis and Description in Social Anthropology." *Advancement of Science*, Vol. 38 (1953).
Fortes, Meyer. *Oedipus and Job in West African Religion*. Cambridge, 1959.
Freud, Sigmund. *The Interpretation of Dreams*. New York, 1955.
Gomme, A. W. *More Essays in Greek History and Literature*. Oxford, 1962.
Gould, Thomas. "The Innocence of Oedipus: The Philosophers on Oedipus the King," Part 3. *Arion*, Vol. 5, No. 4 (Winter, 1966).
Greene, William C. *Moira: Fate, Good, and Evil in Greek Thought*. Cambridge, Mass., 1944.
Greene, William C. "The Murderers of Laius." *TAPA*, 60 (1929).
Harsh, Philip W. *A Handbook of Classical Drama*. Stanford, 1944.
Harsh, Philip W. " 'Ἁμαρτία Again." *TAPA*, 76 (1946).
Jaeger, Werner. *Paideia*, English trans. Gilbert Highet. Oxford, I (2nd ed.), 1945; II, 1943; III, 1944.
Jebb, Richard C. "The Age of Pericles." *Essays and Addresses*. Cambridge, 1907.
Jebb, Richard C. *Sophocles: The Plays and Fragments. Part I: The Oedipus Tyrannus*. 3d ed., Cambridge, 1893.
Jones, Ernest. *Hamlet and Oedipus*. New York, 1949.
Jones, John. *Aristotle and Greek Tragedy*. Oxford, 1962.
Kamerbeek, J. C. *The Plays of Sophocles*, Part 4. Leiden, 1967.
Kanzer, Mark. "The 'Passing of the Oedipus Complex' in Greek Drama." *The Yearbook of Psychoanalysis*, V (1949).

Kirkwood, Gordon M. *A Study of Sophoclean Drama.* Ithaca, 1958.
Kitto, H. D. F. *Form and Meaning in Drama.* London, 1956.
Kitto, H. D. F. *Greek Tragedy, A Literary Study.* New York, 1961.
Kitto, H. D. F. *Poiesis.* Berkeley, 1966.
Kitto, H. D. F. *Sophocles: Dramatist and Philosopher.* Oxford, 1958.
Knox, B. M. W. "The Date of the Oedipus Tyrannus of Sophocles." *American Journal of Philology,* 77 (1956).
Knox, B. M. W. *The Heroic Temper.* Berkeley, 1964.
Knox, B. M. W. *Oedipus at Thebes.* New Haven, 1957.
Lattimore, Richmond. *The Poetry of Greek Tragedy.* Baltimore, 1958.
Letters, Francis J. H. *The Life and Works of Sophocles.* London, 1953.
Lesky, Albin. *A History of Greek Literature,* trans. James Willis and Cornelis de Heer. New York, 1963.
Lévi-Strauss, Claude. "The Structural Study of Myth." *Myth, A Symposium,* ed. Thomas A. Sebeok. Bloomington, 1965.
Livingstone, R. W. "The Exodos of the Oedipus Tyrannus." *Greek Poetry and Life.* Oxford, 1967.
Lucas, D. W. *The Greek Tragic Poets.* New York, 1959.
Lucas, F. L. *Tragedy: Serious Drama in Relation to Aristotle's Poetics.* London, 1953.
Moore, John A. *Sophocles and Arete.* Cambridge, 1938.
Mullahy, Patrick. *Oedipus, Myth and Complex.* New York, 1948.
Murray, Gilbert. *Five Stages of Greek Religion.* New York, 1925.
Nietzsche, Friedrich. *The Birth of Tragedy.* New York, 1953.
Nilsson, M. P. *A History of Greek Religion,* trans. F. J. Fielden. Oxford, 1925.
Nilsson, M. P. *The Mycenaean Origin of Greek Mythology.* New York, 1932.
Nock, Arthur D. "The Cult of the Heroes." *Harvard Theological Review,* Vol. 37, No. 2.
Nock, Arthur D. "Religious Attitudes of the Greeks." *Proceedings of the American Philosophical Society,* 85 (1942).
Norwood, Gilbert. *Greek Tragedy.* London, 1948.
O'Connor, Margaret B. *Religion in the Plays of Sophocles.* University of Chicago Dissertation. Chicago, 1923.
Opstelten, J. C. *Sophocles and Greek Pessimism,* English trans. J. A. Ross. Amsterdam, 1952.
Ostwald, M. "Aristotle on ἁμαρτία and Sophocles' Oedipus Tyrannus." *Festschrift Kapp* (1958).
Pack, R. A. "Fate, Chance, and Tragic Error." *American Journal of Philology,* LX (1939).
Pearson, A. C. *Sophoclis Fabulae.* Oxford, 1923.
Pickard-Cambridge, A. W. *Dithyramb, Tragedy and Comedy.* Oxford, 1927.
Pickard-Cambridge, A. W. *The Dramatic Festivals of Athens.* Oxford, 1953.
Post, C. R. "The Dramatic Art of Sophocles." *Harvard Studies in Classical Philology,* 23 (1912).
Prentice, William Kelly. *Those Ancient Dramas Called Tragedies.* Princeton, 1942.
Rohde, Erwin. *Psyche,* trans. W. B. Hillis. New York, 1925.
Rosenmeyer, T. "The Wrath of Oedipus." *Phoenix,* 6 (1952).
Schlegel, A. W. *Lectures on Dramatic Art and Literature,* trans. J. Black. 2nd ed., New York, 1892.
Sheppard, J. T. *Greek Tragedy.* Cambridge, 1920.
Sheppard, J. T. *The Oedipus Tyrannus of Sophocles.* Cambridge, 1920.
Sheppard, J. T. *The Wisdom of Sophocles.* Philadelphia, 1947.
Thucydides' Account of the Plague in Athens, trans. Benjamin Jowett. *The Greek Historians,* ed. Francis R. B. Godolphin. New York, 1942.
Velikovsky, Immanuel. *Oedipus and Akhnaton: Myth and History.* New York, 1960.
Vellacott, P. H. "The Guilt of Oedipus." *Greece and Rome,* Series 2, Vol. 2, No. 2 (October, 1964).
Versényi, Laszlo. "Oedipus: Tragedy of Self-Knowledge." *Arion,* Vol. 1, No. 3 (Autumn, 1962).
Vlachos, N. "Some Aspects of the Religion of Sophocles." *Reformed Church Review,* Vol. 10, No. 2 (April 1906).
Waldock, A. J. A. *Sophocles the Dramatist.* Cambridge, 1951.
Webster, T. B. L. *An Introduction to Sophocles.* Oxford, 1936.
Webster, T. B. L. *Greek Theater Production.* London, 1956.
Whitman, Cedric H. *Sophocles: A Study of Heroic Humanism.* Cambridge, 1951.
Winnington-Ingram, R. P. "Tragedy and Greek Archaic Thought." *Classical Drama and its Influence,* ed. M. J. Anderson. London, 1965.
Young, Sherman P. *The Women of Greek Drama.* New York, 1953.